THE ENGLISH ROMANTICS.

Peter Landry

www.blupete.com

By the same author

The Essays Of Blupete: Law & Politics (2007)
Biographical Sketches By Blupete: The Thinkers (2007)

To "Dana."

Order this book online at www.trafford.com/07-1001
or email orders@trafford.com

Most Trafford titles are also available at major online book retailers.

Report errors: errata@blupete.com

Note for Librarians: A cataloguing record for this book is available from Library and Archives Canada at www.collectionscanada.ca/amicus/index-e.html

ISBN: 978-1-4251-2859-3

We at Trafford believe that it is the responsibility of us all, as both individuals and corporations, to make choices that are environmentally and socially sound. You, in turn, are supporting this responsible conduct each time you purchase a Trafford book, or make use of our publishing services. To find out how you are helping, please visit www.trafford.com/responsiblepublishing.html

Our mission is to efficiently provide the world's finest, most comprehensive book publishing service, enabling every author to experience success. To find out how to publish your book, your way, and have it available worldwide, visit us online at www.trafford.com/10510

www.trafford.com

North America & international
toll-free: 1 888 232 4444 (USA & Canada)
phone: 250 383 6864 ♦ fax: 250 383 6804 ♦ email: info@trafford.com

The United Kingdom & Europe
phone: +44 (0)1865 722 113 ♦ local rate: 0845 230 9601
facsimile: +44 (0)1865 722 868 ♦ email: info.uk@trafford.com

10 9 8 7 6 5 4 3 2

Table Of Contents:

They are not long, the weeping and the laughter,
Love and desire and hate:
I think they have no portion in us after
We pass the gate.
They are not long, the days of wine and roses:
Out of a misty dream
Our path emerges for awhile, then closes
Within a dream.

– *Ernest Dowson.*

Introduction

The Romantic label, as far as British literature is concerned, is to be pinned to only a thirty-nine year period. We may well mark the beginning of the Romantic period with the year 1793, the year that William Godwin brought out his work, *Political Justice*. Beyond this year we see, finally, regular people reading about and speaking about great topics such as democracy and government. This Romantic movement, though considerably dampened by the Napoleonic Wars (1793-1815), continued throughout the first quarter of the 19th-century and on up to the passing of the *Reform Bill of 1832,* an act which brought very large changes in the British political setup. It was during the Romantic period, as millions began to read, that great literary and political agitators came to the fore. Among these literary and political agitators were Godwin, Bentham, Cobbett, Paine, Brougham, Hallam, and we could go on and on. While each of these men, as mentioned, are to be included in the literary age of which we write, none could be described as poets. And not normally would one think of poets as political agitators. However the best of them were, but usually just in their early careers. The English Romantic Poets who died young, such as Shelley and Byron will always be remembered as great poets who wrote line after line of how things ought to be; they were dreamers who dreamed of a better political state. The ones – and I am particularly thinking of Wordsworth and Southey – who lived on through their middle years, did not hold onto the revolutionary views of their youth.

This volume concerns itself not so much with their poetry as it does with the lives of Wordsworth, Coleridge, Shelley, Hunt, Keats, Southey and Byron.

William Wordsworth

(1770-1850)

William Wordsworth
(1770-1850).

"From Sad Perplexity
To Beauteous Forms — And,
Abundant Recompense."

As the 18th-century closed, and during but the first couple of decades of the next century, there arose an acuteness of apprehension or feeling as to the beauties of nature. Rousseau was the first to emphasize: the natural, the wild, the primitive, the instinctive. This Rousseauish sensibility was to spread beyond the borders of France to Germany and to England. The adherents of this romantic sensibility, while subscribing to a simplicity of manner, often displayed an exaggerated capacity for emotional response. To walk in the country with the express intention of viewing the scenery was common to the romantics of the age. They would take camp stools so to sit at their favorite look offs and contemplate the scene. Often they would look away and use a mirror to see the reflection of the scene. These mirrors were known as a Claude Lorraine glass, named after Claud (of) Lorraine (1600-82), the French landscape painter. These hand held mirrors would be tinted or colored in order to give the viewed scene, these objects of nature, a soft, mellow tinge, like the coloring of that master.

It is in the light of this romantic sensibility that we are to consider the English writers who occupied the literary stage during but a short period, a forty year period, from 1793 to 1833.[1] The literary production of these writers, this eruption into the fashionable world, as Walter Bagehot observed, made an impact on English poetry and English criticism from which they will never recover.[2]

Though there are others to whom in due course I shall turn, William Wordsworth, the subject of this particular portrait, represents English Romanticism like no other of the age.

Wordsworth's Early Days:

The Wordsworths came from North Country stock. Their father John was a lawyer who acted for the Lowther family (Earl of Lonsdale) the predominant Tory power in the region. The family lived at Cockermouth. There were five children. Their mother, at only thirty years of age, died in 1778. Mr. Wordsworth was to find that he could not manage his family and his business all at the same time. Richard and William were sent away to school at Hawkshead. The younger brothers, John and Christopher, were to follow along. Dorothy, the only girl, was sent off to her aunt Elizabeth Threlkald who then resided at Halifax.[3]

William spent nine years at Hawkshead. His experiences there should be compared with the experiences of those who were to become his friends, Samuel Taylor Coleridge and Charles Lamb. Coleridge and Lamb had attended a grammar school in London known as Christ's Hospital. The discipline at Christ's Hospital, in those days, was ultra-Spartan, the mood monastic. All domestic ties were to be put aside. Hawkshead was different. It, unlike Christ's Hospital, provided no accommodations, so those that traveled far to attend were of necessity put up by certain of the townspeople.[4] As for young Wordsworth, he was brought into the home of Anne Tyson, one of the dames at the school. Wordsworth had fond memories of her, and particularly of those winter nights by the Tyson fireside, as he was to describe in his autobiographical work, *The Prelude*. There, at Hawkshead, Wordsworth enjoyed the natural amenities that surrounded him: on Windermere Lake to swim, to fish, to go boating, and in the winter to skate; nutting in the hazelwoods; poaching for woodcock; and all those things that a boy might do in such a natural setting and while in his "glad animal days."

In 1787, Wordsworth came up to Cambridge. This undoubtedly because of his uncle's connections. His Uncle William Cookson was a fellow of St. John's. He spent three years there, "coming down in 1790, without sitting for his degree."[5] During his three years at Cambridge, Wordsworth imbibed the revolutionary views of the day. So too (as it seems like all university students given the chance), Wordsworth ran up bills.

> Like STC [Coleridge] the undergraduate William ran up bills, including debts to his tutor, but without, it seems, experiencing STC's racking qualms of conscience. Like STC, also, William made acquaintance with the contemporary unorthodoxies – the philosophy of Hartley, the polemics of Godwin and Frend, republicanism, all the current intellectual and political movements agitating the universities. Wordsworth's stance was soon Spinozistic, Necessitarian, republican. But whereas STC, encountering these influences, grappled in struggle with them, weighing new ideas against the old and reasoning his way through the problems with which these new ideas confronted him, reveling in the resultant intellectual tussling (having fun with his mind, he called it), Wordsworth adopted radical intellectual and political stances with the unhesitating enthusiasm of callow provincialism in combination with a lazy mind. Coleridge, the youthful polymath, greeted new ideas as a dolphin greets new waters; plunging, leaping, sparing, drenching himself and then flinging off the glittering drops, then diving again to contend joyously with more and more strenuous depths. Wordsworth, in complete contrast, basked on the surface of ideas which he found already thrown up for him. – Lefebure.

The Tempering Of A Poet:

Bills or no bills, during his third summer vacation (1790), Wordsworth somehow managed to find enough money to go off to the continent with a college friend of his, Robert Jones. They landed in Calais on July 13th and returned to England three months later. It would not appear, after that, William ever got back to his studies. That winter he was to be found in London, there to thoroughly take in all the sights.[6] The following spring he was walking around Wales with his friend, Robert Jones. His family tried to get him restarted at Cambridge in the fall of 1791; but his studies to him turned into an "immense wilderness," a wilderness he determined to escape by taking himself off once again to France. He crossed over from Brighton to Dieppe at the end of November. After a few days in Paris he struck south to the Loire. At Orléans, notwithstanding his republican leanings, he was to take up with a military officer by the name of Captain Michael Beaupuy. Beaupuy was one of a band of royalists fighting for what was then, a lost cause. There at Orléans, too, the twenty-one year old Wordsworth was to meet Annette Vallon. Annette, four years older than William, was the daughter of a surgeon who practiced further on down the Loire at Blois. We might suppose Annette was an enthusiast of the New Sensibility as was then sweeping France, where a woman and a man, unlike the age just past, were not afraid to show their fellowship in the new ideals, as for example, upon greeting one another to give one another a Platonic embrace. In the case of William and Annette these Platonic embraces were soon to lead to passionate love making, and, the inevitable – in those days – a pregnancy. Upon the pregnancy becoming obvious,

Annette's family stepped in and forbade any further meeting of the two. That autumn, the French Revolution brought about one of its more ugly scenes, the September Massacres at Paris. William apparently found himself in the middle of this and had real concerns for his safety. He knew he would have to return to England but wanted, before leaving, to have a word with Annette, but that, it seems, was impossible. He left for England very late in the year but not before he did get word that Annette, on December 15th, gave birth to a daughter, Caroline.[7]

Back in England, Wordsworth was to hover about the channel with a view to getting immediately back to France. His biographer, Burra observed: "During the summer he had spent a month of calm and glassy days in the Isle of Wright, waiting for his opportunity which never came then; but he watched in despair the naval preparations for war."[8] Wordsworth slowly and reluctantly came to see the impossibility of his situation: he would have to wait out the war. Little did he know that it would prove to be a very long wait; except for *The Peace of Amiens* (1802-03) during which time Wordsworth did manage to get over to see Annette and Caroline for a short time, as we will see, England and France were to be at war for a 23 year period, ending only with the defeat of Napoleon at *The Battle of Waterloo* in 1815. Thus we would have seen, in 1792, a dejected man, Wordsworth, leaving the southeast coast. He traveled west across England through the Salisbury Plain, where, incidently, he was much moved by the visages of antiquity as is represented by that celebrated ancient stone circle, Stonehenge. From there he traveled alone to Wales, to the valley of the Wye and the ruins of Tintern Abbey. It was in Wales where he met his old friend Robert Jones, and together they carried on to North Wales, there to ascend Snowdon. These three scenes that Wordsworth was to take in during the summer of 1793: Stonehenge, Tintern Abbey and Snowdon – were to make an indelible impression on our budding poet. By 1794, Wordsworth was back in his native north country to be near his family and particularly to be near his sister, Dorothy; to renew, in a sense, the "glad animal days" of his youth.

Thus important years were to pass for Wordsworth. For him, his experiences in France and his utter despondency during that first year back in England, was to be his flaming forge. The quiet events of the following year were to temper the man into what he was to become. Wordsworth's spirit – through the heat, pressure and cooling of these years, from 1793 to 1796 – was to be formed into that of a poet. He achieved a unique perspective and was enabled by his experiences to meld those parts or elements of himself to those of the natural world. De Quincey observed that it is from these years that we "may date the commencement of Wordsworth's entire self-dedication to poetry as the study and main business of his life." (*Recollections* ... .)

A Historical Backgrounder:

France up to the revolution was ruled by an absolute monarch. The French court, the envy of and model for foreign courts, as the 18th-century closed, was bankrupt. The French king, in order to facilitate the business of getting more money out of the people, took a gamble, and called together the States General, it had not been called upon since 1610. Thus there came together, in a legitimate body, a collection of men who were to be a majority who could now act against the ruling classes, those who gave homage to, and were favored by, the French court. No sooner did the members of the States General (mostly Parisians) take their seats, when they defiantly proclaimed that they constituted a National Assembly, and as such was all powerful, or, at least more so than the French king. The French Revolution ensued and the absolute monarchy and its attending aristocratic order collapsed. In July of 1789, the storming of the Bastille took place, after which Louis XVI recognized the legal existence of the Constituent Assembly — as the new National Assembly was called. The assembly adopted the "Declaration of the Rights of Man"[9] and drafted a new constitution, one that did allow for a limited monarchy, such as had existed in England since 1688.[10] The French king was not much impressed with these developments and was of the view that the *Ancient Régime* should but continue. It was not to continue. On January 21st, 1793, as part of its ongoing revolutionary activities, those then in charge of France beheaded Louis XVI. In London, George III, aghast, having sent the French ambassador packing, severed diplomatic relations with France. France invaded England's ally Holland, and, on February 1st, France declared war on England. Austria, Prussia, Spain and Britain formed an alliance against France (the "First Coalition"). Prussia retired after it gobbled up Poland. Spain was to make peace (July 1795), and large parts of Holland and Belgium received France as a friend. This war, according to Edmund Burke was not a regular war between nations. It was, rather, a war of all civilized nations (including the overthrown government of France) against Jacobins. "Whatever were the first motives to the war among politicians, they saw that in its spirit, and for its objects, it was a *civil* war; and as such they pursued it. It is a war between the partisans of the ancient civil, moral and political order of Europe against a sect of fanatical and ambitious atheists which means to change them all. It is not France extending a foreign empire over other nations: it is a sect aiming at universal empire, and beginning with the conquest of France."[11]

In England, the reaction to the goings on in France, at first, were mixed, but the majority, especially when the abuses of the French Revolution were recognized, were ready to support the French Royalists.

The English historian, John Richard Green:

> The cautious good sense of the bulk of Englishmen, their love of order and law, their distaste for violent changes and for abstract theories, as well as their reverence for the past, were rousing throughout the country a dislike of the revolutionary changes which were hurrying on across the channel; and both the political sense and the political prejudice of the nation were being fired by the warnings of Edmund Burke. ... [Burke hated] a revolution founded on scorn of the past, and threatening with ruin the whole social fabric which the past had reared; the ordered structure of classes and ranks crumbling before a doctrine of social equality; a state rudely demolished and reconstituted; a church and a nobility swept away in a night.

There were, of course, people in England, while regretting the blood and destruction of the French Revolution, nonetheless supported the principles for which it stood. These principles were best summed up in Rousseau's expression: "Man is born free; and everywhere he is in chains!" And, the Rousseauish cry: "Liberty, Equality, Fraternity." Most all of the young intelligentsia of the age (for that matter of any age) were for change. After all, was not the existing state, unfair? Where is the justice in the existing system? Things need be set right. These notions were meat and drink to all of the young poets of the age, including William Wordsworth.

In England, in 1793, a political book, like no other, before or since, was to come off the presses. It was *Enquiry Concerning the Principles of Political Justice*, or, more simply, *Political Justice* by William Godwin. It burst upon the scene as a major piece of sedition.[12] It was an attack on aristocracy, property, religion, and even the sacrament of marriage. In 1793, the trials of the "Reform-martyrs," one of whom was Thomas Muir (1765-99) were to unfold. The lot of them were convicted and transported to Botany Bay. In 1794, there was to be the "Trial of the 12 Reformers": Thomas Holcroft, Horne Tooke, Thomas Hardy, John Thelwall and others were brought to trial on the charge of high treason, and, acquitted amid much excitement. These trials were part of the larger government effort to prosecute editors, nonconformists and radicals who were arguing for Parliamentary reform. England, however, was at war; and reform, indeed, even the liberties of the people[13] were to take second place to the grand effort of making England victorious. And, victorious she was to be, due mainly to her superiority upon the oceans of the world.

Literary Collaboration: Wordsworth & Coleridge:

As the year 1794 passed, Wordsworth was to be with his family, and, I should think with his mother's family, the Cooksons at Penrith. It was at Penrith, as the year closed, that he came to find himself nursing a dying friend who had been at Cambridge with him, Raisley Calvert. In January, 1795, the young man died and left an inheritance to Wordsworth, an inheritance which enabled Wordsworth to set out on his life's career which otherwise would not have been possible.[14] He determined, too, at this point, that in life's journey, his sister Dorothy was to be his fellow traveler.

It was during the years, 1794-5, that a very close relationship was to spring up between William Wordsworth and his sister, a relationship unique in the literary world, one that continued until Wordsworth's death in 1850. Just prior to Calvert's death, the pair (William was 24 and Dorothy 22), for many long hours discussed what it was that William was to do with his life. What was clear to Wordsworth was that, "All professions are attended with great inconveniences."[15] Then the Calvert legacy: it enabled Wordsworth to put off a decision as to what he should do to make a living. The decision that William and Dorothy made, now that they could afford to do so, was to live together in a secluded country cottage. As it happened, a friend offered them just such a place, Racedown Lodge, near the Dorset coast. In September of 1795, the Wordsworths took up their residence at Racedown. There William Wordsworth turned to what was to be his life long activity: the writing of poetry.

One of the most famous literary collaborations was that of William Wordsworth and Samuel Taylor Coleridge. When these two first met is a question[16] which likely cannot be answered. By 1797, we see that Coleridge was paying a visit to the Wordsworths at Racedown. Upon meeting Coleridge, the Wordsworths were electrified. We are not to be surprised by this, as Coleridge charmed everyone, at least at first. The diarist, Henry Crabb Robinson who was personally acquainted with Coleridge, wrote: "On politics, metaphysics and poetry, more especially on the Regency, Kant, and Shakespeare he was astonishingly eloquent." After this first meeting, Dorothy got a letter off to her friend Mary Hutchinson. The first thing, as Dorothy was to explain, was William's reading of his new poem *The Ruined Cottage*, with which Coleridge was much delighted. "After tea he [Coleridge] repeated to us two acts and a half of his tragedy *Osorio*. The next morning William read his tragedy *The Borderers*."[17]

The Wordsworths were enthralled with Coleridge; he with them. There were, during the spring of 1797, two or three visits back and forth.[18] Coleridge was then living at Nether Stowey, a Somerset village, under the patronage of the local tanner and literary enthusiast, Tom Poole (1765-1837). Coleridge returned to Nether Stowey from Racedown on June 28th. Upon returning home he told his friends, with much enthusiasm, about the Wordsworths. He immediately set out again to bring the Wordsworths to Nether Stowey. Traveling the fifty mile distance to Racedown, he reappeared back at Nether Stowey on July 2nd with the Wordsworths in tow. Now, as it happened, Charles Lamb was to come up from London to pay his old school chum Coleridge a visit. So, within days of the Wordsworths' arrival at Nether Stowey in came Charles Lamb and his sister. Thus there was to be quite a crowd in the little cottage occupied by the Coleridge family (Coleridge, Sara and their one year old son, Hartley), the Wordsworths, Charles Lamb and his sister. They were all somehow fitted into the small Coleridge cottage. There was to be some relief when the Lambs returned to London, as they had intended to do. The Wordsworths seemed to have little reason to return to Racedown and were quite happy to continue on at Nether Stowey. What the Wordsworths wanted were new accommodations, somewhere near the Coleridges at Nether Stowey. Through the good offices of Tom Poole,[19] benefactor and friend to this growing clutch of literary luminaries, a large home was rented. It was located nearby at Holford Glen, a Queen Anne mansion which was known as Alfoxden. The Wordsworths, who still had a sizable portion of the Calvert legacy in hand, signed a one year lease for the sum of £23. The Wordsworths moved into Alfoxden in July of 1797. Dorothy Wordsworth described it as "a large mansion with furniture enough for a dozen families like ours."

The Alfoxden Days:

In the new year of 1798, the English were feeling glum. Napoleon had successfully invaded Italy, and Spain had joined sides with France. The Austrians, who had stood up to France for awhile, retired from the field. France was left without an enemy on the continent, and England without an ally. Fearing an invasion, England withdrew her ships from the Mediterranean. It was then to become a "French Lake" from January 1797 to May 1798. These were dark times, and the average Englishmen could see French spies everywhere. The regular sort of person that lived around or at Nether Stowey were sure that they had some in their midst. It was that strange group at Alfoxden as headed up by the newcomers. They had to be spies! Soon there was to be a surreptitious but close watch on the Wordsworths and those who came to visit. The mansion apparently came with a few servants. One of them was a female by the name of Mogg who was very suspicious of the new tenants. They talked differently, and to Mogg, this Somerset servant, unfamiliar as she apparently was with the manner and speech of those from the north of England, concluded these tenants must be from France. And they certainly behaved like Papists. Why, they cleaned their clothes on Sunday, and they had the morals of the Continentals, in that "the master of the house had no wife with him, but only a woman that he tried to pass off as his sister." The Wordsworths and their friends also had this habit of going about in the countryside with their friends making observations and writing in note pads which each had ready at hand.[20] Something very sinister was going on here, and Mogg dutifully reported.[21] Word was to get back to the authorities in London about this bunch at Alfoxden and the report was not taken lightly. There was sent out from London a government agent by the name of Walsh. He kept a watch on these strange people: Wordsworth, Coleridge and friends. All of this did not much bother these romantics.[22] The *Alfoxden Circle* "passed the wonderful summer of 1797, with almost ceaseless laughter and high spirits, constant visits, talk and sociability, love and warm happiness, excitement and buoyancy." (Lefebure.)

The "Alfoxden Circle" was to lose one of its more illustrious members, for a time. Coleridge, desperate for money to support himself and his family, had determined to take up a position as a Unitarian minister. A position opened up for him at Shrewsbury, so, there he went to take up his ministry. Coleridge, however, was not to spend much time at Shrewsbury, as, not too long after he left Nether Stowey, a gift of money was to be made to him. The Wedgwoods, in their continuing effort to support the arts, gave a life annuity to Coleridge of £150 per year with no conditions. Such a gift however was not to keep Coleridge at Nether Stowey, as he longed to travel to Germany for further studies. Doubtlessly these plans were discussed with the Wordsworths and a determination was made that all three would travel together to Germany, once the one year lease[23] of Alfoxden was up at the end of June, 1798. It was during this time, it hardly needs to be mentioned, that the two poets collaborated on their work, *Lyrical Ballads*, the manifesto of English Romanticism. Before leaving for Germany, Wordsworth and Coleridge saw to the final arrangements in respect to the publication of *Lyrical Ballads*. These arrangements required, for the most part, their attendance at Bristol where a Bristol bookseller, Joseph Cottle (1770-1853) was putting the book through the press. (They did, during that summer, make a trip to Wales at which time Wordsworth wrote one of his most popular poems, *Tintern Abbey*, written on July 13th, 1798.) By late August the party headed for London, there to make their final preparations for their trip to Germany. On September 16th, Dorothy and William together with Coleridge and a friend of theirs, John Chester, set sail for Germany from Yarmouth arriving at Hamburg on the 19th.[24]

Dove Cottage (1799-1808):

Within 10 days of their arrival at Germany the Wordsworths decided to separate from their companions. We know more about Coleridge's stay in Germany than that of the Wordsworths'. As mentioned they arrived in September 1798. It would appear they were prepared to leave before the year was out, but a severe winter on the continent encumbered travelers. The Wordsworths spent a number of weeks at Goslar. There, at Goslar, few "books were accessible, and the result was a period of great activity in composition." (Burra.) Upon the winter breaking up the Wordsworths were on the move again and were to eventually find their way to the coast and then back to England, arriving there in April of 1799.

It is well, now, to consider events on the continent. Napoleon had managed to slip back from Egypt (autumn of 1799). France was then to make him First Consul (dictator) and the little general re-energized her. Italy was then taken which led to the "Second Coalition" (England, Austria, and Russia) to break up. England was once again left alone to deal with France. Indeed, for a few months during the winter of 1800-01, there was formed a league against England; it consisted of Prussia, Sweden, Denmark and Russia. This "was caused partly by the whim of the Czar Paul [and] partly by two feelings then prevalent in the Courts of Europe, fear of France and jealousy of English naval power." (Trevelyan.) With Nelson's capture of the Danish fleet at Copenhagen during April of 1801, this league against England came to an end.

Once in England, in April of 1799, William and Dorothy, having apparently no particular plan in mind, headed north to Stockton, six miles from Darlington to see Dorthy's old friend Mary Hutchinson who at that time was staying on a farm run by her brother Tom Hutchinson. That October, at William's invitation, Coleridge arrived at the Hutchinson farm. Plans were soon laid for a trip west to the Lake District, to the countryside known by Wordsworth in his youth.[25] Wondering through the Lake District, Wordsworth and Coleridge found their way to Rydal and then to Grasmere. At Grasmere they discovered, on the coaching road descending from Ambleside, a cottage for rent. The cottage was formally an inn, "The Dove and Olive Bough." Wordsworth, then and there, made the determination that this cottage should be his new home. Leaving Coleridge behind, Wordsworth returned alone to the Stockton farm to tell his sister Dorothy of his find.[26] Traveling mostly by foot, in December, Dorothy and William made their way to Grasmere, arriving there on the 20th. They then moved into Dove Cottage, a place that was to be their home for the next eight years.

Catherine Macdonald Maclean of University College, Cardiff, in her book on Dorothy Wordsworth, takes up the subject of Dove Cottage:

> The cottage, which was only a few feet off the road, stood above the lake. Behind it were the towering masses of Nab Scar. The orchard itself was but a slip of the mountain, enclosed and cultivated. It sloped upwards from the house so that from the top of it they could look right over the roof and see the lake. They had a view of the church and Helm Crag and more than two-thirds of the vale. Dorothy instantly built in her imagination a seat and a summer hut in this lofty and gracious place. She clothed the front of the cottage with honey-suckle and roses.[27] ...
>
> Dorothy found that much had to be done before the cottage would be comfortable. One of the rooms upstairs smoked like a furnace; some of the doors had to be mended; most of the rooms needed painting and papering; there was endless sewing to be done. ...
>
> Soon the cottage was made neat and comfortable within-doors. To Dorothy it seemed to have only two serious disadvantages. It was very near the road, and it was so built that sounds passed very distinctly from one part of the house to another.

A more contemporary description of Dove Cottage is that which was given by Thomas de Quincey in his reminiscences. He was to first view it when he met the Wordsworths in August of 1807. De Quincey, incidently, was to become intimately acquainted with Dove Cottage, as, after the Wordsworths left it in 1808, it was to become his home for a period of time.

> A little semi-vestibule between the two doors prefaced the entrance into what might be considered the principal room of the

cottage. It was an oblong square, not above eight and a half feet high, sixteen feet long, and twelve broad; very prettily wainscoted from the floor to the ceiling with dark polished oak, slightly embellished with carving. One window there was – a perfect and unpretending cottage window, with little diamond panes, embowered at almost every season of the year with roses; and, in the summer and autumn, with a profusion of jasmine and other fragrant shrubs. From the exuberant luxuriance of the vegetation around it, and from the dark hue of the wainscoting, this window, though tolerably large, did not furnish a very powerful light to one who entered from the open air.

– *Recollections of the Lakes and the Lake Poets.*

De Quincey was to also give us a glimpse into Wordsworth's diminutive studio as was located upstairs in Dove Cottage. "I was ushered up a little flight of stairs, fourteen in all, to a little drawing-room, or whatever the reader chooses to call it." In it, like most living rooms of the day, there was to be found a fireplace. This upstairs room, itself, "was not fully seven feet six inches, and, in other respects, pretty nearly of the same dimensions as the rustic hall below. There was, however, in a small recess, a library of perhaps three hundred volumes, which seemed to consecrate the room as the poet's study and composing room; and such occasionally it was."

Wordsworth's taking up residence at Dove Cottage heralded a new stage in his poetry writing. It was to be during these days at Dove Cottage that Wordsworth wrote some of his most charming poems of flowers, birds, and butterflies. On April 6th, 1800, Coleridge arrived at Dove Cottage. By this time Coleridge's family problems were becoming more serious. When the heat was on, one of the places to which Coleridge would run was the Wordsworths'. They always welcomed him and were to make little or no reference to his problems, the principal one being, of course, Coleridge's long standing opium habit. The main reason Coleridge was to spend time with the Wordsworths, that spring of 1800, was to assist Wordsworth in the putting together of the 2nd edition of *Lyrical Ballads*.[28] So too, at Dove Cottage, there was to be found William's brother John, who was there that spring for a visit. And also Mary Hutchinson was there for a period of time. By May 4th, Coleridge had left the Lake District in order to see his publisher at Bristol. After Bristol, Coleridge went back to his family who were still at Nether Stowey, not far from Bristol. Things were patched up, such that, on June 29th, Coleridge arrived in the Lake District with his family – Sara (seven months pregnant with Derwent) and four year old Hartley. On July 23rd, the Coleridges were to take up residence at Greta Hall, Keswick, located some thirteen miles or so from Grasmere.

Dorothy and Mary:

Dorothy was 21 months younger than William. She was to lose her mother at age six, her father at eleven. She was separated from her brothers and sent to live with her mother's relatives. Many women of the age, of the ages, share the desires and impulses of the male head of their household. The effect of leaving the business of raising a young impressionable girl by a maiden aunt, Elizabeth Threlkald, is a question we must leave for the psychologists to answer, supposing that they would have enough information to go on. With no father and having been separated from her brothers since the age of six, at the age of fifteen, now a young woman, Dorothy was reintroduced to her brother, William: she fell in love with him, it was to be a deep and an abiding love which was to last a lifetime.[29] William, as we have seen,was off to university (Cambridge) in 1787. Beginning in 1790, he was traveling around a lot, which travels included France in 1792. After returning to England, William wondered through England, in particular through Wales. In 1794 he returned to the countryside he knew as a boy, the Lake District. It is at this point that we may see the beginnings of the close and lifelong relationship as did exist between William and Dorothy. In September of 1795 they determined to live with one another, moving into their first little cottage at Racedown, Dorset. They continued to live together until William's death in 1850. The Wordsworth relationship became a threesome, when in 1802 William married Dorothy's school friend, Mary Hutchinson.

William likely first met Mary when she was but young, at dame school, at Penrith. It seems, however, that the childhood friendship was more between Dorothy and Mary, a friendship that was to continue throughout their lives. As has been seen, during their adulthood, Mary and Dorothy were to pay regular visits with one another, and because of the distances and the difficulty of traveling in those days, these visits would last for weeks on end. When Dorothy and William took up living with one another, these long visits continued, with Mary spending considerable periods of time with both William and Dorothy, beginning in 1795, at Racedown and then, after that, at Dove Cottage at Grasmere. In 1802 – likely inspired by the delightful Coleridge children that now lived nearby – William and Mary married. Thereafter, brother/husband, sister and wife lived together, first at Dove Cottage and then at Allan Bank (1808) and then, for the balance of their years at Rydal Mount (1813): this arrangement worked wonderfully well for all three of them.

Earlier we set forth de Quincey's description of Dove Cottage. Just after giving such a description, he moved along and described how he was to meet two ladies in the cottage. One, "a tallish young woman, with the most winning expression of benignity upon her features ... so frank in air" and, as de Quincey observed, "the native goodness of her manner." De Quincey was describing Wordsworth's wife, Mary. She was "neither handsome nor even comely ... nay, generally ... very plain –

> ... compensatory charms of sweetness all but angelic, of simplicity the most entire, womanly self-respect and purity of heart speaking through all her looks, acts, and movements. *Words* I was going to have added; but her words were few. ... In complexion she was fair, and there was something peculiarly pleasing even in this accident of the skin, for it was accompanied by an animated expression of health, a blessing which, in fact, she possessed uninterruptedly.

Coleridge adored Mary, his "beautiful green willow." Keats described her as Wordsworth's beautiful wife. De Quincey concluded his remarks by praising Mary Wordsworth in glowing terms as having, "a sunny benignity – a radiant graciousness – such as in this world I never saw surpassed." Wordsworth's biographer Burra, wrote: "[Mary] ... served him and protected him, urged him to his poetry, and attended its labor through nearly fifty years of their lives. Writing his letters, copying his poems, nursing Dorothy, keeping the house, she served him with absolute devotion yet lost nothing of her own character, and gave him equally the wit and the criticism which was almost as useful as her love."

As for Dorothy: well, de Quincey sung her praises, too. Dorothy, in the physical comparison, was "shorter, slighter." Unlike most English women, she was of dark complexion, her "face was of Egyptian brown." There was something about her eyes. There was for de Quincey something in them, wild and startling, and hurried in their motion. As for Dorothy's personal characteristics, well, they were quite different from that which de Quincey observed in Mary.

> Her manner was warm and even ardent; her sensibility seemed constitutionally deep; and some subtle fire of impassioned intellect apparently burned within her, which, being alternately pushed forward into a conspicuous expression by the irrepressible instincts of her temperament, and then immediately checked, in obedience to the decorum of her sex and age, and her maidenly condition, gave to her whole demeanour, and to her conversation, an air of embarrassment, and even of self-conflict, that was almost distressing to witness.[30]

Coleridge wrote of Dorothy just shortly after he met her in 1797, in the following terms:

> She is a woman indeed! – in mind, I mean, and heart – for her person is such, that if you expected to see a pretty woman you would think her ordinary – if you expected to find an ordinary woman you would think her pretty! – But her manners are simple, ardent, impressive ... and her taste a perfect electrometer – it bends, it protrudes, and draws in at subtlest beauties and most recondite faults.[31]

During the summer of 1810, Henry Crabb Robinson, on a visit back to his home town, Bury, was to meet Dorothy Wordsworth, who at the time was staying with the Clarksons. This meeting led to an invitation to Rydal Mount which Robinson took up, visiting the Wordsworths in November of that year. Robinson wrote of Dorothy: "Miss W. without her brother's genius or productive power, had all his tastes and feelings, and he was in his youth and in middle age as warmly attached to her as late in life he became attached to his daughter, no one rivalling them in his affections except his admirable wife." (Morley.)

With the signing of the *Treaty of Amiens* on May 25th, 1802, the hostilities between France and England were brought to an end, albeit, only temporarily.[32] The Wordsworths were to take advantage of this lull and, an event to which we have previously referred, made their way to France to visit William's daughter, Caroline and her mother, Annette. Leaving Grasmere on July 9th, they stopped by for a visit with Coleridge (Greta Hall) and the Hutchinsons (Gallow Hill). William and Dorothy stayed in France for a month. The purpose of the trip, plainly, was to get Annette's blessing on an intended marriage.[33] The Wordsworths arrived back at London on August 30th. On October 4th, 1802, William Wordsworth married Mary Hutchinson, at Brompton. By October the 6th the three Wordsworths were settled in at Dove Cottage: William, Mary and Dorothy. Coleridge was to observe of Wordsworth, it seems somewhat enviously: "living wholly among *Devotees* – having every minutest Thing, almost his very Eating & Drinking, done for him by his sister, or Wife."[34] The following year, on June 18th, Wordsworths' first child, a son, John was born.

A Growing Family & Sorrow:

Thus we see William Wordsworth in a happy state; he has income and leisure, and two female *Devotees* who attend to his minutest requirements. This state was to generally continue for the rest of his days, days which were broken up into two principal activities. The one, wondering the pathways overseen by the imposing hills of his beloved Lake Country; and the other, in composing poetry about that which he saw around him.

The Wordsworth household, consisting of brother, sister and wife was soon to grow.[35] As already mentioned, John, the first child was born on June 18th, 1803. Richard (William's older brother) and Dorothy were to stand together as godparents at the little church nearby in what was rather an insular ceremony. Before the summer was out, on August 14th, leaving mother and child at home, Dorothy and William, were off for a tour of Scotland.[36] Their bosom friend, Coleridge, was to join them. All went well for a couple of weeks, when Coleridge left his companions and returned on foot by himself to his home (Greta Hall) arriving there on September 15th. It seems that it was during this trip that Wordsworth was to finally let go at Coleridge for his opium habit. The Wordsworths knew of Coleridge's weakness for drugs, but they said nothing. I guess they might have thought that Coleridge's wife, Sarah said enough for all. But for some reason, Wordsworth on the first part of their Scottish trip lost his patience with Coleridge. It was the first real rent in the Coleridge/Wordsworth friendship; it was downhill thereafter. By 1812 this rupture was to become "profound and complete."

Coleridge's problem was known to family and close friends. Coleridge excused himself, saying simply that he was not well and needed the opium for pain relief. His wife was beside herself, and was at this point making appeals to her brother-in-law, Robert Southey. [Coleridge and Southey had married two of three beautiful sisters, the Fricker sisters. Coleridge married Sara (1770-1845) and Southey married Edith (1774-1837).] In any event, on September 7th, 1803, the Southeys moved into Greta Hall. Robert Southey, thereafter, was to be the principal support of Sara Coleridge and her children. But these events I take up in greater detail when I come to my biographical sketch of Coleridge.

On February 6th, 1804, Wordsworth's younger brother, John, age 33, a captain of an India Merchant Ship, *Earl of Abergavenny*, who had spent a considerable amount of time with William and Dorothy, especially in 1800, much loved, lost his life when his ship was wrecked off the south coast of England, Weymouth. All on board were lost. John was to be described as "a poet in everything but words." He was "the adored friend of everyone who knew him."[37]

Though the sad news of John's death shocked them all, the normal state of happiness of the Wordsworth household was to soon return. On August 16th, 1804, the very year they were to lose John, Wordsworth's second child, Dora was born. Dora was followed, on June 16th, 1806, by Thomas, the third child born to the Wordsworths, so to join three year old John and two year old Dora. Notwithstanding that parts of the household, at times, were noisy, William continued on with what was his occupation, the writing of poetry. His inventory of poems had built up considerably, such that, in May of 1807, Wordsworth's poems were published in two volumes. Things were looking much better, and, needing more room for their growing family, in June of 1808, the Wordsworths moved into their new home, Allan Bank, Grasmere. Another reason that they took a larger place is that it was expected that Coleridge would come to live with them; which apparently he did. During the weekends, Allan Bank was to become a very busy abode, indeed. At times there was as many as seven children (Coleridges and Wordsworths). Sara Hutchinson, who was now, it would appear part of the Wordsworth household (Mrs.

Wordsworth's sister, a lady whom Coleridge was much interested in), was to remark that when Coleridge played with the children, STC made "enough racket for twenty." (Lefebure.) By June 1810, however, Coleridge, fond of his comforts, left Allen Bank (the Wordsworth residence, apparently, was usually in a bit of a rough state, though it never seem to bother them). Coleridge's principal interest, however, it seems plain, while at the Wordsworths, was that he was to be in the good company of Sara Hutchinson. Sara, for her own reasons (I suggest that it was simply because she just could not take Coleridge anymore) had left Allan Bank to return, I think, to her brother's farm in Yorkshire. Coleridge was thus to move back in with his wife at Greta Hall; it was a cohabitation which was to last only about five months. Coleridge took advantage of an offer coming from friends of his, the Montagus – who were just then visiting – to return to London in their carriage and reside with them. Though we will never know exactly what transpired, Coleridge in his conversations on the long ride to London with Montagu determined that Wordsworth had been bad-mouthing him (Coleridge) behind his back. Thus, the breach in the Coleridge/Wordsworth relationship that can be traced back to 1803 when they had traveled to Scotland together, in 1810, opened up, such that their relationship was never thereafter to be the same. Over the next two years, the quarrel between the two poets became a *cause célèbre.*

The year 1812 was to prove to be another sad year for the Wordsworths. First off they came to hear that Coleridge actually was back in the Lake District, for what was to be a rare visit with his family. Greta Hall was but thirteen miles from Allan Bank. Surely, Coleridge would come down to pay them a visit and renew their relationship. The Wordsworths waited expectantly at Grasmere; but Coleridge did not show. The sorrow to the Wordsworths that the relationship that they had with Coleridge had come to an end, was however totally eclipsed when two of the Wordsworth children, that year (1812), were to die: four year old Catherine[38] on June 4th, and six year old Thomas on December 1st. There were then left at this point, to recount, three children: nine year old John, eight year old Dora, and two year old William.

In March of 1813, Wordsworth through the influence of the powerful Lowther family received an appointment as the Collector of Stamps for Westmorland; with it came £400 per year.[39] This additional money allowed the Wordsworths to make a move that they had been contemplating since they first took up residence at Allan Bank, five years earlier. They had continually complained about the smoking chimneys at Allan Bank to its landlord but nothing apparently was done about the problem. The very month that Wordsworth received his appointment as the Collector of Stamps, the family moved to Rydal Mount. It was "two miles away on the Ambleside road, [and] which he rented from the widowed Lady Fleming. The house had superb views, was surrounded by a magnificent wild garden of the kind Dorothy loved, and it was a "gentleman's house." It remained Wordsworth's home until his death 38 years later in 1850."

Throughout these years, Wordsworth continued to write poetry. Indeed, in March of 1815, Wordsworth's "first collected Edition of his works" was to appear. The Wordsworth home was always open to friends and admirers. Thomas de Quincey, would have been a regular visitor,[40] for, as of 1809, he was a resident of Grasmere, indeed he moved into "Dove Cottage" after the Wordsworths moved out. With Wordsworth's growing popularity, visitors would regularly come up from London. Charles Lamb together with his sister, would come up on holidays. So, too, would Crabb Robinson (Robinson and Wordsworth were to become the best of friends). Other luminaries of the age arrived at Rydal Mount, including Walter Scott and William Godwin. One memorable visit made by Godwin, was that made during April 27th & 28th, 1816. While there at Rydal Mount, Wordsworth and Godwin were to have "a fearful quarrel about Waterloo." Godwin, like his followers (Hazlitt, Byron and Shelley), saw it as a catastrophe for progress: whereas Wordsworth and Southey saw it as the putting down of the monstrous ambitions of one man and his deluded supporters – Godwin quit Wordsworth, as Robinson was to report, "with very bitter and hostile feelings." (Johnson.)

As we have seen Wordsworth began his continental travels early. Leaving university behind, but twenty years of age, he made a tour of the continent with his friend Robert Jones. Wordsworth loved to travel and did so throughout the whole of his life. He made a number of trips to Scotland, there to visit Scott. He traveled to the continent during the years: 1820, 1823, and 1828. His trip of 1820 ran on for months (July-November). On this trip he had with him: Dorothy, Mary, Mr. and Mrs Monkhouse, and Crabb Robinson. When in Paris Wordsworth paid a visit to Annette and Caroline (by then married). During his 1828 trip, Wordsworth toured the Rhine with Dora (then 24 years of age) and, interestingly, with Coleridge. During 1837 Wordsworth made his last continental tour. He was then to travel again with his friend Crabb Robinson. In Italy they paid a visit to the graves of Keats who died at age 26, and Shelley who died at age 30. Keats and Shelley were very much alive to the social and political questions of the time, and, dying young, were to do so with Rousseauian beliefs yet in their hearts. Like Wordsworth and Coleridge, in their time, Keats and Shelley made imagination the supreme gift so that "what the Imagination seizes as beauty must be truth." There, stood Wordsworth and Robinson, in an Italian grave yard, Wordsworth 67 years of age, Robinson, 62. While Keats and Shelley died with romantic hopes; Wordsworth and Robinson, growing old, had gradually traded their romantic beliefs for the practical realities of the world. A retrospective story of the romantic poets of the early 19th-century might be told with this grave side scene. But I must break away from this sad reverie and write a few words about the relationship of these two men: Wordsworth and Robinson.

Wordsworth's Relationship With Robinson:

> Crabb Robinson became a familiar friend of the whole Wordsworth household, a constant visitor to Rydal, and an intimate with all who frequented the Mount. He traveled with Wordsworth on various occasions – in Wales, in Scotland, in Switzerland, Germany, and Italy. The friends met in Herefordshire at the home of Miss Fenwick's relatives, and in London, where they visited in the same houses. They heard frequently from each other by letter when they were separated, and their respect and love for each other increased year by year. – Edith Morley.

Morley continues and points out that Wordsworth owes, in no small measure, his fame to the tireless promotional activities of Crabb Robinson. The fact of the matter is that Wordsworth's poems in the early days were not read at all. "At home and abroad, in writing and in conversation, by gifts of the poems, by quotation and by exposition, Robinson did what could be done by heart-felt praise to make converts to the poetry he was among the first to estimate justly." Robinson's message to all who would listen was the same: Wordsworth was "the greatest man now living in this country." Robinson's admiration was not, however, uncritical. "He saw the weaknesses of Wordsworth's work just as he saw faults and his narrowness as a man." The two men were "fundamentally opposed in their religious outlook and in their political views," subjects which both men took very seriously. Wordsworth was an orthodox member of the Church of England, "who could not tolerate talk of church reform"; Robinson was a Unitarian.[41] Robinson was part of an emerging liberal movement, a Whig; Wordsworth, while very much a revolutionary in his younger days came around to be very much the Tory and supported the aristocratic establishment. To Wordsworth – "Rash experiments in such serious matters as government, education and religion were the most dangerous modes of proceeding that could possibly be adopted."

Edith Morley in her work made the comparison: Robinson to Wordsworth:

> Wordsworth instinctively revolted against the unknown; Robinson was attracted to it. The subject of 'animal magnetism,' or 'mesmerism' as it is now called, is a case in point. Of an entirely different order was the poet's typically insular attitude to foreigners, their habits, and their strange tongues. Crabb Robinson suffered on more than one occasion, when they were fellow-travellers, from Wordsworth's bad manners and British insolence when he was abroad. Thus he provoked rudeness from a waiter or a guide, or incurred retaliation from a landlord, who made him pay for his unreasonableness when the bill was presented. On the other hand, Wordsworth intensely disliked Robinson's habit of entering into

conversation with strangers, in a foreign language, at table d'hôte or in the diligence. The poet liked getting up and going to bed early, and he was not particularly fond of town sight-seeing. As he grew older, Crabb Robinson hated Wordsworth's country hours, and he could not bear to leave unseen any sort of curiosity – old buildings, pictures, sculpture, attracted him as much as the beauties of nature, which were his companion's preponderating interest. The long Italian journey became towards the close somewhat of a trial to both men, and though Crabb Robinson never suffered anything comparable with Wordsworth's moodiness, yet there were occasions when even he was hard put to it to maintain his normal equilibrium and cheerful spirits. Not too much should be made of passing breezes: that neither man was unduly ruffled is sufficiently proved by the fact that, after a very short interval at home, they set out again together for another tour of England. There is, besides, the warm and obviously heartfelt praise of Crabb Robinson in Wordsworth's dedication to him of the Italian poems, to show that disagreement was not serious. That it existed is added testimony to the mutual love and respect which rendered the friendship genuine, and unspoilt by anything approaching insincere adulation or toadying on the part of Crabb Robinson.

The Contemporary Critics:

Leigh Hunt was a member of the "seditious press," and, for his ferocious attack on the Prince Regent, was to spend time in an English prison. In one of Hunt's articles,[42] he held up Wordsworth to ridicule; not so much for his poetical judgments, but for his political ones. "Mr Southey," he had said, "and even Mr Wordsworth, have both accepted offices under government, of such a nature as absolutely ties up their independence. ... and yet they shall all tell you that they have not diminished their free spirit a jot. In like manner they are as violent and intolerant against their old opinions, as ever they were against their new ones, and without seeing how far the argument carries, shall insist that no man can possess a decent head or respectable heart who does not agree with them. ... The persons of whom we have been speaking have been always in extremes, and perhaps the good they are destined to perform in their generation, is to afford a striking lesson of the inconsistencies naturally produced by so being. Nothing remains the same but their vanity."[43]

In his autobiography, Hunt was to come again to the subject of Wordsworth:

> [Wordsworth] ... had a dignified manner, with a deep and roughish but not unpleasing voice, and exalted mode of speaking. He had the habit of keeping the left hand in the bosom of his waistcoat; and in this attitude, except when he turned round to take one of the subjects of his criticism from the shelves (for his contemporaries were there also) he sat dealing forth his eloquent but hardly catholic judgments.

William Hazlitt wrote:

> Mr Wordsworth, in his person, is above the middle size, with marked features, and an air some what stately and Quixotic. ... He has a peculiar sweetness in his smile, and great depth and manliness and rugged harmony in the tones of his voice. His manner of reading his own poetry is particularly imposing; and in his favourite passages his eye beams with preternatural lustre, and the meaning labours slowly up from his swelling breast. ... In company, even in a *tête-à-tête*, Mr. Wordsworth is often silent, indolent, and reserved. If he is become verbose and oracular of late years, he was not so in his better days. He threw out a bold or an indifferent remark without either effort or pretension, and relapsed into musing again.[44]

John Keats:

> I am sorry that Wordsworth has left a bad impression wherever he visited in town by his egotism, vanity, and bigotry. Yet he is a great poet, if not a philosopher.[45]

In 1797, Wordsworth (then twenty-eight) and Coleridge (twenty-six), were to compile and see to the publication of *Lyrical Ballads*. *Lyrical Ballads* is one of the landmarks in literature, heralding, as it did, the period which we know in literature as English Romanticism. *Lyrical Ballads* was a volume of poetry which opened with Coleridge's magical "Ancient Mariner" and ended with Wordsworth's "Tintern Abbey." Wordsworth's "Tintern Abbey" was of country scenes and people, written in plain language and style; and, as for Coleridge's "The Rime of the Ancient Mariner," – well, it was a tale with a supernatural theme not common to the writings up to that date.[46] The *Lyrical Ballads* was not, by any means, an immediate hit with the public; the first reviews were unenthusiastic and sales were meager.

Wordsworth defined poetry as follows: "Poetry is the breath and finer spirit of all knowledge; the impassioned expression which is in the countenance of all science." For Wordsworth – and the same can also be said of Shelley, Keats, and Coleridge – "Nature is an inexhaustible source and provocative of lovely imaginings. Wordsworth conveys the loneliness of the mountains, Shelley, the tameless energies of wind, Keats the embalmed darkness of verdurous glooms and winding mossy ways, with an intensity which made all other Nature poetry seem pale." Professor Herford continued, "... the poets of English Romanticism had definite limitations. They lacked vision for the world of man, save under certain broad and simple aspects – the patriot, the peasant, the visionary, the child. They lacked understanding of the past, save at certain points on which the spirit of liberty has laid a fiery finger."

The *Lyrical Ballads* were, to Hazlitt, an unaccountable mixture of simple and abstruse poems, at which fools laughed and wise men scarcely understood. And while that was Hazlitt's observation in one essay, in another he was to write that *Lyrical Ballads* contained beautiful work which is most difficult to criticize as it represented a new school, and, as such, could not be compared to any previous standard or theory of poetical excellence. But generally, Hazlitt was of the view that Wordsworth endeavored to "aggrandize the trivial, and add the charm of novelty to the familiar. ... Reserved, yet haughty, having no unruly or violent passions (or those passions having been early suppressed), Mr. Wordsworth has passed his life in solitary musings or daily converse with the face of nature. ... He has dwelt among pastoral scenes ..."[47]

William Hazlitt was tough on Wordsworth, but it should be noted he liked Lord Byron's work even less. Wordsworth's poetry was "pleasing and permanent": Lord Byron's poetry was like that of its creator, possessed of "pomp and pretension." Hazlitt likened Wordsworth's poetry to that of "a vein of ore that one cannot exactly hit upon at the moment, but of which there are sure indications." I quote from "My First Acquaintance with Poets."

> He [Coleridge] lamented that Wordsworth was not prone enough to believe in the traditional superstitions of the place and that there was something corporeal, a-matter-of-fact-ness, a clinging to the palpable, or often to the petty, in his poetry, in consequence. His genius was not a spirit that descended to him through the air; it sprung out of the ground like a flower, or unfolded itself from a green spray, on which the goldfinch sang. He said, however (if I remember right), that this objection must be confined to his descriptive pieces, that his philosophic poetry had a grand and comprehensive

spirit, in it, so that his soul seemed to inhabit the universe like a palace, and to discover truth by intuition, rather than by deduction.

By 1815 – the year in which the *Battle of Waterloo* was to take place – Hazlitt was in full cry. It just so happens, that a draft of Wordsworth's new poem, "Excursion," meant for Charles Lamb in London, fell into Hazlitt's hands. Hardly had the new poem been published, when Hazlitt ripped it up: "The Excursion, we believe, fell still-born from the press. There was something abortive, and clumsy, and ill-judged in the attempt." Hazlitt was not alone in his criticism of Wordsworth. In 1815, Wordsworth's *The White Doe of Rylstone* was published and Jeffrey[48] was to opine, "This has the merit of being the very worst poem we ever saw imprinted in a quarto volume."

What Hazlitt wrote of Wordsworth was not all bad:

> He takes a subject or a story merely as pegs or loops to hang thought and feeling on; the incidents are trifling, in proportion to his contempt for imposing appearances; the reflections are profound, according to the gravity and aspiring pretensions of his mind. ... No storm no shipwreck startles us by its horrors; but the rainbow lifts its head in the cloud, and the breeze sighs through the withered fern. No sad vicissitude of fate, no overwhelming catastrophe in nature deforms his page: but the dew-drop glitters on the bending flower, the tear collects in the glistening eye. ... The vulgar do not read them [Wordsworth's writings]; the learned, who see all things through books, do not understand them; the great despise. The fashionable may ridicule them: but the author has created himself an interest in the heart of the retired and lonely student of nature, which can never die. ... He has described all these objects [of nature] in a way and with an intensity of feeling that no one else had done before him, and has given a new view or aspect of nature. He is in this sense the most original poet now living, and the one whose writings could the least be spared: for they have no substitute elsewhere. ...

> However we may sympathize with Mr. Wordsworth in his attachment to groves and fields, we cannot extend the same admiration to their inhabitants, or to the manners of a country life in general. We go along with him, while he is the subject of his own narrative, but we take leave of him when he makes pedlars and ploughmen his heroes and the interpreters of his sentiments. It is, we think, getting into low company, and company, besides, that we do not like. We take Mr. Wordsworth himself for a great poet, a fine moralist, and a deep philosopher; but if he insists on introducing us to a friend of his, a parish clerk, or the barber of the village, who is as wise as himself, we must be excused if we draw back with some little want of cordial faith.

During the years, 1799-1802, William Hazlitt had made an intimate, soul searching acquaintance with the poetry of Coleridge and Wordsworth. Then, these poets were Hazlitt's heros. This study had succeeded his eventful visit with them in 1798. Hazlitt had walked miles from his home to visit them at Nether Stowey. Hazlitt recognized these two men as being part of the new sensibility, Rousseauish sensibility. Part of the youth movement, who thought that there was something seriously wrong with existing social conventions and that matters ought to be changed: somehow, by somebody. As the years passed, Hazlitt was to continue to hold Coleridge in considerable awe, but like so many of his contemporaries, thought Coleridge had thrown his talents away in favor of drugs. As for Wordsworth: well, Hazlitt was of the view – and he was not alone – that Wordsworth had sacrificed or betrayed his principles for his own private interest. Hazlitt's criticisms of the man cut a wide swath including Wordsworth's political beliefs and his poetry, too. In 1815 – at a time when Hazlitt's grand hero, Napoleon, was absolutely and finally defeated on the field of battle – we see where Hazlitt wrote of Wordsworth:

> He tolerates nothing but what he himself creates ... He sees nothing but himself and the universe. He hates all greatness, and all pretensions to it but his own. His egotism is in this respect a madness; for he scorns even the admiration of himself, thinking it a presumption in any one to suppose that he has taste or sense enough to understand him. He hates all science and all art; he hates chemistry, he hates conchology; he hates Sir Isaac Newton; he hates logic ... he hates all poetry but his own; he hates Shakespeare ... he thinks everything good is contained in the *Lyrical Ballads*, or, if it is not contained there, it is good for nothing; he hates music, dancing, and painting; he hates Rubens, he hates Rembrandt, he hates Raphael, he hates Titian, he hates Vandyke; he hates the antique ... He is glad that Buonaparte is sent to St. Helena, and that the Louvre is dispersed ...[49]

This was hard stuff that was printed for public consumption and had to cut Wordsworth and his friends, terribly. It has to be put in the context of Hazlitt's political opinions, which, were decidedly unpopular, for, "though he had never shared the rhapsodical dreams of Coleridge, the extravagant hopes of Wordsworth, or the petulant sedition of Southey and Landor." Hazlitt was a "Child of the Revolution," a "Champion of Freedom" and the rights of the people. "He followed Bonaparte's career 'like a lover.'" (Birrell.) I am obliged, however, to leave my dissertation on Hazlitt go, to return another day.

Wordsworth admitted that his notions on the subject of government had, for him, changed through the years, and that it should be no surprise that the notions of an enthusiastic youth are different from those of a matured man, one who would take a "profit by reflection." Certainly, Wordsworth was readily able to reflect and to take a profit from the contemporary events in France—the excesses of the revolution and the tyranny of Bonaparte. "To Wordsworth tyranny could be exercised not only by individuals like Bonaparte, but the hydra-headed collective of masses of ignorant, maddened people. He had the born countryman's fear of huge cities – 'For upwards of 30 years the lower orders have been accumulating in pestilential masses of ignorant population.'" (Johnson.)

Hazlitt's main point, however, and a convincing one at that, was this:

> The philosophers, the dry abstract reasoners, submitted to this reverse pretty well, and armed themselves with patience 'as with triple steel,' to bear discomfiture, persecution, and disgrace. But the poets, the creatures of sympathy, could not stand the frowns both of king and people. They did not like to be shut out when places and pensions, when the critic's praises, and the laurel wreath were about to be distributed. They did not stomach being sent to Coventry, and Mr. Coleridge sounded a retreat from them by the help of casuistry and a musical voice. – 'His words were hollow, but they pleased the ear' of his friends of the Lake School, who turned back disgusted and panic-struck from the dry desert of unpopularity, like Hussan the camel-driver,
>
> 'And curs'd the hour, and curs'd the luckless day,
> When first from Shiraz' walls they bent their way.'
>
> They are safely inclosed there. But Mr. Coleridge did not enter with them; pitching his tent upon the barren waste without, and having no abiding place nor city of refuge!' ("Mr. Coleridge.")

The Later Years:

As we have now seen, William Wordsworth was to certainly have his critics, mostly, his fellow writers who were interested in selling their articles to the papers. Generally, though, those in political power and the common people that were to follow along, especially in his later years, all, were to honor Wordsworth. The railway, something that Wordsworth had resisted, at least in respect to the Lake District, was eventually to "run to Windermere, and enthusiasts poured all over his garden." (Burra.)

In 1839, Wordsworth was granted a honorary degree by Oxford, Doctor in Civil Law. With Southey's death, Wordsworth was offered the Laureateship, which, while he at first declined, he was to accept with assurances from the Lord Chamberlain that it was to be but an honor bestowed for past services and that it was not expected he should render any services in the future.

At Wordsworth's age fifty-four, in 1824, the romantic world that he had know was fully behind him. Signs of the new modern age were now about him. New industries were envisioned: railway, gas, steamship, iron, and coal. Companies were being organized for them all, most legitimate but not all. London then experienced a bull market which ran from summer 1824 to autumn 1825. Speculators elbowed in with dreams for sale; a credit crunch and, in turn, an economic disaster followed. In 1827, the first allied peace keeping mission, with Admiral Sir Edward Codrington in charge, sailed into Navrino Bay, Turkey, and on the 20th of October 1827 the *Battle of Navrino* ensued, which while lasting only four hours, took the lives of 8,000 Turks and Egyptians. The allies lost only 178 men. This battle was to be the last of the great sea battles between the square sailed fighting ships. In 1830, there was to be another general election in Britain. The Duke's government was swept away and Earl Charles Grey (1764-1845) came in. It was his task to frighten, persuade and cajole the King, the Lords and the borough-owners into giving up their power; he had only to point to the European continent. In 1832 the *Great Reform Bill* was introduced into parliament, and, upon its passing, power was taken from the landed aristocracy and immediately taken up by the political jobbers.

In September of 1830, Wordsworth made his fourth tour of Scotland during which he was to pay a visit to his literary friend at Abbotsford. Again, I should think, Wordsworth and Scott would commiserate with one another, nodding their heads, expressing their horror of all reform: civil, political or religious. It was to be the last meeting: in 1832 Scott died. Dorothy, the lady, as de Quincey was to observe, who paced by Wordsworth's "side continually through sylvan and mountain tracks, in Highland glens," the lady who "first couched his eye to the sense of beauty" and "humanized him by the gentler charities, and engrafted, with her delicate female touch" and whose graces were to subdue Wordsworth's "ruder growths of his nature"—Dorothy, was now ill. Her illness started in 1829; an illness that was to last many years. All along, Mary Wordsworth was to take loving care of Dorothy.[50] In 1834, Wordsworth was to hear of the deaths of two old friends: Coleridge and Lamb. Three years later, as we mentioned earlier, Wordsworth was to make his last continental tour with his friend Crabb Robinson, including Italy, there to visit the graves of Keats and Shelley. In 1843, Southey died and was buried at Keswick. He had been the Poet Laureate of England since 1813, and with his death, the English government immediately pressed the honor upon Wordsworth. Then there were two events of great importance to Wordsworth's life, which involved his daughter for whom he had a great love: the one in 1841 and the other 1847. I can do no better then to set forth the description given by Edith Morley:

> The poet was not enthusiastic about the proposal that his beloved Dora should wed a middle-aged widower who was also a Roman Catholic and without means. But when he found that her heart was in it, the only stipulation he made was that Quillinan should be in a position to support her. When, four years later, that natural proviso was not met, the poet made the couple an allowance out of his own

small income, and the wedding took place in 1841. By that time Dora's precarious health was already undermined, and she survived her marriage for less than six years, which were chequered by constantly recurring illness. She died in July 1847 [but 43 years of age], and Wordsworth never recovered from the shock. It is pitiful to read in letters to and from Crabb Robinson, and in his journals, of the old man's bursts of grief, his silences, and his inability to settle to any occupation.

Wordsworth remained vigorous through his later years. At 60 years of age, Dorothy was to write, "he is still the crack skater on Rydal Lake, and, as to climbing of mountains, the hardiest and the youngest are yet hardly a match for him." Dorothy was also to write, "In comparison I can perceive no failure, and his imagination seems as vigorous as in youth." However trouble with his eyes limited him and his output of poems dropped accordingly.

William Wordsworth was to die at eighty years of age. Though I dare say the authorities would have readily agreed to place his remains with the rest of the literary lights in the Poets Corner of Westminster Abby – Wordsworth was buried, appropriately, in the small churchyard of Grasmere.

Conclusions:

Paul Johnson:

Wordsworth was not a bookish man. Wordsworth's library was pitifully small; he read the mountains and lakes and his fellow Westmorlanders and Cumbrians. He was absurdly self-centered, vain, narrow in many ways, a little grasping in others, but he was from first to last a local patriot. He nailed his colors to the mast of freedom and independence. He saw the yeoman-farmers of the dales – called, significantly enough, "statesmen" – as essentially free even if they observed a proper respect for grand local families like the Lowthers and deferred to these families' views on national issues. His feeling for the dalesmen made him identify with the Swiss:

that was why Bonaparte's enslavement of the Swiss finally turned Wordsworth against revolutionary republicanism and the aggressive, conquering spirit that went with it.

Whatever one might have to say about Wordsworth's poetry or his politics, one thing is plain: all those who were in close communion with Wordsworth – his neighbors, friends and family – had the highest respect and deepest affection for him. Even his contemporaries gave him due praise. Hazlitt: "His style is vernacular: he delivers household truths. He sees nothing loftier than human hopes, nothing deeper than the human heart. ... [Wordsworth believed in] the healing power of plants and herbs and 'skyey influences,' this is the sole triumph of his art. ... his poetry is founded on setting up an opposition ... between the natural and the artificial..." And, "The current of his feelings is deep, but narrow; the range of his understanding is lofty and aspiring rather than discursive. The force, the originality, the absolute truth and identity, with which he feels some things, makes him indifferent to so many others. The simplicity and enthusiasm of his feelings, with respect to nature, render him bigoted and intolerant in his judgments of men and things."

Wordsworth's poems will live on no matter the observations, then and now: he rather thought they would. Relatively early in his career he was to write Lady Beaumount about the destiny of his poems. They would, Wordsworth's poems, long after his death, console the afflicted and add sunshine to the lives of those who were to take the time to read them. They would "teach the young and the gracious of every age to see, to think, and feel ..."

“Tintern Abbey”
(Last Lines)

If I were not thus taught, should I the more
Suffer my genial spirits to decay:
For thou art with me here upon the banks
Of this fair river; thou my dearest Friend,
My dear, dear Friend; and in thy voice I catch
The language of my former heart, and read
My former pleasures in the shooting lights
Of thy wild eyes. Oh! yet a little while
May I behold in thee what I was once,
My dear, dear Sister! and this prayer I make,
Knowing that Nature never did betray
The heart that loved her; ‘tis her privilege,
Through all the years of this our life, to lead
From joy to joy: for she can so inform
The mind that is within us, so impress
With quietness and beauty, and so feed
With lofty thoughts, that neither evil tongues,
Rash judgments, nor the sneers of selfish men,
Nor greetings where no kindness is, nor all
The dreary intercourse of daily life,
Shall e’er prevail against us, or disturb
Our cheerful faith, that all which we behold
Is full of blessings. Therefore let the moon
Shine on thee in thy solitary walk;

And let the misty mountain-winds be free
To blow against thee: and, in after years,
When these wild ecstasies shall be matured
Into a sober pleasure; when thy mind
Shall be a mansion for all lovely forms,
Thy memory be as a dwelling-place
For all sweet sounds and harmonies; oh! then,
If solitude, or fear, or pain, or grief,
Should be thy portion, with what healing thoughts
Of tender joy wilt thou remember me,
And these my exhortations! Nor, perchance –
If I should be where I no more can hear
Thy voice, nor catch from thy wild eyes these gleams
Of past existence – wilt thou then forget
That on the banks of this delightful stream
We stood together; and that I, so long
A worshipper of Nature, hither came
Unwearied in that service: rather say
With warmer love – Oh! with far deeper zeal
Of holier love. Nor wilt thou then forget,
That after many wanderings, many years
Of absence, these steep woods and lofty cliffs,
And this green pastoral landscape, were to me
More dear, both for themselves and for thy sake!

Samuel Taylor Coleridge
(1772-1834)

Samuel Taylor Coleridge
(1772-1834).

"Wrecked in a Mist of Opium."[1]

In height he might seem to be about five feet eight (he was, in reality, about an inch and a-half taller, but his figure was of an order which drowns the height); his person was broad and full, and tended to corpulence; his complexion was fair; though not what painters technically style fair, because it was associated with black hair; his eyes were large, and soft in their expression; and it was from the peculiar appearance of haze or dreaminess which mixed with their light that I recognised my object. This was Coleridge.[2]

Early Days:

Samuel Taylor Coleridge was the youngest son of the Reverend John Coleridge, the vicar of Ottery St. Mary, a parish in the southern quarter of Devonshire.[3] Coleridge's father had been married twice; by his first wife he had three children and by his second wife he had ten. De Quincey recalls – a situation which might explain much about Coleridge's principal difficulty in life, his addiction to opium – that Coleridge was persecuted by his mother. How this persecution manifested itself, is something that we do not know. This so-called persecution may have been, indeed, but the memory of a correction or chastisement given to a child by a mother occupied in the business of ministering to several young children all at the same time, a correction or chastisement which was misinterpreted by an overly sensitive young mind. In any event, "STC" – as he often referred to himself, "ess-tee-see," – was sent off to dame-school (an elementary school) and kept there until 1778. When STC was ten years old, his father suddenly collapsed and died. A local judge, who had known his father, took a particular interest in the young Coleridge and arranged for him to be interviewed for a position at a prestigious preparatory school in London known as Christ's Hospital. He was thus to become a "Blue coat boy." (The well recognized uniform of the boys from Christ's Hospital was a long blue habit and yellow stockings.) "The discipline at Christ's Hospital in those days was ultra-Spartan, the mood monastic. All domestic ties were to be put aside."[4] It was here, at Christ's Hospital, that Coleridge was to first meet, as a fellow student, Charles Lamb.

In October of 1791, Coleridge was installed at Cambridge (Jesus College) as a sizar.[5] I am not in a position to give details of Coleridge's first two years at Cambridge, hopefully it will be sufficient to write that his heart was not in his studies; further, he ran up bills both with his tutors and with the townspeople. His mounting debts and his looming academic failure were to take a toll on Coleridge, not the least of which was his increasing use of opium to which we will refer, further on. Things became so distressing for Coleridge that he took longer and longer leaves of Cambridge, usually to go to London for the high life. His family was to hear of his situation, his brother in particular. A sum of money was gathered up and sent off to young Coleridge, the principal purpose of which was to pay off the bills that he had run up with his tutors (it would not appear they had much knowledge of the bills which Coleridge had run up in the various shops about town). With money in his pocket, instead of settling up with his creditors, Coleridge took himself off to London, once again, a place Coleridge or no man could tire of. With his money gone, he returned to Cambridge in a situation which was but worse. Creditors pressed him but he had no one to whom he could turn, certainly he thought he had exhausted the patience of his family. During December of 1793, England and France then being at war, Coleridge ran off; and, using a fictitious name, signed up with the 15th, or King's Regiment of Light Dragoons. What possessed Coleridge to become a cavalry soldier, is hard to say. He likely lied about his knowledge of horses; in any event, his officers were soon to know about Coleridge's inexperience in equestrian matters. He proved to be a flop in the army as much as he was a flop at university. He was soon to be more miserable than ever and contrived to get an indirect message to his brother. Arrangements were made. Coleridge, with some difficulty, was bought out of the army; his bills were paid off (I suppose directly this time); and he was delivered back to Cambridge a much chastened man – "rescued, admonished, forgiven, and turned over a new leaf." (Lefebure.)

Coleridge's return to Cambridge occurred in April of 1794. During this second stint at Cambridge, Coleridge is seen to be more industrious – not in pursuing the regular courses, but rather, as so many young men were doing at the time, imbibing revolutionary ideas. These young men, as young men always have, talked long and hard about how society in its existing formation was rotten and dreamt how things might be changed. It was during these times, in June of 1794, that Coleridge was to meet Robert Southey. Southey was enrolled at Oxford and Coleridge was visiting with a fellow student from Cambridge. The two hit it off. Together with other fellow students, the two were soon dreaming of a new society which they hoped they themselves might set up: a pantisocracy.

Pantisocracy:

A pantisocracy, as was dreamt up by Coleridge and Southey, is a societal setup based on the doctrine of aspheterism, viz. that there ought to be no private property. The pantisocrats were devotees of William Godwin. Godwin had brought out his work *Enquiry Concerning the Principles of Political Justice*, or more simply, *Political Justice* in 1793. Godwin foresaw a time when "there will be no war, no crimes, no administration of justice, as it is called, and no government. Besides this, there would be neither disease, anguish, melancholy nor resentment. Every man will seek with ineffable ardour the good of all."

Professor C. H. Herford:

> ... Godwin saw in government, in law, even in property, and in marriage, only restraints upon liberty and obstacles to progress. Yet Godwin was not, strictly speaking, an anarchist. He transfered the seat of government from thrones and parliament to the reason in the breast of every man. On the power of reason, working freely, to convince all the armed unreason of the world and to subdue all its teeming passion, he rested his boundless confidence in the 'perfectibility' of man'—.

Thus Godwin believed it was impossible to be rationally persuaded and not act accordingly, and that therefore, man could live in harmony without law and institutions; he believed in the perfectibility of man. This, of course, is the pantisocracy which Coleridge and Southey felt they could take steps to create. It would be a society of men that would exclude the notion of property rights that in its place was to be "fraternal equality and a participatory government by all, for all." If, the schemers thought, "fear, selfishness, deceit and desultory hatred" could not be eliminated amongst themselves, then, by proper steps, it might be eliminated from their offspring. That being done everything would work just fine and the participants would then lead happy and productive lives. For pantisocracy to work, it was thought, it was necessary that things get started by a collection of individuals dedicated to its principles, isolated from those who might corrupt the system. It was determined that "twelve gentlemen of good education and liberal principles" should embark for America with twelve ladies. They determined, after a year's preparation, that they would set sail for America in April of 1795. Something was to get in the way of these dreams and plans: it was in the delightful forms of the Fricker sisters.

Interrupted Plans: The Fricker Sisters:

We have seen that Coleridge and Southey had first met in June of 1794 through the acquaintance of mutual friends. Coleridge had come over to Oxford on a visit from Cambridge. Upon meeting, the two became fast friends. The intended visit of a couple of days turned into a visit of a couple of weeks as plans were laid for a pantisocracy. On parting the two determined that they would soon meet up again. Coleridge was to make a tour with his Cambridge friends to Wales, the object being to recruit a few new pantisocrats. Southey, with the same object, left for his native Bristol. By August, the two had met up at Bristol, and Southey was soon making the rounds in order to introduce his new Cambridge friend. One of the households visited was that of the Fricker family. This family was headed up by a widow who ran a dress shop in Bristol and consisted of three very attractive older girls, a younger girl and a younger boy.

Southey was already courting one of the Fricker sisters, Edith (1774-1837). His friend Robert Lovell (1770-96) in 1794 married Mary (b.1771). The oldest, Sarah (1770-1845), and Coleridge were almost immediately attracted to one another; a match which Southey was to actively promote. The Fricker sisters were to be the ideal mates envisioned in a pantisocracy. Things were very pleasantly falling into place. Bristol was to be from where the pantisocratic plans were to be finalized and from where the founding members would board a sailing ship for America. An essential beginning was to find some money: none of these young people had any: maybe they could publish certain of their writings, maybe their poetry, maybe a play. In any event, though it would seem he had now formed the attention to make the Bristol area his home base, Coleridge was obliged to leave Bristol in order to take care of certain outstanding matters. So, we would have seen at the first of September in 1794, Coleridge leaving Bristol "to a flutter of Fricker handkerchiefs and the republican salutes of his fellow Pantisocrats." (Lefebure.) He was headed back to his studies at Cambridge via London. Once back in Cambridge a "period of frenetic indecision" was to ensue. He had made commitments to Southey and to Sarah Fricker, but once away from them he was not so sure he should follow through.

More than one of the pantisocrats were to have doubts about whether the envisioned community would ever come into being. Coleridge had his doubts; but really it was Southey who was the first to come out with it, and suggested, instead of going off to America, maybe they could find a farm in Wales and try to establish a community there. But Southey was to soon give up on the idea of pantisocracy all together. The plans of these young men did not much impress Southey's family; it was thought that Robert should go to the ministry, or, if not that, then he should read for the bar. In the meantime, it was suggested, that Robert should take a little time to think about things; he should go to Portugal and have an extended visit with an uncle. Southey agreed. He gave up his ideas of pantisocracy. This decision, however, did not entail giving up his idea of marrying Edith Fricker. The marriage of Robert Southey and Edith Fricker took place in November of 1795, with considerable secrecy, in the parish church of the Fricker family, St Mary Redcliff, Bristol. Immediately after the ceremony Southey departed for Lisbon, alone. But I run ahead of my story.

Last we saw Coleridge, he had left Bristol in August of 1794 to go to Cambridge via London. Coleridge might have well carried on with his studies; but throughout the balance of the year (1794) and into the next, he was to spend as much time in London as anywhere else. It was during this time, it is speculated, that Coleridge was to first meet Wordsworth. There thus began one of the most noteworthy literary collaborations, ever. Throughout these months letters were exchanged with Southey, and Coleridge was to learn that his fellow pantisocrat had lost his enthusiasm in respect to putting himself in an egalitarian colony. Coleridge returned to Bristol: he wanted to face Southey, and, I think, he needed to be with Sarah Fricker.[6] He made his way back to Bristol likely in the early spring of 1795.

The friendship of Coleridge and Southey deteriorated through the winter as their correspondence that winter shows. Indeed, their friendship was pretty much at an end as their arguments became "increasingly fierce and personalised." (Holmes.)

For Coleridge this was a profound shock. He had lost the friend whom he had come to regard as his 'Sheet Anchor.' He wrote with sudden hysteria of Southey's "catalogue of lies," and his low, dirty, gutter-grubbing" compromise with the world. In fact it was this intense emotional clinging, as well as his 'indolence,' which finally repelled Southey and convinced him that Pantisocratic partnership – even farming in Wales – would never work. – Holmes.

That October, the 4th, 1795, Coleridge married Sarah Fricker at the church of St Mary Redcliff, Bristol. Robert Southey was not present; nor was any of Coleridge's family, indeed, a year was to pass before Coleridge brought his wife to visit his family at Ottery. That fall they spent their first happy months in a cottage at Clevedon not far from their family and friends, just west of Bristol. In time, Coleridge was to make his excuses to Sarah on how he would have to spend time away from her (it was to become a regular scene between the two of them) as he had pressing literary business, elsewhere. Initially this literary business was to be conducted in Bristol, however, Coleridge did travel about, often giving talks – making a little money there, a little money here. In such a way he was to come into contact with Tom Poole (1765-1837) who lived at Nether Stowey, a community just south of Bristol. Poole was a literary enthusiast who had inherited from his father a successful tannery business at Nether Stowey. Poole was a well respected member of the community. Poole was charmed by Coleridge.[7] Hearing, I suppose, that the accommodations at Clevedon, a small cottage, was not now to Coleridge's liking, Poole proposed that he could lend to Coleridge and Sarah a cottage just beyond his garden gate. The invitation was taken up, and the Coleridges moved to Nether Stowey. This was to occur in December of 1796. Prior to that, during September of 1796, Sarah was delivered of her first child, a son, Hartley. With this event, given that their wives were sisters, it is seen that Southey and Coleridge were to partially makeup.

By this time, the close of 1796, the dreams of the pantisocrats had come to an end. They had resolved to pass their lives like regular people as opposed to living on a collective commune. Brailsford, in his work in the area, was to make reference to this most famous literary tale:

> It is a tale which every student of literature has delighted to read, how Coleridge and Southey, bent on founding their Pantisocracy, on the banks of the Susquehana, came to Bristol to charter a ship, and whilst they waited, dimly aware that they lacked the funds for the adventure, anchored themselves in English homes by marrying the Fricker sisters.

Wordsworth and Germany (1797-1800):

This collaboration, that of Wordsworth and Coleridge, and the movements of these two poets, especially, are matters which I took up under my treatment of Wordsworth. They may have first met in London during the winter of 1794/1795, of that we cannot be sure. What we do know is that in March of 1797, Wordsworth had traveled with his friend Basil Montagu to Bristol from Racedown (where, then, Wordsworth and his sister were living) and a visit was paid to Coleridge at Nether Stowey. In June of that year Coleridge had returned to Stowey from a visit which he had in turn paid to the Wordsworths. Within days of that, Coleridge had set out once again to Racedown.

On July 2nd, the Wordsworths, at the urging of Coleridge, left Racedown in order to come to Stowey to live. While spending a number of days in the cramped quarters of the Coleridge household, Wordsworth, again with the help of Tom Poole, before July was out, had made arrangements to rent a mansion (Alfoxden) located nearby to Coleridge.

Practically, from their first meeting, the two were discussing their views on poetry. The results of these discussions was momentous for English poetry, for, in 1798, there was published *Lyrical Ballads*, a volume of poetry to which they both had contributed. It opened with Coleridge's magical "Ancient Mariner" and ended with Wordsworth's "Tintern Abbey." It took some time before *Lyrical Ballads* came off the press, indeed, at the time that happened, Coleridge and Wordsworth were in Germany. The book was not, by any means, an immediate hit with the public. One of Coleridge's biographer's, Molly Lefebure, writes: "The first reviews were unenthusiastic and sales were meagre. Wordsworth's poems, upon the whole, were not unkindly treated by the leading reviewers, but "Ancient Mariner" was ill-received. Southey, in the *Critical Review* for October 1798 declared dourly: 'Genius has here been employed in producing a poem of little merit.'"

There now comes a question to be asked, the answer to which requires me to make a short digression. How were Wordsworth and Coleridge, as full time poets, able to live? It was certainly not from the sales of their works, at least, not in these beginning years. Wordsworth, as we might see from the brief sketch made of him, had very fortunately come into some money by way of an inheritance from a school friend, one that was to keep him going for a number of years. As for Coleridge: he had the good fortune of making the acquaintance of the

Wedgwoods. The Wedgwood family, of course, was a family of potters; they had pursued the making of pottery as an art for a number of generations before the lives of the poets of which we write. Josiah Wedgwood (1730-1795) in his turn as the head potter in this old family business, in 1763, patented a cream colored ware, Queen's ware, which became very popular. His designs became know as Wedgwood ware and included his well known blue with the raised designs in white. In 1769 Josiah built a plant at Hanley which was known as "Etruria." It would certainly seem that the family became very rich. Josiah had three sons: John, who became a banker; Josiah, who succeeded his father in the operation of the business; and Thomas, though a chronic invalid, was a dilettante, a supporter of the arts. What is known, is that both John and Tom Wedgwood were to visit the poets, and, in particular, were to spend five days at Alfoxden. They were not so impressed with Wordsworth, indeed they formed a very indifferent opinion of him; but, not so of Coleridge, of him, they were very much impressed. Recognizing that if Coleridge was to be kept at his literary work full time, it would be necessary that he should receive some financial help: the Wedgwoods determined to assist Coleridge in his artistic endeavors.

Coleridge, now with a wife and child to support and another on the way, determined to go to work as a Unitarian minister. His first appointment was at Shrewsbury. He had actually started preaching in Shrewsbury when he received word, in January or February of 1798, from his friends back at Nether Stowey that the Wedgwoods had arranged a life annuity in the amount of £150 per year with no conditions.[8]

Such a gift however was not to keep Coleridge at Nether Stowey, as he longed to travel to Germany for further studies. Doubtlessly these plans were discussed with the Wordsworths and a determination was made; all three would travel together to Germany, once the one year lease of Alfoxden was up, viz. the end of June, 1798. It was during this time, it hardly needs to be mentioned, that the two poets collaborated on their work, *Lyrical Ballads*, the manifesto of English Romanticism.

Before leaving for Germany, Wordsworth and Coleridge saw to the final arrangements in respect to the publication of *Lyrical Ballads*. These arrangements required, for the most part, their attendance at Bristol were a Bristol bookseller, Joseph Cottle (1770-1853) was putting the book through the presses. (They did, during that summer, make a trip to Wales at which time Wordsworth wrote one of his most popular poems, "Tintern Abbey," written on July 13th, 1798.) By late August the party headed for London there to make their final preparations for their trip to Germany. On September 16th, Dorothy and William, together with Coleridge and a friend of theirs, John Chester, set sail for Germany from Yarmouth arriving at Hamburg on the 19th.

I should mention that a few months before Coleridge set off for Germany, a second child was born to the Coleridges, a son, Berkeley, this was during May of 1798. Thus Coleridge was to leave behind, his wife and two small children (two year old Hartley and the infant Berkeley) – just so Coleridge could go study in Germany. Coleridge was to stay in Germany for almost a year coming back to England in July of 1799. He and the Wordsworths did not in fact stay together for long in Germany, the Wordsworths determined to go their separate way within days of their arrival and were to arrive back in England a few months later without Coleridge. While in Germany, Coleridge had acquired a tolerable sufficiency in the German language; further, he was to acquire a permanent bent for German philosophy and criticism. And, while writing his family at regular intervals with expressions of how he so missed them, Coleridge, given his gregariousness, made the rounds visiting all the fashionable places in Germany which included his attendances to a great number of dinners and balls. In his absence, his infant son Berkeley died. Leaving Germany during July of 1799, Coleridge returned to England. I am sure he must have gone down to Nether Stowey to see Sarah and his surviving son, however we soon see where Coleridge was off again. This time to find the Wordsworths, who, just then, were staying at a farm in Yorkshire, Stockton-on-Tees. He arrived at the Hutchinson farm on October 26th. It was then, for the first time, he met the Hutchinson sisters: Mary who was to become Wordsworth's wife and Sara, the younger of the two, who was to become the object of Coleridge's attention for a considerable period of time. By December 19th, however, Coleridge was in London where he took lodgings (21, Buckingham Street). Things were now better with the Coleridges, as we see that Sarah and young Hartley had come to London to be with Coleridge: Sarah was soon pregnant again. In London, Coleridge turned to newspaper work. He wrote for the *Morning Post* making contributions between December 7th, 1799 and April 21st, 1800. He was on the political beat, and, as such, attended at the House of Commons to report on the debates. He also went to the theater in his capacity as a drama critic. During this period, Coleridge was socializing both with the Godwins and the Lambs.

The Lake District (1799-1806):

Coleridge was forever pulled to London, when he was not there; and when there, forever pulled to the countryside. This competition, this pull when at one place to go to another, was not unlike the relationship Coleridge had when it came to the women in his life. He would arrive, having longed to be at home with Sarah, and for days or weeks all would be well, sweetness and happiness, then, he would find himself dreaming of another. And then, soon again he would be off on the top of a coach drawn by horses, soon again to be at another place, a move which would quell his longings – but, only for a little while.[9] He managed in 1800 for a short period of time to combine his two loves, but he never lived long in London with Sarah. Midway through 1800 while at London, Coleridge was struck, once again, with his memories of Wordsworth and of the Lake District; he determined he should return.[10] Coleridge traveled there with Wordsworth a few months after they had gotten back from Germany. Indeed, he was with Wordsworth when they had discovered Dove Cottage. The Lake District, its lakes and the mountains, was where Wordsworth had spent his boyhood, a place which Wordsworth was always talking about. It was the previous autumn, 1799, that Coleridge and Wordsworth had walked west from the Hutchinson farm in the Yorkshire dales, having both just spent some pleasant time with the Hutchinson sisters. They walked along the dales and into the Lake District at a time when the surrounding woods were ablaze. There they made visits to the places of Wordsworth's youth: Brampton, Windermere, Hawkshead, Rydal, and, of course, Grasmere. The day was "soft and grave" when they came to Grasmere, "a purple light lay on the waters, indescribably beautiful. Coleridge spoke of the two lakes as 'divine sisters' ... Coleridge was beginning to understand more fully the tyrannous sublimity of whose hauntings William so often had spoken, the imperious brooding and influences from sun and sky, water and mountain wind, that could make a man their slave." (Maclean.) He left this scene for London, there, to stay with Sarah and their little boy throughout the winter, 1799/1800. He was to find out that Wordsworth and his sister had traveled to Grasmere that past December, there to take up their residence at Dove Cottage. By the spring of 1800, Coleridge could stand it no longer: he took himself to Grasmere.

At the first of March, Sarah, then three months pregnant, had left Coleridge in London intending with little Harley to visit friends at Kempsford. A month later, on April 6th, Coleridge arrived at Dove Cottage. Ostensibly, he had gone to assist Wordsworth in the putting together of the 2nd edition of *Lyrical Ballads*. At this time, too, at the Wordsworths' there was to be found Wordsworth's brother, and, at least, one of the Hutchinson sisters, Mary. By May 4th Coleridge left in order to see the publishers at Bristol. That June, the 29th, Coleridge was back at the Wordsworths' arriving this time with Sarah and Hartley. On July the 23rd, the Coleridges took up residence at Greta Hall, Keswick. That September, a third child (it will be recalled that their second had died) was born to the Coleridges, a son, Derwent.

The domestic regularity which seemed to prevail during the balance of 1800 and for most of 1801 was splintered again by disputes and mutual recriminations, such that Coleridge felt obliged to escape by going to London, there to work for the *Morning Post*. It was during this time, in 1801, in London, Coleridge was to see much of Humphry Davy. In fact he made his first acquaintance of Davy back in 1799, at Bristol. It was when Davy was in charge of a laboratory, known as the Pneumatic Institution, which a Dr. Beddoes had set up. So once again, we see Coleridge leading the life of a bachelor; his residence then was to be found at No. 10, King Street, Covent Garden. In March of 1802, Coleridge returned to the north country, *en route* he was to pay a visit at the new Hutchinson farm at Gallow Hill, his objective being to spend some time with the sisters, Mary and Sara. Sarah Coleridge, when Coleridge was to finally make it back to her at Keswick, was not much impressed by Coleridge's diversions. That year, incidently, on October 4th, William Wordsworth married Mary Hutchinson. The Wordsworths and Coleridge through these years, notwithstanding Coleridge's problems, were to get along famously. During August of 1803 the three of them (Wordsworth, his sister Dorothy and Coleridge) set off for a tour through Scotland. All went well for a couple of weeks, then Coleridge left his companions and returned on foot by himself to his home (Greta Hall) arriving there on September 15th. It seems that it was during this trip that Wordsworth let go at Coleridge for his opium habit.[11] It was the first real rent in the Coleridge/Wordsworth friendship; it was downhill thereafter; by 1812 this rupture was to become "profound and complete."

Within months Coleridge determined that he must leave his family, once again. (He imagined he had health problems; and, I daresay, he did. To Coleridge, his health problems led to an increasing use of opium; in truth his health problems were likely due to his excessive use of opium – we will return to this subject, shortly.) Coleridge arrived in London on January 24th, 1804, having left Grasmere on the 14th. He had expressed to his family[12] and friends that all he needed was a warmer climate for a few months and his health would thereby improve. In this regard, Coleridge was to accept a position as a secretary to Sir Alexander Ball (1757-1809), the Governor of Malta. On March 27th, he set off from London on the Portsmouth mail-ship. He arrived at Malta on May 18th. Thus Coleridge was to be out of England (mostly in Malta) for better than two years.[13] By the spring of 1806, Coleridge was touring Italy with a friend (Thomas Russell). During August, 1806, having fled from Italy in June before Napoleon's triumphant advance, Coleridge returned to England and "threw himself upon that universal refuge, the Lambs."[14] So, in October of 1806, we would have seen at Greta Hall, Sarah Coleridge and the children all joyfully excited at the prospect of seeing Coleridge after his long absence. They were expecting a change in Coleridge; and, maybe, life as a real family would be finally established. Coleridge arrived and the joy and laughter was soon to give way to argument, temper and tears: Coleridge wanted a permanent separation.

Opium Use:

Most people know little of Coleridge's writing. They will know of his "The Rhyme of Ancient Mariner,"and, maybe too, of his "Christabel" or of "Kubla Khan"; but for what Coleridge is most known, is – well, he was a druggy. Coleridge took up the use of opium as a young man; it became a life long addiction. He was by all accounts a brilliant man, a delightful conversationalist; but Coleridge's career, his life, was ruined by the use of opium. His opium habit was a misery to him and to his friends. His addiction meant that "his existence became a never-ending squalor of procrastination, excuses, lies, debts, degradation, failure." (Lefebure.)

Opium use in English society in the 19th-century was completely acceptable when it was used at a time a person was in a painful circumstance, such as when suffering from a tooth ache. Most all households had a bottle of laudanum, viz. opium dissolved in alcohol. No one thought ill of a person for keeping such a remedy handy or using it on occasion.[15] The local chemists would prepare their own favorite medical potions, and there indeed was a variety of ingredients; but always there was added a liberal dose of opium.

> There were nationally famous and long-established preparations like Dover's Powder, that mixture of ipecacuanha and powdered opium originally prescribed for gout ... An expanding variety of commercial preparations began to come on the market at mid-century [18th]. They were typified by the chlorodynes – Collis Browne's, Towle's and Freeman's. The children's opiates like Godfrey's Cordial and Dalby's Carminative were long-established. They were everywhere to be bought. There were local preparations, too like Kendal Black Drop, popularly supposed to be four times the strength of laudanum – and well known outside its own locality because Coleridge used it.[16]

An understanding of the wide spread use of opium will lead one to conclude that it was not the mere use of opium that lead to Coleridge's ruin but rather his extensive and continuous use of the stuff. Keats, Byron, Shelley, Scott: they all took it, laudanum, off and on. Bristol, at the close of the 18th-century, was at the center of a luminous drug circle revolving around a Dr. Beddoes, who had among his patients: Tom Wedgwood; James MacIntosh; Charles

Lloyd; and, of course, Coleridge. The writer Thomas de Quincey was as much known for his drug use as anyone else, but it did not take the same toll on him as it did on Coleridge. De Quincey freely made reference to his usage of drugs, and, in his *Recollections*, tells how Coleridge got hooked:

> ... a toothache had obliged me [de Quincey] to take a few drops of laudanum. At what time or on what motive he had commenced the use of opium, he [Coleridge] did not say; but the peculiar emphasis on horror with which he warned me against forming a habit of the same kind, impressed upon my mind a feeling that he never hoped to liberate himself from the bondage my belief is that he never did.

Coleridge's Writings:

That Coleridge was able to produce such literary works as he did, notwithstanding his life's problems, was due to a natural talent that at times came to the surface of his drug induced hazes, a natural talent that was undoubtedly developed early during his days at Grammar School. As has been mentioned, Coleridge attended a school at London known as Christ's Hospital. At that time there was a Head Master by the name of the Reverend James Bowyer. Coleridge wrote of him in *Biographia Literaria*:

> He would often permit our exercises, under some pretext of want of time, to accumulate, till each lad had four or five to look over. Then placing the whole number *abreast* on his desk, he would ask the writer, why this or that sentence might not have found as appropriate a place under this or that other thesis: and if no satisfying answer could be returned, and two faults of the same kind were found in one exercise, the irrevocable verdict followed, the exercise was torn up, and another on the same subject to be produced, in addition to the tasks of the day. ... He sent us to the University excellent Latin and Greek scholars, and tolerable Hebraists. Yet our classical

knowledge was the least of the good gifts, which we derived from his zealous and conscientious tutorage.[17]

Coleridge contribution, only contribution to *Lyrical Ballads*, was that work for which Coleridge will ever be remembered, "The Rhyme of the Ancient Mariner."[18] By March of 1801, Coleridge had lost much of his confidence. In a letter to Godwin, dated March 1801, Coleridge wrote, "The poet is dead in me, My imagination ... lies like the cold snuff on the circular rim of a candlestick." In July of 1802 he wrote to Southey, "All my poetic genius ... is gone."[19] Besides his "Ancient Mariner," I suppose, the other works of which we must make note is "Christabel" and "Kubla Khan." All of these works, these poems, were casted with exotic and/or supernatural themes. I set forth a few lines for a taste:

"Ancient Mariner":

The ship was cheered, the harbor cleared,
Merrily did we drop
Below the kirk, below the hill,
Below the lighthouse top, (pt. I, st. 6.) ...
The fair breeze blew, the white foam flew,
The furrows followed free;
We were the first that ever burst
Into that silent sea. (pt. II, st. 5.) ...
Water, water, everywhere,
Nor any drop to drink. (pt. II, st. 9.) ...
Alone, alone, all, all alone;
Alone on a wide, wide sea., (pt. IV, st. 3.) ...
Oh sleep! it is a gentle thing,
Beloved from pole to pole. (pt. V, st. 1.) ...
Like one that on a lonesome road
Doth walk in fear and dread,
And having once turned round walks on,

And turns no more his head;
Because he knows a frightful fiend
Doth close behind him tread. (pt. VI, st. 10.)

"Kubla Khan":

In Xanadu did Kubla Khan
A stately pleasure dome decree:
Where Alph, the sacred river, ran
Through caverns measureless to man
Down to a sunless sea.
So twice five miles of fertile ground
With walls and towers were girdled round.

"Christabel":

And the spring comes slowly up this way. (pt. I, l. 22.) ...
The one red leaf, the last of its clan,
That dances as often as dance it can. (pt. I, l. 49.) ...
And constancy lives in realms above;
And life is thorny; and youth is vain;
And to be wroth with one we love
Doth work like madness in the brain. (pt. II, l. 410)

Coleridge's Philosophy:

John Stuart Mill thought Coleridge to be one of "the two great seminal minds" of early 19th-century England, the other being Bentham; though, unlike Bentham, Coleridge "asserted the primacy of the transcendent imagination."

William Hazlitt:

All his [Coleridge's] ideas ... are like a river, flowing on forever, and still murmuring as it flows, discharging its waters and still replenished –

And so by many nooks it strays,
With willing sport to the wild ocean![20]

The philosopher which had the greatest impact on Coleridge was David Hartley (1705-57). Hartley, an English philosopher, was educated at Jesus College, Cambridge, and became a fellow; it will be recalled that Coleridge went there during the years 1791-4. George Berkeley (1685-1753) also had a significant impact on Coleridge's thought, especially in the earlier years.[21] At another point in his life, Coleridge delved into the philosophy of the Dutch philosopher, Spinoza.

"It was early in the year, 1801, that the intellect of Kant first took hold of him [Coleridge], as he significantly expresses it, with 'giant hands'."[22] In Kant's system, we are but only able to comprehend observable phenomena and this was but parts of an interconnected whole that cannot be comprehended by the human mind. As Coleridge put it: the universe of which we are conscious is but "merely a mass of little things." Now, I shall observe, by way of commentary, that the view that we as humans are capable of only comprehending but parts of the universe, may be perfectly correct. The difficulty is met when we see people going about filling in the blanks out of their pure imaginations and thus to proceed to build "castles in the air" which the rest of us are unable to falsify. As for Coleridge, it is almost needless to add, his imagination was fueled by opium.

Years of Bondage (1808-16):

We may mark the time just after Coleridge came back from Germany as the time when Coleridge was to permanently separate from his wife and children. After that time he was to go back to Grasmere, but only for visits with his family, or, more likely, long stay-overs with the Wordsworths. In June of 1808, the Wordsworths had moved into their new home, Allan Bank at Grasmere, a much larger place than their previous abodes. One of the reasons that the Wordsworths made the move was that they anticipated that Coleridge might come to live with them; and apparently he did. During the weekends Allan Bank was to become a very busy place, indeed. At times there was as many as seven children: three Coleridges (down on a visit with their father) and four Wordsworths. Living there, in addition, was Sara Hutchinson to whom Coleridge was particularly attracted. It would appear that Sara Hutchinson was part of the Wordsworth household at this time. It will be recalled that her sister Mary, married Wordsworth the previous year. Sara Hutchinson was to remark that when Coleridge played with the children, STC made "enough racket for twenty." (Lefebure.)

It was during this period that Coleridge brought out a weekly paper, *The Friend*, the first of its number was dated June 1st, 1809; and the last, after 27 editions, March 15th, 1810. He apparently continued to work out of the Wordsworth residence and likely went up to Greta Hall, nine miles away or so, in order to pick up or deliver his three children. In February, Sara Hutchinson took her leave of the Wordsworth household at Allan Bank. That June, fond of his comforts (the Wordsworth household, apparently, was usually in a bit of a rough state, though it never bothered them), especially now since Sara Hutchinson had left, Coleridge took his leave of Allan Bank. He moved back in with his wife at Greta Hall, but this particular period of cohabitation lasted but five months. In October Coleridge took advantage of an offer coming from Basil Montagu and his wife who were just then visiting the Lake District. Seeing how unhappy Coleridge was, the Montagues offered to him a seat in their carriage and thus to come to London with them and once there to reside with them. Given the domestic habits of these two very different people (Montagu would not even countenance the use of wine at his table) the arrangement of Coleridge living with the Montagues in London did not last long; the Montagues and Coleridge parted company almost immediately. We know that on April 15, 1816, Coleridge moved in with Dr. Gillman and lived there for the balance of his life. Prior to moving in with the Gillmans, between the years 1812-16, Coleridge, this eccentric man of genius, mostly resided with the Morgans, whom he had known in Bristol. They first resided near Bath then later at Calne, Wiltshire. He got on better with the Morgans, mainly because the Morgans were so patient with Coleridge; "it would probably be no exaggeration to say that without their devoted friendship and support he could not have survived."[23]

There is another thing to be said about the carriage trip that Coleridge took with Basil Montagu in the fall of 1810 *en route* to London. Though we will never know exactly what transpired, Coleridge in his conversations with Montagu determined that Wordsworth was bad-mouthing him (Coleridge) behind his back. Problems, as we have seen, started back in 1803 when the pair of them with Dorothy had made a trip to Scotland; now, in 1810, this rent turned into an open breach. Over the next two years, the quarrel between the two poets became a *cause célèbre*.

All through these times Coleridge supported himself both by lecturing and writing. On April 15th, 1816, as already mentioned, Coleridge took up residence in Highgate, London, at the home of Dr. James Gillman.

It was intended that Coleridge should receive extended medical help in respect to his long-standing opium addiction; it was to be a last ditch effort. Gillman, in exchange for the pleasure of his company – Coleridge could be most charming and intellectually engaging – was to somehow wean Coleridge off of his opium habit, well, if not off the drug altogether then, more likely, down to timed and manageable doses. The plan was that Coleridge was to stay with Gillman for a month; he stayed with Gillman until his death in 1834.[24]

Conclusions:

In analyzing the character of Coleridge in the first part of his essay, "Mr. Coleridge," William Hazlitt, as he so often did, put his finger immediately on the point. The point is that the making of a good work, does not depend on genius, but it most certainly depends on a disconnected consciousness focused on the job at hand. "It is hard to concentrate all our attention and efforts on one pursuit, except from ignorance of others; and without this concentration of our faculties no great progress can be made in any one thing." Hazlitt, in the latter part of his essay deals with this point in greater length, and applied it to Coleridge. Hazlitt compared Coleridge to one of the literary lights of that age, William Godwin.

> No two persons can be conceived more opposite in character or genius ... Mr. Godwin, with less natural capacity and with fewer acquired advantages, by concentrating his mind on some given object, and doing what he had to do with all his might, has accomplished much, and will leave more than one monument of a powerful intellect behind him; Mr. Coleridge, by dissipating his, and dallying with every subject by turns, has done little or nothing to justify to the world or to posterity the high opinion which all would have ever heard him converse, or known him intimately, with one accord

entertain of him. Mr. Godwin's faculties have kept at home, and plied their task in the workshop of the brain, diligently and effectually: Mr. Coleridge's have gossiped away their time, and gadded about from house to house, as if life's business were to melt the hours in listless talk. Mr. Godwin is intent on a subject, only as it concerns himself and his reputation; he works it out as a matter of duty, and discards from his mind whatever does not forward his main object as impertinent and vain.

Mr. Coleridge, on the other hand, delights in nothing but episodes and digressions, neglects whatever he undertakes to perform, and can act only on spontaneous impulses without object or method. 'He cannot be constrained by mastery.' While he should be occupied with a given pursuit, he is thinking of a thousand other things: a thousand tastes, a thousand objects tempt him, and distract his mind, which keeps open house, and entertains all comers; and after being fatigued and amused with morning calls from idle visitors [he] finds the day consumed and its business unconcluded. Mr. Godwin, on the contrary, is somewhat exclusive and unsocial in his habits of mind, entertains no company but what he gives his whole time and attention to, and wisely writes over the doors of his understanding, his fancy, and his senses –'No admittance except on business.' He has none of that fastidious refinement and false delicacy, which might lead him to balance between the endless variety of modern attainments. He does not throw away his life (nor a single half hour of it) in adjusting the claims of different accomplishments, and in choosing between them or making himself master of them all. He sets about his task (whatever it may be), and goes through it with spirit and fortitude. He has the happiness to think an author the greatest character in the world, and himself the greatest author in it.

Mr. Coleridge, in writing an harmonious stanza, would stop to consider whether there was not more grace and beauty in a *Pas de trois*, and would not proceed till he had resolved this question by a chain of metaphysical reasoning without end. Not so Mr. Godwin. That is best to him, which he can do best. He does not waste himself in vain aspirations and effeminate sympathies. He is blind, deaf, insensible to all but the trump of Fame. Plays, operas, painting, music, ball-rooms, wealth, fashion, titles, lords, ladies, touch him not. All these are no more to him than to the magician in his cell, and he writes on to the end of the chapter through good report and evil report. *Pingo in eternitatem* is his motto. He neither envies nor admires what others are, but is contented to be what he is, and strives to do the utmost he can. Mr. Coleridge has flirted with the Muses as with a set of mistresses: Mr. Godwin has been married twice, to Reason and to Fancy, and has to boast no short-lived progeny by each. – *The Spirit of the Age*.

Just after he first got to know Coleridge, during the winter of 1810, Henry Crabb Robinson wrote in his diary:

It was after my first day's sitting with him that I wrote thus to my brother: He kept me on the stretch of attention and admiration from ½ past 3 till 12 o'clock. On politics, metaphysics and poetry, more especially on the Regency, Kant, and Shakespeare he was astonishingly eloquent. But I have made one remark on him: tho' he practises all sorts of delightful tricks and shews admirable skill in riding his hobbies, yet he may be easily unsaddled. I was surprised to find how easy it is to obtain from him concessions which lead to gross inconsistencies. Tho' an incomparable declaimer and speech-maker, he has neither the readiness nor the acuteness required by a colloquial disputant, so that with a sense of inferiority that makes me humble in his presence, I do not feel in the least afraid of him. Rough said yesterday that he is sure he would never have succeeded at the bar even as a speaker. – This I wrote after the first sight of him. I used afterwards to compare him as a disputant with a serpent – easy to kill if you assume the offensive, but if you let him attack, his bite is mortal. Some years after this, when I saw Mme de Staël in London, I asked her what she thought of him. That, she replied, he is very great in monologue, but he has no idea of dialogue

Robinson was to make this observation on Coleridge's lecturing technique, one that was more of a general observation of Coleridge, viz. Coleridge had a splendid intellect but it was "vitiated by want of method and concentration."

Colerige's lectures do high honour to him as a man of genius, but are discreditable to him (perhaps I might use without injustice a stronger word) as a man who has a duty to discharge; for either he wants judgment to know what he ought to introduce in his lectures, or is overpowered by very culpable indolence and will not qualify himself to do justice to his subject, his hearers or himself. His pretended lectures are unmethodical rhapsodies, moral, metaphysical and literary; abounding in brilliant thoughts, fine flashes of rhetoric, occasionally profound and salutary truths, but they are not a scientific or constructive course of reading on any one subject a man can wish to fix his attention on.

Robinson compares Wordsworth to Coleridge:

One I believe the greatest man now living in this country and the other a man of astonishing genius and talents, though not harmoniously blended as in his happier friend to form a great and good man.[25]

From de Quincey's *Literary Reminiscences*:

Coleridge, as is notorious, whenever he happened to be in force, or even in artificial spirits, was even more than brilliant; to use a word too often abused and prostituted, he was even magnificent beyond all human standards; had a felicitous conversational specimen from him, was sometimes the most memorable chapter in a man's whole intellectual experience through life.

Hazlitt:

This gentleman [Coleridge] belongs to the class of eclectic philosophers; but whereas they professed to examine different systems, in order to select what was good in each, our perverse critic ransacks all past or present theories, to pick out their absurdities, and to abuse whatever is good in them. ... He refers the great excellence of the British Constitution to the prerogatives of the Crown, and conceives that the old French Constitution must have been admirably defended by the States-General, which never met, from the abuses of arbitrary power. He highly approves of *ex-officio* informations and special juries, as the great bulwarks of the liberty of the press; taxes he holds to be providential relief to the distresses of the people and war to be state of greater security than peace. He defines Jacobinism to be an abstract attachment to liberty, truth, and justice; and finding that this principle has been abused or carried to excess, he argues that Anti-jacobinism, or the abstract principles of despotism, superstition, and oppression, are the safe, sure and undeniable remedy for the former, and the only means of restoring liberty, truth, and justice in the world. ... He judges of men as he does of things. He would persuade you that Sir Isaac Newton was a money-scrivener, Voltaire dull, Bonaparte a poor creature, and the late Mr. Howard a misanthrope; while he plays a willing homage to the Illustrious Obscure, of whom he always carries a list in his pocket. He is at cross-purposes with himself as well as others, and discards his own caprices if ever he suspects there is the least ground for them. Doubt succeeds to doubt, clouds rolls over cloud, one paradox is driven out by another still greater, in endless succession. He is equally averse to the prejudices of the vulgar, the paradoxes of the learned, or the habitual convictions if his own mind. He moves in an unaccountable diagonal between truth and falsehood, sense and nonsense, sophistry and common-place, and only assents to any opinion when knows that all the reasons are against it. A matter of fact is abhorrent to his nature: the very air of truth repels him. He is only saved from the extremities of absurdity by combining them all in his own person. Two things are indispensable to him – to set out from no premises, and to arrive at no conclusion. The consciousness of a single certainty would be an insupportable weight upon his mind. He slides out of a logical deduction by the help of metaphysics: and if the labyrinths of metaphysics did not afford him "ample scope and verge enough," he would resort to necromancy and the cabala. He only tolerates the science of astronomy for the sake of its connection with the dreams of judicial astrology, and escapes from the *Principia* of Newton to the jargon of Lily and Ashmole. All his notions are floating and unfixed, like what is feigned of the first form of things flying about in search of bodies to attach themselves to; but his ideas seek to avoid all contact with solid substances. Innumerable evanescent thoughts dance before him, and dazzle his sight, like insects in the evening sun. Truth is to him a ceaseless round of contradictions: he lives in the belief of a perpetual lie, and in affecting to think what he pretends to say. His mind is in a constant state of flux and reflux: he is like the Sea-horse in the Ocean; he is the Man in the Moon, the Wondering Jew. – The reason of all this is that Mr. Coleridge has great powers of thought and fancy, without will or sense. He is without a strong feeling of the existence of any thing out of himself; and he has neither purposes nor passions of his own to make him wish it to be. All that he does or thinks is involuntary; even his perversity and self-will are so. – *Political Essays.*

We have seen where on April 15th, 1816, Coleridge moved into the London home of Dr. James Gillman. This was done so that Gillman might help Coleridge with his long-standing opium addiction. With help from the Gillmans, Coleridge became at least stabilized, such that he was finally able to get certain of his works into print.[26] In 1816, Murray published three of Coleridge's works: *Chrisabel*, *Kubla Khan*, and *The Pains of Sleep*. It came out as one, a 64 page pamphlet. In 1817, *Biographia Literaria* was published. In 1825, his *Aids to Reflection* came out. Friends, both new and old came to pay visits to Coleridge at the Gillman residence. It would not appear that he traveled much beyond that point where Dr. Gillman could not keep an eye on him. As already mentioned, Coleridge in 1828, then 56 years old, did get together with Wordsworth and Wordsworth's daughter Dora, the three taking a tour of the Rhine. By 1832, however, Coleridge's health was in a serious state. It was then that Robinson made a note in his diary that Coleridge was "horribly bent and looked seventy years of age." On July 25th, 1834, Coleridge died.[27] His Epitaph, which he wrote himself, reads as follows:

Beneath this sod
A poet lies, or that which once seemed he
Oh, lift a thought in prayer for STC!
That he, who many a year, with toil of breath,
Found death in life, may here find life in death.

The image that we are left with is that, though possessed of a brilliant intellect, Coleridge was a person without a will who abandoned himself to his drug addiction at the expense of his family and friends, and possibly the literary world, as he wrote little of importance beyond his earlier works.

> His usual tearing high spirits, enormous charm, beautiful manners, inherent sweetness of nature goodness of heart, dazzling conversation, over-whelming intellectual capacity and vast erudition made it seem incredible that this gifted 'Heaven-eyed creature' should possess feet of a substance not so much resembling clay, as pulp.
>
> – Lefebure.

For people who write such things, they live their life almost to the end then write their biography. For Coleridge, he first wrote his biography in the form of his epic poem, "Ancient Mariner," then he lived it.

Alone, alone, all, all alone,
Alone on the wide wide sea!
And never a saint took pity on
My soul in agony.
The many men, so beautiful!
And they all dead did lie:
And a thousand thousand slimy things
Liv'd on; and so did I.

Percy Bysshe Shelley

(1792-1822)

Percy Bysshe Shelley
(1792-1822).

"I had rather not have
my hopes and illusions
mocked by sad realities."[1]

Thorton Hunt, who had met Shelley, wrote:

> [Shelley was an heir] to fortune and title, while yet a boy he revolted against tyranny, dogma, and falsehood, so openly and uncompromisingly that his family disowned him as far as it might, society looked askance at him, and only they welcomed him who were at issue with the dominant idolatry of that period, now passed away. ... and refusing a family condonation, a seat in Parliament, and higher honours in prospect, he sought his life in poetry made real; wedding the daughter and intellectual heiress of *Political Justice*, and literally leading her clear mind into his own path of classic study and exalted speculation. As he advanced towards its midst he drew around him men older in years, more trained in the world; and more accustomed to embody their thoughts in definite aims, whether of social action or worldly success.
>
> – As quoted by Blunden, *Leigh Hunt and his Circle.*

In about the year 1816, Horace Smith paid a visit to the twenty-four year old Shelley who was just then starting to make a reputation for himself. Smith described Shelley as follows:

> I beheld a fair, freckled, blue-eyed, light-haired, delicate-looking person, whose countenance was serious and thoughtful, whose stature would have been rather tall had he carried himself upright; whose earnest voice, though never loud, was somewhat unmusical. Manifest as it was that his preoccupied mind had no thought to spare for the modish adjustment of his fashionably made

clothes, it was impossible to doubt even for a moment that you were gazing upon a *gentleman*, ... one that is gentle, generous, accomplished, brave.

— As quoted by Blunden, *Shelley, A Life Story*.

Childhood:

Sir Bysshe Shelley (1731-1815) was known as a rich old eccentric. He was one of three boys[2] born in the American colonies, New Jersey. The family moved back to England, Sussex, when Bysshe was only a boy. Getting a good start from his family and marrying well, Bysshe became a rich and influential man. From his first marriage there was produced a son. (Bysshe was married at least twice and had a number of offspring.) This son was Timothy (1753-1844), our poet's father. Timothy went up to Oxford, where in 1778 he was awarded his Bachelor's and in 1781 his Master's. After Oxford, Timothy studied law as a student at Lincoln's Inn. Shelley's biographer, Edmund Blunden, deduced that Timothy was "a steady, punctilious young man." (*Shelley* ... .) In 1790, Timothy became the Member of Parliament for Horsham. In October of 1791, Timothy married Elizabeth Pilfold and the couple moved into one of the Shelley estates, Field Place, Warnham, located 40 miles from London. On August 4th, 1792, there was born to the couple their first child, Percy Bysshe.[3]

Shelley, to use Blunden's words, was "brought up in the air of riches and responsibility and the confidence that wishes can be fulfilled ..." After attending a preparatory school (Sion House Academy), in 1804, he was enrolled at Eton. There, he received a sound training in the classics of ancient Greece and Rome. His belief "that wishes can be fulfilled" when fitted together with the grounding that he received in classical myth and mystery will maybe give the reader a better understanding of the poetry which Shelley came to write.[4]

Oxford:

In 1810, the father brought the son to his *Alma Mater*, Oxford. Timothy was pleased with the prospects of his eldest; he had no idea of the difficulties ahead. Blunden wrote:

> Calling on the son of his old boarding-house-keeper, Mr. Shelley found that another son whom he had known was now in business as a bookseller; he marched off with Bysshe to the shop and ordered him to buy his books and stationary there. The handsome shop was almost opposite University College. To Henry Slatter and his partner he said, 'My son here has a literary turn; he is already an author, and do pray indulge him in his printing freaks.'

Shelley was soon settled in at Oxford. His rooms were located "in the south-west corner of the principal quadrangle." A fellow student, Thomas Jefferson Hogg, of whom we shall shortly hear more, wrote of these rooms:

> Books, boots, papers, shoes, philosophical instruments [we would call them scientific, these days], clothes, pistols, linen, crockery, ammunition, and phials innumerable, with money, stockings, prints, crucibles, bags and boxes, were scattered on the floor and in every place ... An electrical machine, an air-pump, the galvanic trough, a solar microscope, and large glass jars and receivers, were conspicuous amidst the mass of matter..
>
> – Blunden, *Shelley, A Life Story*.

Hogg also gave us a picture of the young of Shelley:

> His clothes were expensive ... but they were tumbled, rumpled, unbrushed. His gestures were abrupt, and sometimes violent,

> occasionally even awkward, yet more frequently gentle and graceful. ... His features, his whole face, and particularly his head, were, in fact, unusually small; yet the last appeared of a remarkable bulk, for his hair was long and bushy, and in fits of absence, and in the agonies (if I may use the word) of anxious thought, he often rubbed it fiercely with his hands, or passed his fingers quickly through his locks unconsciously, so that it was singularly wild and rough.[5]

Notwithstanding Shelley's possession of "philosophical instruments," in the days under review, it is not likely that Oxford was a place where intensive scientific investigation was carried out in respect to the natural world. It was still very much an educational institution under the strictures of religion. Every student, in order to gain admission, was obliged to sign the Thirty-nine Articles of the Church of England. Robert Southey observed that "Oxford is a school for divinity, and for nothing else." The religious propensity of the times, as was fully reflected at Oxford, proved to be the rock which Shelley ran up upon.[6]

Within months of his arrival at Oxford, during the Christmas vacation Shelley delivered to his printers "a short specimen of logic" which bore the title "The Necessity of Atheism." It was printed up as a pamphlet and nowhere did the writer's name appear. To write and publish such a work, denying the existence of God, at the first of the 19th-century, was inevitably to bring on trouble. This was especially so, since, to make a lark out of it, Shelley sent a copy of the pamphlet to everybody who was anybody at Oxford. He also sent a copy to every bishop in England. Though by reading the work no one could tell who wrote it, apparently Shelley made no secret of its authorship to his friends; soon it got around to the administrators of the university that the work was that of young Shelley. On March 25th of that year (1811), a meeting of the overseers was convened and Shelley was asked to appear before them. Shelley was given the chance to deny that the work was his; he refused to give it or to answer any of the questions put to him. It was, as Blunden pointed out, a "conflict of traditions and tempers." (*Shelley* ... .) A bitter decision was made then and there: Shelley was expelled from Oxford. Thomas Jefferson Hogg, Shelley's student friend, much to his credit, took sides and supported his friend. Hogg, knowing that Shelley was at the meeting, got a message through to the university officers that he wished to appear before them directly Shelley should leave the room. After being invited in he proceeded to tell the officers that should they expel Shelley, they should expel him as well. They obliged Hogg and sent both of the boys packing. The next day, Shelley and Hogg took the coach to London.

One can but imagine what the family thought about these developments. Their blond-haired boy expelled from Oxford? It most certainly must have been on account of the influence of his friends, bad friends, and in particular Mr. Hogg, who was now living with Shelley at London. A message was sent to Shelley. It offered condolences and a suggestion that he take some time off and go on a voyage through the Greek Islands, then, presumably after such a change and rest, he might once again take up his studies. There was, however, a condition, he could not take Mr. Hogg along with him. Shelley refused the offer. Then his father suggested he should come home to Field Place and there he might be put into "the care and society" of a gentleman tutor, a person to be picked by his father. Shelley also refused this offer. Shelley was now fixed in his political belief that the power in the country lay in the hands of those who are most distinguished by birth, fortune, or of a privileged order such as those associated with the Church of England. Shelley had rebuked the latter and was expelled from Oxford; he now rebuked his family, one of high birth and good fortune. Shelley, having spurned his father's advances, was cast out of the family as he was out of Oxford; he was thereafter to be on his own. Shelley never was to change his political beliefs and was never to be reconciled to his family.

Harriet:

Harriet Westbrook was the daughter of a retired coffee house proprietor. Her family lived in London. Harriet attended the same school (at Clapham) as did certain of Shelley's sisters. No matter that Shelley was shut out of his father's house, his sisters would come to London to see their older brother and likely during school holidays they would go along to the Westbrooks. One of these intended visits, for whatever reason, did not come off; so, the sisters asked Shelley if he would bring a present to Harriet. Thus Shelley was to meet Harriet. The young couple were soon making plans for marriage. The two – she was only sixteen and he nineteen – with the help of an uncle, went off to Scotland. At Edinburgh, on August 28th, 1811, Shelley and Harriet were married.[7] However pleased they were that their Harriet married into such a distinguished family, the Westbrooks, devote Methodists, were taken aback by Shelley's declared atheism. In the meantime, back at Field Place the family were now quite convinced that their first born had gone mad: communications between Shelley and the family were all relayed through the family lawyer.

Shelley was restless and infected with wanderlust; it came on immediately with his marriage and lasted throughout his life. It was impossible for him to settle down in any one place for long; he led a nomadic life. After leaving Edinburgh the couple spent time with his old university friend Tom Hogg who was then at York.[8] After a short stay at York they were off to Keswick and with some help from Southey they moved into rental accommodations. Then, in February of 1812, they were off to Ireland. Shelley had decided to help the Irish people. In another of his "printing freaks," Shelley wrote a piece, "Address to the Irish People" and made it into a pamphlet; he then proceeded to scatter 4,000 of them throughout Dublin. What the Irish people needed, so Shelley wrote, was "Catholic Emancipation" and "the restoration of the old liberties and happiness of Ireland." Leaving Ireland in April of 1812, the couple went back to England via Wales. By June, the couple were living at Lynmouth in a cottage with "roses on the walls, a thatched roof, a sea view [and] a screen of mountains." (Blunden, *Shelley ....*) It was during this time that Shelley wrote *Queen Mab*.[9] It would not appear that the couple remained long at Lynmouth, for, by November of 1812, following up on the letters he sent earlier in the year, Shelley was making extended visits to the Godwin household in London.

Napoleonic Background:

These were historically interesting times. In May of 1812, the British prime minister, Perceval was assassinated. Lord Liverpool succeeded him. Liverpool appointed Lord Castlereagh as the Foreign Secretary, and, as such, became the soul of the coalition against Napoleon who had been waging war on most all of his European neighbors, including Great Britain, since 1793. In the early part of this 23 year long war with Napoleon, Britain's policy, up to 1801, "was twofold: it was a naval policy and a policy of subsidy." (Rosebery.) The money spent on her navy paid handsome dividends. Britain kept its position as an international trader and turned the island nation into a financial powerhouse. And though there were real worries that Napoleon might cross the channel[10] and get at them, those worries melted away like a dream when Lord Nelson and his captains destroyed both the Spanish and French fleets at Trafalgar in 1805. However, in that same year, the *Battle of Austerlitz* took place (Austerlitz is a place located in modern day Czechoslovakia) which ended up with Napoleon having decisively defeated the armies of Russia and Austria, each with its emperor at its head. A decisive point in this long war with Napoleon came when, in support of a Spanish rising, during July of 1808, Arthur Wellesley (later to become known as the Duke of Wellington) led the first small British force of 9,000 men into the Peninsula of Spain, a gateway into the hostile fortress of Napoleonic Europe. Up to this point all that Britain sent was money, and lots of it, to its allies such as Austria. In August of 1808, Wellesley defeated the French under Junot at Vimeiro. Finally, the people of Great Britain and those of Europe were to understand that the French armies of Napoleon were not invincible. Though Wellington met with some success in Spain, Britain at that point (1808) had established but a toehold on Napoleonic Europe; there were years of fighting to come. Indeed, it is one of the great questions of history as to whether Napoleon would have ever been overcome by his enemies had it not been for his one big mistake –

invading the vast northern territory of Russia. By the winter of 1812/13, news came of Napoleon's retreat from Moscow and his struggle to retain a hold on central Europe. During forty days in May and June of 1813, the British troops drove the French armies over the Pyrenees and out of Spain; after years of being the military might in Europe, Napoleon's back was broken. In April of 1814, Paris was captured; and the war, or so everybody thought, was at an end. Napoleon, like everything else he did in his life, was to leave the world stage with dramatic flare. With his capture, Napoleon was sent into exile on the island of Elba. Elba proved to be no prison for him. On March 1st, 1815, Napoleon made his way from Elba to Paris and the "Hundred Days" began. He rallied his armies once again, then, on June 18th, 1815, the *Battle of Waterloo* unfolded. Napoleon's defeat brought 23 years of war between Britain and France, finally, to an end.

Political Justice:

One of the works with which the supporters of the populist movement of the 19th-century grounded themselves was that written by William Godwin, *Political Justice*. The work was published in 1793. It was considered to be a major piece of sedition. It was an attack on the established institutions of the aristocracy, such as property and religion. *Political Justice*, however, was not to light any political fires in England. As it happened, just as *Political Justice* appeared, so too did the beginning of the Napoleonic Wars. War does not allow much scope to a nation to perfect its ideas of liberty. It was only after the war, after 1815, that the populist movement again began to take hold.

It will be no surprise, given the course of his life thereafter, to learn that Shelley read *Political Justice*. Indeed, during his school days he became a Godwinian. Godwin, in his philosophy, followed along in the footsteps of Rousseau and the nostalgia for the simple and the primitive. Godwin could foresee for mankind a perfect equality and happiness; he believed in the perfectibility of man; he believed that it would be impossible to be rationally persuaded and not act accordingly, and that therefore man ultimately could live in harmony without laws and institutions. Such institutions as government, law, property and marriage, Godwin figured, were restraints upon liberty and obstacles to progress.

Shelley was to have a personal connection to Godwin; but, before we come to that, as necessary background, we make a note on Godwin's family. In 1796, Godwin was to meet Mary Wollstonecraft (1759-97). (Mary Wollstonecraft, in 1792, wrote "the first great feminist manifesto," *Vindication of the Rights of Women.*[11]) Finding that they had conceived a child together, Godwin, though no believer in the institution, took a practical route and wed Wollstonecraft during March of 1797. On August 30th, 1797, Mary was born; and, within two weeks of that, presumably of complications due to childbirth, Wollstonecraft was dead. Godwin was left with two small children on his hands, the infant Mary and Fanny Imlay (born 1794, a child which Mary Wollstonecraft had by Gilbert Imlay). In 1801, Godwin married a second time. His second wife was Mary Jane Clairmont who came to the marriage with two children, Charles and Jane (b.1798). Godwin and Clairmont went on to have one child together, William (b.1803).[12]

As mentioned, Shelley, when but a school boy, took a deep interest in Godwin's writing. A number of years passed, when, not even sure that his hero was alive, Shelley dispatched a letter to Godwin in January of 1812. Godwin got a reply off within days inquiring about his young admirer's background. Shelley was delighted that he had made this connection to Godwin and wrote a second letter. In this second letter, Shelley let slip that he was heir to an estate that, in time, would provide £6,000 a year.[13] This last little piece of information was of considerable interest to Godwin. Godwin was always hard up for cash and was ready to put the touch on anyone who he thought could make a small "loan" to him.[14] It was plain that Godwin would be delighted if Shelley could come up to London and would greet this rich young poet with open arms.

In the summer of 1813, Shelley saw to the private publication of *Queen Mab*. He continued his vagabond ways going from place to place to live, even though there was now a young child with whom they must contend. (In June of 1813, Harriet gave birth to her first born, a girl, Eliza Ianthe.) During the months from July to October they stayed at Bracknell in Berkshire just west of London. In the fall of the year they determined to go to the Lake District, but not finding suitable accommodations went further north to Edinburgh. In December, they (Shelley, Harriet and Eliza Ianthe) moved yet once again and by the end of 1813 they were living near Windsor. It might be interesting to speculate what transpired between Shelley, his bride, the bride's sister (the meddlesome Eliza) and the families (the Westbrooks and the Shelleys) during the winter of 1813/14. During this time the relationship between Shelley and his family turned around for the better. He and his father actually had a friendly meeting in London while the lawyers worked out a deal in respect to his inheritance.[15] Apparently, one of the matters that put the families out of joint was the Scottish marriage. To put it right, and as part of a larger bargain which is suspected was struck between Shelley and the families, the couple were married once again on March 20th, 1814, in St. George's church, at London, Hanover. Part of the deal, too, it seems, was that the couple was finally to get rid of Harriet's sister, Eliza, for whom Shelley had no like, at all, and who had been chaperoning the couple since first Shelley met Harriet.[16] Everything seem to be falling in place. Shelley and Harriet, it appeared, were headed for leading a normal life in harmony with their respective families. Enter Mary Godwin.

Mary and Jane:

We saw where, during the early part of 1812, that the twenty-year old Shelley was writing letters to Godwin, who had become to Shelley, through his readings of *Political Justice*, a monumental icon of human liberty. By November of 1812, the 20 year old Shelley had made his way to London to visit the 52 year old Godwin. Thereafter, Shelley was making extended visits to the Godwin household. I do not know how frequently Shelley made visits, we might suppose not too frequently given that during this period, 1812-14, Shelley, Harriet and Eliza (Harriet's sister) were moving about a great deal. It was not until 1814, on June 18th, to be precise, that Shelley was to first lay eyes on Mary Godwin. She was then 17 and he 22. Shelley had showed up at Godwin's house to give to him the proceeds of a loan which Shelley had arranged (one of a number of transactions during which Godwin dunned money out of Shelley).[17] Mary had just returned from Scotland where she had been attending school. He was immediately taken and transported by her – "a dream from heaven." Harriet was just then some distance away, at Bath. Shelley during the balance of June and into July was escorting both Mary and her younger half-sister, Jane (or, Claire, as she came to be known) around various places including the grave site of Mary's illustrious mother, Mary Wollstonecraft. During this time Shelley wrote letters to Harriet and made no secret of his attraction to Mary. In July, on Shelley's suggestion, Harriet came up to London. Shelley brought Harriet to the Godwins so that she might meet everyone. The suggestion, which Harriet thought came from Mary (she blamed Mary), was that, forgetting about all the social implications of the arrangement, the three should just live together. The suggestion literally made Harriet sick.

While Harriet was sick over Shelley's involvement with Mary Godwin, Mary was over the moon. Letting Harriet stew over the matter (she was then about four months pregnant), Shelley and Mary, together with Claire,[18] now that war in Europe had come to an end, determined to go to the continent. So off they went for a six week trip. They left, it would appear, without taking their leave of anyone in particular. Shelley arranged for a carriage and the girls (Mary was seventeen, Claire was sixteen) slipped out of their parents' house and off they drove to Dover. After a windy trip over the channel they arrived at Calais. Through France they traveled and then on to Switzerland. From Switzerland Shelley wrote Harriet inviting her to come to Switzerland where he would find her a "sweet retreat among the mountains."

By September the 13th the three were back in London. Shelley was without money and needed some so that he might rent a place for himself and the girls; he went to Harriet and she gave him £20 to tie him over.[19]

That November, 1814, Harriet gave birth to her second child, a son, Charles Bysshe. Though a week passed before Shelley was to hear the news, it was an event which drew him to Harriet's side. The meeting was unhappy. No doubt the older and scolding sister, Eliza, was hovering in the background.[20] Shelley was soon back with Mary who then was but two months off from being delivered of her child by Shelley.[21] The new year brought news of the death of Shelley's grandfather, the 84 year old, the rich and eccentric, Sir Bysshe. Though it is less than clear, Sir Bysshe's death brought Shelley that much closer to his inheritance. It was at this time that the lawyers were brought in so that the father might settle with the son. A deal was struck whereby Shelley was to give up his rights to the family estate in exchange for a tidy monthly sum to continue throughout his life. Harriet was to get £200 a year, and a further and immediate payment was made to get rid of her outstanding bills.[22]

So the year of 1815 passed, and in that year, for Shelley, three matters were put on a level footing: his separation with Harriet was formalized, his financial future was fixed, and his relationship with Mary was stabilized. The turmoil in Shelley's life had ebbed. It will be remembered, too, that in 1815, Napoleon was finally defeated and the long years of war had come to an end. Unemployed ex-servicemen walked the streets. Markets slumped for lack of demand. Men in all walks of life began to agitate for political reform. Shelley who was now coming into his own as a poet, wrote *Alastor*, "a masterpiece in blank verse."[23] The work, published in 1816, reflecting a more tempered view of things, condemned the self-satisfaction of the idealist who dreamt of the perfect society but who were powerless to change the conditions with which the poor and the disadvantaged were afflicted, seemingly, in all events.

Last Years In England:

In January of 1816 Mary gave birth to her second child, William. Within months of the birth of William, Shelley made a determination to go to Geneva, principally, it seems, so that he could meet Byron who just that April, having fallen out of favor with the public, had removed himself from England. Shelley, Mary and Claire[24] set out for Switzerland that May. Byron and Shelley were to meet at Geneva for the first time. Though their characters and ideals were different, the two poets were attracted to one another and recognized each other's genius. Shelley admired Byron the poet, Byron liked Shelley the man.[25] At the end of August, Shelley and his female companions left Geneva for England. Once back in England, Mary and Claire, together with the baby and a Swiss nurse went to stay at Bath. Shelley stayed on for a period of time at London as he had business to transact.[26] At the end of September, Shelley was at Bath (5 Abby Churchyard) to be with Mary, the baby and Claire.

Shelley, in 1816, was to make friends with Leigh Hunt. Hunt, together with his brother, had established one of the most famous newspapers of the time, the *Examiner*. In the paper, Hunt was given to express his liberal views. Such expressions of liberalism was to get he and his brother into trouble with the government, which was more interested in prosecuting the war against Napoleon than with civil liberties at home. Both of the Hunt brothers were tried and found guilty "for a libel on the prince regent." They both received a two year term of imprisonment, 1813-15. "I first saw Shelley," Hunt explained in his *Autobiography*, "during the early period of the *Examiner*, before its indictment on account of the Regent; but it was only for a few short visits, which did not produce intimacy. ... He was then a youth, not come to his full growth; very gentlemanly, earnestly gazing at every object that interested him, and quoting the Greek dramatists." Shelley, always a man to support a good cause, sent "a large sum of money" to Hunt at his home address, known as the "Vale of Health" at Hampstead: thereafter, "an affectionate correspondence began." (Blunden, *Leigh Hunt and his Circle*.) On December 6th, 1816, Shelley arrived at Hunt's home at Hampstead and was ushered in as a member of the family. To Shelley, Hunt dispensed enthusiasm and encouragement and most importantly gave Shelley (he was to do the same for the young John Keats at the same time) access to the columns of the *Examiner*.

In the meantime, there, in the background, was Harriet and the two children, all of whom Shelley had effectively deserted.[27] The loss to her was a great one and she suffered more than we will ever know. Thomas Love Peacock (1785-1866), a friend of Shelley's, was to write of Harriet:

> Her manners were good; and her whole aspect and demeanour such manifest emanations of pure and truthful nature, that to be once in her company was to know her thoroughly. She was fond of her husband, and accommodated herself in every way to his tastes. If

they mixed in society, she adorned it; if they lived in retirement, she was satisfied; if they traveled, she enjoyed the change of scene.

– As quoted by Blunden, *Shelley* ...

In December of 1816, Harriet's body was pulled out of a pond located in Hyde Park, "The Serpentine." On December the 30th, Shelley married Mary.[28]

Within days of Harriet's death, her family, the Westbrooks brought a petition before the court of Chancery which would effectively deprive Shelley of any say in respect to his two children, who were then three and half years old (Eliza Ianthe) and two (Charles Bysshe). Eliza Westbrook, Harriet's elder sister was undoubtedly the driving force behind the move to shut Shelley out. There were any number of stories, mostly true, which the court was to hear which went to the suitability of Shelley as a father. The children were made wards of the court and went to live with a mutually acceptable family, Dr. and Mrs. Hume.[29] Shelley was given limited visitation rights but it would not appear that he exercised these rights to any great degree and not at all after he left for Italy in March of 1818.

In spite of these listed miseries, or maybe because of them, Shelley wrote poetry. He was now coming into his best years. In 1817, he wrote "Rosalind and Helen" and "The Revolt of Islam" and (in part) "Prince Athanase." In the new year (1817) Shelley took a house[30] at Hampstead, so to be near Leigh Hunt. Hunt had just seen to the publication of his, "The Story of Rimini." Hunt's enemies (he had many due to his writings in the *Examiner*) criticized the poem's "idiosyncratic, colloquial style and the sympathetic treatment of incestuous adultery."

Italy:

There are a number of good reasons for Englishmen to go and live in Italy. There is the cheapness of living, the sunshine and the classical culture. Avoidance of creditors has always been one of the chief reasons. Shelley's spending habits, marked by great generosity to his friends, was to get him into serious financial trouble.[31] By 1817, his sources of credit dried up. Though it certainly seems that he had a substantial and regular income, it simply did not match his outgo. As the year closed, matters were in the extreme. Bailiffs were arriving to take inventory. Shelley, leaving Mary and the children in the big house they had rented, Great Marlow, started to hide out in various places throughout London.

In February of 1818, after packing up many of their possessions, the Shelleys moved out of their large house at Great Marlow and handed the premises over to new tenants. They spent the next few weeks in London making the rounds. On March 9th, the two children, six month old Clara and 26 month old William, together with Claire's child she had by Byron, 14 month old Allegra, were brought to St Giles-in-the-Fields, there to be christened; it was but a sop which the atheistic Shelley gave to the families.[32] The following day, March 10th; Shelley, Mary, Claire, the children and servants made their way to Dover. After waiting a couple of days for the weather to clear they all boarded the *Lady Castlereagh* and were blown across the channel to Calais. Shelley had left England for good.

Traveling overland, via Lyons, they entered Italy at Susa and were soon at Milan. At Milan correspondence was entered into between Shelley and Byron who was then in Venice. Byron demanded that Allegra be delivered to him. Sad as it was for her mother, realizing that Allegra's future depended on satisfying Byron, Allegra[33] was sent off to Venice with her nurse on April 28th. A couple of days later the Shelleys left for Pisa. Though intending to stay at Pisa,[34] the Shelleys were soon drawn to Venice, mainly for Claire's sake so that she might check up on Allegra.[35] By September the Shelleys were occupying Byron's summer place at Este, he having moved to Venice for the winter season (Este is located just north of Venice). It is during this period of time that Clara, Shelley's one year old died. Shelley, now having reached the full height of his genius, was writing his best poetry, including: "Lines Among the Euganean Hills" and the first act of *Prometheus Unbound.* In November, Shelley, ever so true to his vagabond ways, determined to live awhile at Naples; and, on the way, take in the sights of Rome[36] and Pompeii. In March of 1819 the Shelleys were on the move again – they arrived at Rome where they stayed to June 10th. While at Rome, Shelley wrote the second and third acts of *Prometheus Unbound.* It was at this time, on June 6th, while at Rome, that his son William died. Alone now without children, leaving Rome, they traveled north to take up residence at Leghorn (Livorno), on the western coast not far from Pisa. Then in October, north again to Florence, there to take up residence at Palazzo Marino, 4395 Via Valfonda. Mary then gave birth, on November 12th, to Percy Florence. All along, Shelley was writing: *A Philosophical View of Reform*, *The Mask of Anarchy*, "Peter Bell the Third," "Ode to the West Wind" and the third act of *Prometheus Unbound.*[37]

In January of 1820, the Shelleys moved to Pisa. In June, they moved to the west coast, to Leghorn. The worst of the hot weather can be avoided when on the sea coast.[38] In August they moved to San Giuliano, near Pisa. On October 31st, Shelley moved his household back to Pisa. During the year, Shelley continued to be productive and wrote "The Witch of Atlas" and "Oedipus Tyrannus." That summer a book of his poems came out which included: "The Cloud," "The Skylark," "The Hymn of Pan," "Arethusa" and the "Song of Proserpine." In the new year, 1821, Lord Byron came to be part of the literary group around Shelley. Byron regularly entertained by throwing dinner parties that lasted to three in the morning. During the months of January and February, Shelley wrote "Epipsychidion."[39] On February 23rd, the young poet whom Shelley had befriended back in England, died at Rome.[40] This event caused Shelley to write one of his finest poems, "Adonais," an elegy on John Keats.[41]

That fall, in 1821, Shelley and Byron struck upon an idea that they could enter into a joint literary venture. They would, from Italy, launch a new magazine, *The Liberal*. The implementation of this plan (mainly promoted by Shelley) would allow Shelley to achieve an objective he long had: to get his friend Leigh Hunt to come out from England to Italy. Hunt, due to his involvement with the *Examiner*, a successful London magazine which he and his brother had set up in 1808, would be a valuable person to have in the setup and production of the new magazine which Shelley and Byron envisioned. Hunt, however, had a large family and no funds. This problem was to be surmounted. Shelley and Byron (with independent aristocratic means, the both of them) would provide money sufficient, and a house. Mary Shelley was to write directly to Marianne Hunt: "Italy will not strike you as so divine at first; but each day it becomes dearer and more delightful; the sun, the flowers, the air, all is more sweet and more balmy than in the Ultima Thule that you inhabit." (As quoted by Blunden, *Leigh Hunt ...*) In January of 1822, Shelley, writing from Italy, sent to Hunt by "return of post" £150. In his letter Shelley writes:

> Lord Byron has assigned you a portion of his palace, and Mary and I had occupied ourselves in furnishing it ... We had hired a woman cook of the country for you, who is still with us. Lord B. had kindly insisted upon paying the upholsterer's bill, with that sort of unsuspecting goodness which makes it infinitely difficult to ask him for more ...[42]

During January of 1822, Edward John Trelawny (1792-1881) joined the circle at Pisa.[43] He was quite the character. Mary Shelley described him:

> A kind of half Arab Englishman whose life has been changeful as that of Anastasius and who recounts the adventures of his youth as eloquently and well as the imagined Greek ... he is a strange web which I am endeavouring to unravel ... he is six feet high – raven black hair which curls thickly and shortly like a Moor's – dark grey expressive eyes, overhanging brows, upturned lips and a smile which expresses good nature and kindheatedness ...[44]

Shelley's Death:

Summer was coming, and as usual, the Shelleys sought a new place to live in 1820, a place with cool sea breezes, a place where Shelley might be inspired to write his poetry. Such a place was found and the household moved to San Terenzo, on the Bay of Spezzia. The house was called the Casa Magni.[45] It stood alone on the edge of the sea under steep and wooded slopes. There were only two ways, then, to get to Casa Magni: by sea which came to the front steps or by paths that led in from Lerici on the south and from the north where there was a small fishing village, San Terenzo. The views in all directions were beautiful, however, as spectacular as they surely were, Mary was uncomfortable with the surroundings. Claire was with them just as she mostly was from the very start. So, too, were Edward and Jane Williams. The Williamses and the Shelleys had became fast friends earlier in the year, indeed, they occupied the ground floor of where the Shelleys had lived at Pisa, Tre Palazzi. It was just shortly after they had moved into Casa Magni that news had come that the five year old Allegra, Claire's child by Byron, had died at the convent in which Byron had eventually placed her. This news had set a very sombre mood for the household.

The weeks passed at Casa Magni. Williams who had been in the navy taught Shelley how to sail.[46] During this time, in June of 1822, Shelley worked on what must have been the last of his works, *The Triumph*. On June 15th, the Hunt family arrived in Italy, touching first at Genoa. A message had been gotten through to Shelley that his friend had, at long last, arrived. It was expected that they should soon be at Leghorn. On July 1st, Shelley and Williams set sail at Casa Magni. After a seven and half hour sail, covering a distance of approximately fifty miles going south along the coast, Shelley and Williams arrive in the *Don Juan* at Leghorn. The next day Shelley met Leigh Hunt. Shelley wanted to see that his literary friend with his wife and children were comfortably settled at Pisa where Byron had offered the downstairs floor of his palace for their use. Shelley could not stay long with the Hunts at Pisa. Mary had not been well and he wanted to return to her as soon as possible. On July 8th, having returned to Leghorn, Shelley set out for the return sail up the coast to Casa Magni. Trelawny was just then at

Leghorn taking care of Byron's sailboat, the *Bolivar*. It was not Trelawny's intention to sail all the way to Casa Magni; he was, however, ready for a short sail in the larger *Bolivar* and to accompany the *Don Juan* out into the bay.[47] Having sailed alongside for a period of time the crew of the *Bolivar* waived goodby to the *Don Juan*, and, coming about, made for port. Arriving back at Leghorn, Trelawny tied the *Bolivar* up. We now turn to Trelawny, who, in stirring prose, explained the scene and the anxiferous events thereafter.

Although the sun was obscured by mists it was oppressively sultry. There was not a breath of air in the harbor. The heaviness of the atmosphere and an unwonted stillness benumbed my senses. I went down into the cabin and sank into a slumber. I was roused up by a noise overhead, and went on deck. The men were getting up a chain cable to let go another anchor. There was a general stir amongst the shipping; shifting berths, getting down yards and masts, veering out cables, hauling in of hawsers, letting go anchors, hailing from the ships and quays, boats sculling rapidly to and fro. It was almost dark, although only half past six. The sea was of the color and looked as solid and smooth as a sheet of lead, and covered with an oily scum; gusts of wind swept over without ruffling it, and big drops of rain fell on its surface, rebounding, as if they could not penetrate it. There was a commotion in the air, made up of many threatening sounds, coming upon us from the sea. Fishing craft and coasting vessels under bare poles rushed by us in shoals, running foul of the ships in the harbor. As yet the din and hubbub was that made by men, but their shrill pipings were suddenly silenced by the crashing voice of a thunder squall that burst right over our heads. For some time no other sounds were to be heard than the thunder, wind and rain. When the fury of the storm, which did not last for more than twenty minutes, had abated, and the horizon was in some degree cleared, I looked to seaward anxiously, in the hope of descrying Shelley's boat amongst the many small crafts scattered about. I watched every speck that loomed on the horizon, thinking that they would have borne up on their return to the port, as all the other boats that had gone out in the same direction had done.

Trelawny continued to give his eye-witness account of the time Shelley was lost at sea.

> I sent our Genoese mate on board some of the returning crafts to make inquiries, but they all professed not to have seen the English boat. ... During the night it was gusty and showery, and the lightning flashed along the coast; at daylight I returned on board and resumed my examinations of the crews of the various boats which had returned to the port during the night. They either knew nothing or would say nothing. My Genoese, with the quick eye of a sailor, pointed out on board a fishing-boat an English-made oar that he thought he had seen in Shelley's boat, but the entire crew swore by all the saints in the calendar that this was not so. Another day was passed in horrid suspense. On the morning of the third day I rode to Pisa. Byron had returned to the Lanfranchi Palace. I hoped to find a letter from the Villa Magni; there was none. I told my fears to Hunt, and then went upstairs to Byron. When I told him his lip quivered, and his voice faltered as he questioned me.

Mary had no way of knowing, on the 8th, that Shelley had set sail. The days passed and the concern of the three woman at Casa Magni turned into worry. (There at Casa Magni waiting for the return of the boat was Mary; her half-sister, Claire; Jane Williams; and, of course the only surviving child of Mary and Shelley, the two and a half year old Percy Florence Shelley.) A letter had come in from Pisa; it was from Hunt. It sat there on the table for a day or two before Mary determine to open it up. Hunt enquired whether the trip back home went well. The worry of the women now turned into great panic. In the meantime Trelawny was searching the coast. He was aware of the storm that likely overtook Shelley and Williams, maybe they were stranded, maybe blown over to Corsica. Then Trelawny got the news. There was debris found. Then, on July 18th, accounts came in of bodies being found on the shore. The bodies that the sea had cast up were separated from one another by a number of miles. Of the body found at Viareggio, on it being described, Trelawny was of no doubt that it was that of Shelley's. It was the body of a tall person of slight figure and in one pocket of the jacket worn was a volume of Aeschylus (the classic Greek poet) and in the other a copy of Keats' poems. Trelawny went and broke the news to the two widows who had been going back and forth through these days, from Lerici to Pisa (where Byron and Hunt were headquartered) – hoping against hope.

The bodies had been buried – which under the law, the local authorities were required to do – buried in the sand where they had been found. Decomposing bodies are a hazard to public health; and so the ground was opened up and quicklime thrown in with the bodies. What Jane Williams wanted was for her husband's remains to be sent back to England. Mary Shelley wanted Shelley's remains to be buried at Rome in the English (Protestant) burying ground where their three and a half year old son, William had been buried in 1819. The health laws were such that bodies could not be moved. Principally through the efforts of Trelawny, who took charge of the entire matter, permission was obtained from the authorities to burn them. On August 15th, in a specially constructed furnace, Williams's body was dug out of the sand at the mouth of the Serchio and burned. Three days later, in the company of Byron and Hunt,[48] on August 18th, the badly decomposed body of Shelley was dealt with in the same manner. Wine, oil and salt were thrown on the pile, and with them the volume of Keats which Shelley had last consulted: all except for some white ashes went up in smoke.[49]

Conclusion:

Shelley learned his lessons in England. With his move to Italy, he left behind "his crude romances of political martyrdom"[50] and turned to writing his best work, such as: "Lines among the Euganean Hills," "Ode to the West Wind," "Adonais," and, of course, *Prometheus Unbound.* But Shelley's poetry was not, however, the best of English poetry[51] as might be claimed by his friend Byron or of one of an earlier age such as Alexander Pope. Hughes, in his work on Shelley, called him the poet of sorrow. "Even in the quieter years in Italy, sorrow was still constant to him: in the 'hunt of obloquy', now at greater distance, but all the while in cry; in the deaths of his two children; and in an increasing sense of wrongness in his own life and in the world."

To William Hazlitt, Shelley was a hot brained dreamer:

> The shock of accident, the weight of authority make no impression on his [Shelley's] opinions, which retire like a feather, or rise from the encounter unhurt through their own buoyancy. He is clogged by no dull system of realities, no earth-bound feelings, no rooted prejudices, by nothing that belongs to the mighty trunk and hard husk of nature and habit, but is drawn up by irresistible levity to the regions of mere speculation and fancy, to the sphere of air and fire, where his delighted spirit floats in 'seas of pearl and clouds of amber.' There is no *caput mortuum* of worn-out, threadbare experience to serve as ballast to his mind; it is all volatile intellectual salt of tartar, that refuses to combine its evanescent, inflammable essence with anything solid or anything lasting. Bubbles are to him the only realities: – touch them, and they vanish. Curiosity is the only proper category of his mind, and though a man in knowledge, he is a child in feeling.[52]

To this epilog I add a few words as to what became of Mary Shelley[53] and her half-sister, Claire. Within a day, the women moved from Casa Magni. For the two months that they lived there, they had a foreboding of the dreadful event which had overtaken them. Mary had some money and soon made arrangements to return to England. So too, she paid for the expenses so that Claire could join her brother Charles in Vienna. Claire was an accomplished linguist knowing five languages. Such a knowledge made her an ideal governess and was to work as such, as I understand, for the balance of her working life. (Indeed, even when Shelley was alive, she spent time at Florence as a governess.) Claire stayed with her brother in Vienna for a number of months, then, in 1823, she took herself to Russia. For a year she was at St. Petersburg then for another four years in Moscow. In 1828, Claire returned to England there to spend a year, after which she went to Germany, Dresden. In the 1840s she was settled in Paris. All along, when granted leave by the family for which she was working, she would return to England for a visit. In 1870 Claire moved to a place she knew well as a young woman, Florence. There at Florence, Claire died in 1879, in her eighty-first year.[54] As for Mary Shelley: as mentioned, she returned to England in 1823 with her son, Percy Florence. Shelley's father gave her a small pension, mainly because of his grandson and heir. The payments to Mary were made on terms including that she should not involve herself in the publication of Shelley's work, of which Sir Timothy did not approve. Mary Shelley, of course, had proven herself to be a successful writer with her first and most impressive novel, *Frankenstein* (1818). She continued to write, though, as agreed, not under the name of Shelley. She wrote novels for a while then travel guides. She lived to age 53

Mary was to write of her Shelley:

> He had been from youth the victim of the state of feeling inspired by the reaction of the French revolution; and believing firmly in the justice and excellence of his views, it cannot be wondered that a nature as sensitive, as impetuous, and as generous, as his, should put its whole force into the contempt to alleviate for others the evils of those systems from which he himself suffered. Many advantages attended his birth; he spurned them all when balanced with what he considered his duties. He was generous to imprudence, devoted to heroism.
>
> —In her introduction to *The Complete Poetical Works of* … .

Trelawny told a story about his friend. It seems that there was a Scottish family that was living in Italy, and on a walk one time with Shelley, Trelawny determined to pay them a call and entered their home with Shelley whom he did not introduce, at least not as Shelley, fearing I suppose that they would take an immediate dislike to a person who had been described in the periodicals of the day as being satanical, a person to be despised and hated.

> The ladies – for there was no man there – were capital specimens of Scotswomen, fresh from the land of cakes – frank, fair, intelligent, and, of course, pious. After a long and earnest talk [they were new to Italy and Shelley told them of his impressions of Italy] we left them, but not without difficulty, so pressing were they for us to stop to dinner.
>
> When I next visited them, they were disappointed at the absence of my companion; and when I told them it was Shelley, the young and handsome mother clasped her hands, and exclaimed,
>
> 'Shelley! That bright-eyed youth! – so gentle, so intelligent – so thoughtful for us! O, why did you not name him?'
>
> 'Because he thought you would have been shocked.'
>
> 'Shocked! – why, I would have knelt to him in penitence for having wronged him even in my thoughts. If he is not pure and good, then there is no truth and goodness in this world. His looks

reminded me of my own blessed baby – so innocent, so full of love and sweetness!'

'So is the serpent that tempted Eve described,' I said.

Leigh Hunt
(1784-1859)

Leigh Hunt
(1784-1859).

Leigh Hunt is known to us all a fresh and airy essayist, a fresh and airy poet, a liberal thinker in the morals both of society and of politics (hardly a politician in the stricter sense of the term), a charming, companion, a too-constant cracker of genial jacosities and of puns.[1]

Together with his elder brother, John, Leigh Hunt established one of the most famous newspapers of the time, the *Examiner*. The *Examiner*, a Sunday paper, was one in which Leigh Hunt was given to express his liberal views. Such expressions of liberalism were to get the Hunts into trouble with the government of the day, which was more interested in prosecuting the war against Napoleon than with civil liberties at home. The Hunts were tried and found guilty "for a libel on the prince regent"; both of the Hunt brothers were imprisoned for two year terms, 1813-15. Thus, the Hunts were martyrs to the new age of reform, though, as for Leigh Hunt, he is more to be remembered as a literary figure if not for his writing, then for his connections. It was through the *Examiner* that he introduced to the world Keats and Shelley. In 1822, Hunt left England to be with his literary friends, Shelley and Byron who were then in Italy. No sooner did he arrive when Shelley died tragically in a boating accident. In 1825 — the government having taken the pressure off of those who expressed views contrary to it — Hunt returned to England to carry on for the balance of his life with his literary pursuits.

Early Life (1784-1808):

The Hunt family had, many years back, established themselves in the English colony of Barbados. Leigh's father, Isaac Hunt (1752-1809) was sent from Barbados to Philadelphia for his education after which he was called to the Pennsylvania bar. At Philadelphia Isaac met and married Mary Shewell the daughter of a merchant. Isaac Hunt came out full square against those who fought for the independence of the American colonies. As Leigh Hunt wrote in his *Autobiography*, my father "entered with so much zeal into the cause of the British Government, that, besides pleading for loyalists with great fervour at the bar, he wrote pamphlets equally full of party warmth, which drew on him the popular odium." Once the outcome of the American War became obvious, Isaac Hunt took his family to England, where he intended to build a new life.[2]

Issac Hunt was not able to practice law in England. Legal work as a profession was reserved for the well connected. However, his education and oratory skills made Issac a candidate for the church. He became a preacher. This was an understandable course, as his father and his grandfather had been men of the cloth in Barbados. It was the Duke of Chandos, James Henry Leigh, who having heard him preach employed Isaac Hunt as a tutor to his nephew. Thus, we will better understand that Issac's fifth son, born on October 19th, 1784, was named James Henry Leigh Hunt.

Leigh's father earned little income from preaching and tutoring; it was only ever to be but a minor supplement to a small loyalist pension. The father, too, was one of those souls, forever possessed with plans but not the gumption to put any of them into effect. Leigh Hunt wrote in his *Autobiography*, "[my father] was always scheming, never performing; always looking forward with some romantic plan which was sure to succeed, and never put into practice." Thus, the Hunt family had money problems; indeed, the first room of which Leigh Hunt had any recollection was the one his father occupied in debtor's prison.

Leigh attended Christ's Hospital at London[3]; he become a "Blue Coat Boy."[4] Attending first in 1792, he spent eight years at Christ's Hospital. At age fifteen Leigh traded in his school uniform for "a coat and neckcloth." "I was then first deputy Grecian,[5] and I had the honour of going out of the school in the same rank, at the same age, and for the same reason, as my friend Charles Lamb.[6] ... For some time after I left school, I did nothing but visit my shoolfellows, haunt the book-stalls, and write verses." Eventually, due to a good connection, Hunt was to get a job as a clerk in the war office, though at the same time Leigh took an increasing interest in the business which his older brother had established. John Hunt, eight years older than Leigh, had become a printer. The brothers decided in 1805, while Leigh was yet with the war office,[7] to establish, as a joint venture, a newspaper, *The News*. I know nothing of this publication, but, for whatever reason, it did not seem to be published beyond 1808. In that year the brothers established a political weekly, one that was to make their reputation, the *Examiner*.[8] "The main objects of the *Examiner* newspaper," as Hunt described, "were to assist in producing Reform in Parliament, liberality of opinion in general (especially freedom from superstition), and a fusion of literary taste into all subjects whatsoever." The *Examiner* had not been established for more than a year before it drew the attention of those who ran the government. Soon thereafter, prosecutions were instituted against the Hunt brothers as the proprietors of the *Examiner*.

Seditious Liable (1808-15):

During the last part of the 18th-century, between the opening years of the American Revolution and the beginning of the French Revolution, journalism, or rather the power of journalism, came of age. As literacy spread and the population grew, reading was becoming an increasingly popular pastime; publishing was becoming a big business. With the turning of the century there were to be found on the streets of London newspapers, such as: the *The Morning Chronicle*, *The Morning Post*, *The Morning Herald*, and *The Times*. Public opinion from this point was to be molded by what was written in the public press.[9] And because of the better established periodicals, such as has been just mentioned, there came "a new tone of responsibility and intelligence." (Green.) In the beginning years of the 19th-century, however, the state of journalism was to shift with the coming of the "radical press," a press, against which, having been thoroughly shaken by the American and French revolutions, the aristocratic institutions in England took action.

> The differences and animosities were fully reflected in the radical press, which included Henry White's *Independent Whig*, T.J. Wooler's *Black Dwarf*, the Hunt Brothers' (Leigh and John) the *Examiner*, Cobbett's *Political Register*, and the many scurrilous sheets with names like *The Cap of Liberty* and *Medusa*. Such publications abused each other as often as they did the government. The government and its friends studied them nervously, from time to time, and occasionally prosecuted, though doing so had become much more difficult since Charles James Fox's 1792 amendment to the law of libel, which allowed the jury (as opposed to the judge) to decide whether the words complained of were libelous. Juries, especially those in the London area, were usually unpredictable, notably in cases involving freedom of the press. In the years 1808-21 the authorities embarked on 101 prosecutions for seditious liable, and as often as not failed to get a conviction. — Johnson.

From its very first edition, those who made up the aristocratic institutions perceived the *Examiner* to be a threat. As Hunt set out in his *Autobiography*: "In the course of its warfare with the Tories, the *Examiner* was charged with Bonapartism, with republicanism, with disaffection to Church and State, with conspiracy at the tables of Burdett, and Cobbett, and Henry Hunt."[10] The first prosecution against the Hunts came about in consequence of some remarks in respect to a British army officer in that he showed favoritism and was guilty of corruption. The prosecution against the paper prompted an internal investigation in the services, which, in turn, brought on a move by the prosecution to drop the charges. Within the year, yet another prosecution was brought against the Hunts because of a less than complimentary set of words about the old king; also, at the same time, charges were brought against a Mr. Perry of the *Morning Chronicle*. Perry's case came up first and he obtained an acquittal, which led to the dropping of the charges against the Hunts.

During 1812, the Hunts were once again brought into a court of law. In that year, on March 22nd, there appeared in the *Examiner* a ferocious attack on the Prince Regent. The Hunts considered that he "was a violator of his word, a libertine over head and ears in disgrace, a despiser of domestic ties, the companion of gamblers and demireps, a man who has just closed half a century without one single claim on the gratitude of his country, or the respect of posterity!" They could not escape this one. The government attempted to negotiate a settlement but the Hunts were uncompromising. The prosecution proceeded, and, in the result, both brothers were convicted. On February 3rd, 1813, the sentence was pronounced. Because of my interest in things legal, I set out the pronouncement of the sentencing judge, Mr Justice Le Blanc, who addressed the defendants in the following terms:

– 'John Hunt and Leigh Hunt, you have been tried and convicted by a jury of your country, of printing and publishing a scandalous and defamatory libel upon his royal highness the prince regent. The libel is contained in the information, and ... is expressed, in the newspaper of which you, John Hunt, were the printer, and you, Leigh Hunt, the editor ... What were the motives which induced you either to compose, or to adopt the composition of others, and which in your minds appeared honourable, and not with any design to slander from personal malice, it is impossible for me to conceive; but this one may venture to pronounce, that no man filling the character of a good subject could, with any motive but a bad one, print a libel of this description, attacking and vilifying the head of the government of the country; because the individual occupying that station, standing at the head of the government of a nation, is not to be held up in public newspaper, in the manner you have held up the prince regent, as an object of detestation and abhorrence, which you endeavour to persuade your readers that he is. Whether your motive was to gratify the mischievous curiosity of the public – to satisfy the diseased taste of the people, greedy to catch at anything which, by destroying the respect due to the constituted authorities, pulls down those at the head of affairs to the lowest possible level – if such were the motive which you call not malicious or dishonourable, the court cannot pronounce. But when they have before them men who have been convicted of offences like the present, it behoves those who are entrusted with the administration of criminal justice to protect that government under which we all live, and to support the head of that government, without which the present state of society could not exist. In passing, therefore, the sentence of the court, it is necessary to keep in view that which is ever an object of criminal justice – to hold forth to the world, that those who are found in your situation, must answer to the country for the mischief which their publication must necessarily occasion, since the effect of it is to destroy the bonds of society, by holding up the government to disgrace and contempt. We must point out wholesome examples to others, to deter them from being guilty of offences similar to that of which you have been convicted.

The sentence of the court upon you, therefore, is, that you severally pay to the king a fine of £500 each; that you be severally imprisoned for the space of two years; you, John Hunt, in the prison in Coldbath-fields, and you, Leigh Hunt, in the New Jail for the county of Surrey in Horsemonger-lane; that at the expiration of that time, you each of you give security in £500 and two sufficient sureties in £250 for your good behaviour during five years, and that you be further severally imprisoned until such fine be paid, and such security given.'

The defendants bowed, and withdrew from the court in custody.

Hunt's prison term was not as one might imagine it; he was not confined to one small dingy room to live on water and bread and to stare continuously at a brick wall with a small barred window. No, Hunt was not uncomfortable[11] in prison; he was able to have his friends and family with him.[12] He was able to continue to carry out his journalistic work. His experience in prison, however, was to permanently change Leigh Hunt.

At night-time the door was locked; then another on the top of the staircase, then another on the middle of the staircase, then a fourth at the bottom, a fifth that shut up the little yard belonging to that quarter, and how many more, before you got out of the gates, I forget: but I do not exaggerate when I say there were ten or eleven. The first night I slept there, I listened to them, one after another, till the weaker part of my heart died within me. Every fresh turning of the key seemed a malignant insult to my love of liberty. I was alone, and away from my family. – *Autobiography.*

Imprisonment, viz. the condition of being kept in captivity and forcibly deprived of personal liberty, is an experience – thankfully, I can only but imagine – which impacts greatly on the life of the imprisoned person. There is no question, notwithstanding that he made the most of it, Leigh Hunt was indelibly marked by the experience: as he himself declared many years later in his *Autobiography*, "I have never thoroughly recovered the shock given my constitution." Upon his release from prison, in 1815, Hunt turned from things political to things literary.

The Poets: And A Sojourn In Italy (1816-25):

Ann Blainey writes of Hunt's immediate post-prison life:

> At the end of 1816 he moved to the favorite of all his homes: Hampstead, the site of his mother's grave and the place to which, above all others, he felt strongly attached. The place – near enough to London for visiting friends, bookshops, and theaters but sufficiently rural to provide peace and quiet – soothed his jangled nerves and he entered into a happy and fruitful period. The focus of his life was changing. Previously it had centered on his brother John and the *Examiner* to the detriment of his wife and babies. In prison he became a different person, his priorities committed less to John and the paper and more to his wife and three children, and to those literary friends who had so faithfully supported him through his sentence.[13]

Among his literary friends were two young men, who, it can be claimed, were first introduced by Hunt to the literary world. "I first saw Shelley," Hunt explained in his *Autobiography*, "during the early period of the *Examiner*, before its indictment on account of the Regent; but it was only for a few short visits, which did not produce intimacy. ... He was then a youth, not come to his full growth; very gentlemanly, earnestly gazing at every object that interested him, and quoting the Greek dramatists." It appears that the two did not hit it off until 1816, after Hunt had come out of prison and after his,

"The Story of Rimini" was published in 1816. It was shortly after that, that Shelley, from an aristocratic family of means, sent "a large sum of money" to Hunt at his home address, known as the "Vale of Health" at Hampstead: thereafter, "an affectionate correspondence began." On December 6th, Shelley arrived at Hunt's home at Hampstead and was ushered in as a member of the family. So too, and quite independent of Shelley, the young John Keats, a medical student at the time, arrived at Hunt's home. Both of these young men were to get the same warm reception. To both Keats and Shelley, Hunt dispensed enthusiasm and encouragement; and most importantly he gave them access to the columns of the *Examiner*. Thus, it is to Leigh Hunt that we might give thanks for our current day knowledge of Shelley and Keats. Though it was indeed fortunate for them to have taken the trouble to meet Hunt, their friendship with this writer and newspaper editor came with a built in set of enemies. As we shall see on our biographical sketch on Keats, the association he had with Hunt made him a particular target of critics.

In 1816, Hunt had his long narrative poem, "The Story of Rimini" published. It had a mixed reception. His friends liked it well enough, but Hunt's enemies criticized the poem's "idiosyncratic, colloquial style and the sympathetic treatment of incestuous adultery." The *Quarterly Review* and *Blackwood's Edinburgh Magazine*, Tory magazines, seemed to have led the attack.[14] Hunt's style was a matter of taste, but the reference to his acceptance of sexual liberty was a matter of fact. Hunt himself, it seems, was faithful to Marianne, a simple woman and by whom he had numerous children; but his young poetic friend, Percy Bysshe Shelley was ready to get it on with any attractive woman who happened to be in his company and had a little time on her hands.

Paul Johnson:

> Shelley was soon renting a big house in Great Marlow, for an extended family consisting of himself; the pregnant Mary [Mary Wollstonecraft/Godwin, Shelley's second wife]; her stepsister Claire Clairmont with the baby, Allegra, whom she just had by Byron; as well as Leigh Hunt and his wife Marianne, also pregnant; and Marianne's sister Bess. They built an alter to Pan in the woods, and the atmosphere was heavy with sexual innuendo. Mary was correcting the proofs of *Frankenstein* and Shelley was writing *Laon and Cynthia*, whose theme was incest.[15]

The worshippers at Great Marlow were not to stay together for long, for, in February of 1818, the Shelleys with Claire and the children left for Italy, so to join Lord Byron. Hunt was probably encouraged to come along; but he, with no money and a growing family, could hardly go off to Italy as much as he might like to do so.[16] By September of 1821, however, Hunt was summing up the reasons why he too should go off to Italy: his health, Marianne's tuberculosis, his declining interest in the *Examiner*, the cheapness of living and education in Italy, the sunshine, and the classical culture. An additional incentive was offered: the three (Shelley, Byron and Hunt) could get up a new literary/political journal which they could all do from Italy. Hunt was without money, but that problem too was surmounted; Shelley and Byron (with independent aristocratic means, the both of them) would provide money sufficient, and a house. Mary Shelley was to write directly to Marianne Hunt: "Italy will not strike you as so divine at first; but each day it becomes dearer and more delightful; the sun, the flowers, the air, all is more sweet and more balmy than in Ultima Thule that you inhabit."[17]

In January of 1822, Shelley, writing from Italy, sent to Hunt by "return of post" £150. In his letter Shelley writes:

> Lord Byron has assigned you a portion of his palace, and Mary and I had occupied ourselves in furnishing it ... We had hired a woman cook of the country for you, who is still with us. Lord B. had kindly insisted upon paying the upholsterer's bill, with that sort of unsuspecting goodness which makes it infinitely difficult to ask him for more ...

On May 13th, 1822, the Hunt family[18] went aboard a sailing vessel, the *David Walter*, which set sail for Italy; the vessel arrived at Genoa on June 15th, it then sailed down to Leghorn arriving there on the first of July. Within days of Hunt's arrival in Italy, Shelley died in a boating accident. The death of Shelley left Leigh Hunt without his chief ally in respect to the forthcoming publication of the planned periodical, *The Liberal*. Byron was to soon lose interest in *The Liberal*.[19] Its first number did appear in September of 1822. It was a work doomed to failure, mainly, I suppose, due to Shelley's death: it was criticized as "a miscellany of disconnected writings without the momentum of a controlling mind." Shelley's contribution to the publication was key to its success. Still, it might have had a bit of a run, but Byron had lost interest, it seems, even before Shelley's tragic and unexpected death. With Shelley having died, and with Byron's whims and Hunt's penniless state; it will be no surprise to read that *The Liberal* came onto the streets a sickly child. It was blasted by certain editors, such as those at the *Quarterly*, as just being more drivel from "The Cockney School of Poetry."[20]

It is of course history, and a matter to be taken up in connection with my biographical sketch of the man, but Lord Byron left Italy and went off to Greece in 1823, there to die, at the age of 36, in pursuit of his final romantic dream. So, there it is: Hunt's reasons for being in Italy, to be with Shelley and Byron, went up and disappeared, like thick-flaming shots from a funeral pyre. Hunt would then have gladly returned to England but he lacked passage money; further, he could not face the prospect of being arrested for debt, or of trying to resolve the growing argument with his brother, John (from whom he had borrowed heavily) over the proprietorship of the *Examiner*.

In September of 1825, having received "a literary advance" from England, Hunt and his family (there was by this time seven children) departed overland for Calais; on October 12th, the family took a "steamboat" at Calais. For Hunt, with the death of Shelley and Byron, an era had come to an end; in any event, Leigh Hunt was glad to take his leave of Italy.

> To, me. Italy had a certain hard taste in the mouth. Its mountains were too bare, its outlines too sharp, its lanes too stony, its voices too loud, its long summer too dusty. I longed to bathe myself in the grassy balm of my native fields. — *Autobiography*.

Later Years (1826-59):

Leigh Hunt, with a large family and little money coming in from his writing,[21] suffered from poverty most all of his days; though in his later days matters improved. There were, of course, authors of the time who did not suffer from the miseries of poverty; I am thinking particularly here of Southey, Wordsworth and Scott. Because they accepted government positions, they were subject to being in a state of dependance, and thought to be quite ready to please and humor their Patrons. That could not be said of Hunt, or, by way of further example, of Hazlitt or of Keats.[22] That certain of his contemporaries, who started out as reformers, sold themselves to officialdom, so to live a more comfortable life, must have galled Hunt.

> 'Mr Southey', he [Hunt] had said, 'and even Mr Wordsworth, have both accepted offices under government, of such a nature as absolutely ties up their independence. Mr Coleridge, in pamphlets and newspapers, has done his best to serve likewise; and yet they shall all tell you that they have not diminished their free spirit a jot. In like manner they are as violent and intolerant against their old opinions, as ever they were against their new ones, and without seeing how far the argument carries, shall insist that no man can possess a decent head or respectable heart who does not agree with them. ...The persons of whom we have been speaking have been always in extremes, and perhaps the good they are destined to perform in their generation, is to afford a striking lesson of the inconsistencies naturally produced by so being. Nothing remains the same but their vanity'. — Howe.

In later years Hunt's fortunes improved. A new generation of young writers saw him as the survivor of the glamorous poetic world of Keats, Shelley, and Byron. Budding writers, one of whom was Charles Dickens, organized a private pension and agitated for a government pension which was first paid to Hunt in 1847.

In the meantime, in 1835, Hunt moved to Chelsea – it having that combination of town and country which he loved. It was on his suggestion that Thomas Carlyle became Hunt's neighbor in Cheyne Row; and Carlyle was to become one of Hunt's closest friends. Hunt's door was always open to his friends; at the right moment he may be caught at his supper and the recommendation by

Hunt would be immediately made to partake of his fare, "dried fruit, bread, and water." Most visitors came away appalled by the thriftless gypsiness of the Hunts' chaotic household. Hunt floated above it all in his flowered "wrapping gown," reading the classics and discoursing on the beauty of nature, and always through his words and acts expressing the philosophy of positive enjoyment. He wrote ceaselessly: essays, articles, poems, literary guide books to London, reworkings and recyclings of former works, and a number of anthologies which he rounded out with essays often on literary criticism. Hunt published his *Autobiography* in 1850. Carlyle was to observe that it was "by far the best of autobiographic kind I can remember to have seen in the English language."

In the mid-1840s his eldest daughter and his second son (a delinquent child who had grown into a delinquent adult) had died, however, their deaths did not hurt him as much as that of Vincent, his youngest son and favorite child. The last illness of tubercular Vincent was in the autumn of 1852, it was a time when Hunt and his beloved son became closer than ever. Hunt's grief at Vincent's death was extreme.

The publication of Charles Dickens' novel, *Bleak House*, was to cause quite a stir in the Leigh Hunt circle. In the work, there was a character, "airy, improvident and objectionable"; his name was Harold Skimpole. The character of Skimpole was, without doubt, based on Leigh Hunt. This characterization of Hunt by Dickens was to greatly effect Hunt and his friends; Dickens' denials and apologies only partly fixed up the rift that *Bleak House* had caused between Dickens and a number of his literary contemporaries.[23]

In his later years, as his *Autobiography* will show, Hunt allowed that he was "ratherish unwell." Though he occasionally got out to go to the theater or to dinner he became increasingly more sedentary. In January, 1857, Marianne died. "She [Marianne Hunt] was a limited, consumptive girl beset by chronic poverty, illness, and a family of ten children; and he was an impractical, insecure, and intensely demanding man whose intellect and friends were beyond her."[24] Thorton Hunt, Leigh Hunt's eldest son, who was to go on to become an accomplished man of letters in his own right, was to write of his parents: "Fate joined him with one who shared his taste for plastic art, with a greater natural aptitude, but without culture or the power of acquiring it; with childlike sense of verse, never matured; with an almost equally childlike sense of economy which the bookworm long believe to be nearly perfect. ... they were actuated by motives so different, that lengthening years only made them, in the longer portion of their faithful and unsevered union, strangers."

Concluding Remarks:

The artist, Benjamin Robert Haydon, a contemporary of and an early friend of Leigh Hunt's wrote in his *Autobiography*:

> He [Hunt] had been educated at Christ's Hospital, and was not deficient in classical knowledge, but yet not a scholar. Then we were nearly of an age; he being only three years older than myself, and he had an open affectionate manner which was most engaging, and a literary, lounging laziness of poetical gossip which to an artist's mind was very improving. At the time of our acquaintance, he really was, whether in private conversation or surrounded by his friends, in honesty of principle and unfailing love of truth, in wit and fun, quotation and impromptu, one of the most delightful beings I ever knew.[25]

William Hazlitt was of the view, what our thoughts of Leigh Hunt, as came to us through his writings, were but improved through personal acquaintance:

This is a charge that none of his friends will bring against Mr. Leigh Hunt. He improves upon acquaintance. The author translates admirably, into the man. Indeed, the very faults of his style are virtues in the individual. His natural gaiety and sprightliness of manner, his high animal spirits, and the vinous quality of his mind, produce an immediate fascination and intoxication in those who come in contact with him, and carry off in society whatever in his writings may to some seem flat and impertinent. From great sanguineness of temper, from great quickness and unsuspecting simplicity, he runs on to the public as he does at his own fire-side, and talks about himself, forgetting that he is not always among friends. His look, his tone are required to point many things that he says: his frank, cordial manner reconciles you instantly to a little over-bearing, over-weening selfcomplacency. 'To be admired, he needs but to be seen': but perhaps he ought to be seen to be fully appreciated. No one ever sought his society who did not come away with a more favourable opinion of him: no one was ever disappointed, except those who had entertained idle prejudices against him. He sometimes trifles with his readers, or tires of a subject (from not being urged on by the stimulus of immediate sympathy); but in conversation he is all life and animation, combining the vivacity of the school-boy with the resources of the wit and the taste of the scholar. The personal character, the spontaneous impulses, do not appear to excuse the author, unless you are acquainted with his situation and habits: like some great beauty who gives herself what we think strange airs and graces under a mask, but who is instantly forgiven when she shews her face.[26]

And finally, Leigh Hunt wrote of himself:

I am not conscious of having given praise for policy's sake, or blame for malignity's; and I never will. A strict adherence to truth, and a recurrence to first principles, are the only things calculated to bring back happier times of our literature and constitution; and however humble as an individual, I have found myself formidable as a lover of truth, and shall never cease to exert myself in its cause, as long as the sensible will endure my writings, and the honest appreciate my intentions. – *Autobiography*.

Leigh Hunt died on August 28th, 1859 in his 75th year; he was buried in the place of his choice, Kensall Green Cemetery.

John Keats

(1795-1821)

John Keats
(1795-1821).

"Lover of loneliness,
Of upcast eye,
And tender pondering!"[1]

His father, Thomas Keats, managed the stable at an inn[2] known as the "Swan and Hoop" located in the north-end of London, in the Hampstead area. Thomas was to marry his employer's daughter, Frances Jennings. Four children were born to the union: the oldest was John, born in 1795, followed along by George, Tom and Frances (Fanny). The parents died early, the father as a result of a fall from a horse in 1804, the mother of tuberculosis in 1810. After their father's death, the mother having remarried,[3] the Keats children moved in with grandmother Jennings.

John Keats attended school at Enfield (in the general neighborhood of the Jennings household) where he was befriended by the schoolmaster's son, Charles Cowden Clarke.[4] Clarke, eight years older, had a considerable influence on the young Keats. In 1810, the same year during which his mother died, John, at the tender age of fifteen, was to leave school. He was then to be apprenticed, "with a premium of £210," to Mr. Hammond, a surgeon of some repute at Edmonton.[5] For whatever reason (it is not clear why) Keats left Hammond before he completed his apprenticeship. On the first of October, 1815, Keats entered Guy's Hospital. He remained at Guy's Hospital for only six months, leaving so to devote his time exclusively to the writing of poetry, thus to join the "beggar-clan."[6]

From Medicine To Poetry:

Leigh Hunt ran a newspaper in London, the *Examiner*. It had been established in 1808. Hunt, as the editor, together with his brother, as the printer, in a case that was to be a *cause célèbre* was convicted in 1813 of having libeled the Prince Regent. Their sentence – considered harsh even in those days – in addition to paying a large fine was that each brother was to spend two years in prison. Upon him coming out of prison in 1815, Leigh Hunt was less inclined to political commentary and turned more to literary composition. In 1816, Hunt had his long narrative poem, "The Story of Rimini" published. While this work had a mixed reception, it was to bring two young poets to his door step.[7] The young poets, of course were Percy Bysshe Shelley and John Keats. Hunt dispensed enthusiasm and encouragement to both Keats and Shelley, and, most importantly, gave them access to the columns of the *Examiner*. That December (1816) there appeared in the *Examiner* an article written by Hunt entitled "Young Poets"; two of the young poets to whom he made reference was Shelley and Keats.

Keats' interest in poetry did not suddenly come upon him. Charles Cowden Clarke, his mentor during his school days, had obviously sparked that interest. In spite of his full time devotion and industry to the writing of it, his poetry might never have come into vogue if Keats did not have the combined assistance of Hunt and Shelley. Hunt was to be his avenue to getting his work published. Shelley was a charming personality, who, notwithstanding that he was in 1816 only twenty-four years old (Keats, twenty-one) had had experience in the writing and publication of poetry.[8] In March of 1817 John Keats published his first book of poetry. His next project was to be somewhat different, for he had in his brain the germ of his first large work, a poetic fantasy.

The most talked about and renowned poetic fantasy of these times was Coleridge's "The Rime of the Ancient Mariner," and while it had been first published in 1798 it was yet, eighteen years later, sending up a wash along the banks of literature. For an epic poem which gave an accounting of a poet's travels, Keats would have had freshly before him Byron's *Childe Harold. Childe Harold* was published in 1812 and it had established Byron's reputation. *Childe Harold* was written while Byron traveled east through Europe and then to Greece. In 1816, when the young Keats determined to write poetry, Byron was in Geneva writing the third canto of *Childe Harold* and also writing the first two cantos of *Don Juan*, his masterpiece, an epic-satire. It happened that in the months of May through to August of 1816 Shelley had traveled to Geneva and was to meet and then to spend time, with his two female traveling companions, cavorting on the banks of Lake Geneva with Lord Byron. Back in England, that autumn of 1816, Shelley, as we have seen, was to meet John Keats and the two of them were to spent time together. I think it safe to conclude that Shelley[9] was enthusiastically telling of his first meeting with Lord Byron and of his continuing work on *Childe Harold* and how he was beginning a new work, *Don Juan*. What I think became plain to Keats is that it would be necessary, following the examples of both Byron and Shelley, to get out on the road.[10] Thus Keats strapped on his knapsack and set out to the southeast of England; so to soak up the essential qualities and properties of the places he was to visit; so to gain the needed material and inspiration; so to write poetry.

On April 15th, 1817, then at Southampton, Keats wrote his brothers: "I did not know the Names of any of the Towns I passed through all I can tell you is that sometimes I saw dusty Hedges sometimes Ponds ..." On April 17th, he was on the Isle of Wright. ("On the Sea – It keeps eternal Whisperings around ...") From there he traveled up to Margate. At Margate, on May 10th, he wrote Hunt and Shelley: "Does Shelley go on telling strange Stories of the Death of Kings?" Then, still at Margate, he wrote his artist friend, Haydon,[11] "I read and write about eight hours a day." It was during these travels along the south coast of England between the Isle of Wight and Margate that Keats was writing his first major work and did indeed complete Books I and II of *Endymion.* Still at Margate, on May 17th, he wrote his publishers, Taylor and Hessey: "I found my brain so overwrought that I had neither Rhyme nor reason in it – so was obliged to give up for a few days ... This evening I go to Canterbury – having got tired of Margate."

At some point in his travels during the springtime of 1817, Keats met for the first time Benjamin Bailey (b.1791). We don't know much about Bailey, except that he seems to have been from the upper class.[12] By September, Keats was at Oxford staying with Bailey where he completed Book III of *Endymion.*[13] By October 8th, Keats had returned to Hampstead.[14]

It was in the fall of 1817, it would appear, that Keats was invited by his friend, Charles Armitage Brown[15] to move in with him. Brown was located at Hampstead not far from where Keats was born. The house, Wentworth Place[16], was a pair of semi-detached residences which shared a garden. Keats paid Brown £5 a month for board and lodging and had his own small sitting room at the back of the house with a bedroom above.

Hob-nobbing In London (1818):

On November 22nd, 1817, Keats wrote letters to two of his friends, John Reynolds and Benjamin Bailey. Both of these letters were postmarked Leatherhead, a place which is across the Thames in south London. "My Brother Tom is much improved – he is going to Devonshire – whither I shall follow him – at present I am just arrived at Dorking [south again of Leatherhead] ..." By December 21st John is writing his brothers who were then located at Teignmouth. John's letter is dated at Hampstead. It would seem that a decision was made by the brothers to get Tom as far south as they might, as Tom, like their mother, seven years before, was now suffering from the effects of tuberculosis. John, it seems, accompanied his brothers Tom and George part way with the promise to join them as soon as he could. John Keats was obliged to return and stay at London as his work, *Endymion* had reached the editing stage and there was a publisher waiting. With the opening of 1818, January 5th, we see where John wrote his brothers at Teignmouth. John heads up his letter, "Featherstone Building." During this time he is dealing with his publisher and revising his *Endymion* and making the rounds at London. He attends the lectures that William Hazlitt was then giving at London. Keats is a regular visitor at Haydon's (the artist, Benjamin Robert Haydon) who had moved from Great Marlborough Street to his new studio at Lisson Grove North, there to party with Wordsworth, Lamb, and others. On January 23rd, at London, Keats wrote "I have sent my first book [*Endymion*] to the Press ." "I have seen a good deal of Wordsworth. Hazlitt is lecturing on Poetry at the Surrey institution – I shall be there next Tuesday." On February 21st, in a letter from Hampstead, to his brothers,

Keats gives us his feelings about Wordsworth: "Wordsworth has left a bad impression where ever he visited in town by his egotism, vanity, and bigotry." In a later letter, dated in March to Haydon, he wrote, that "Wordsworth went [from London to the Lakes?]. I can't help thinking he has returned to his Shell – with his beautiful Wife and his enchanting Sister." In another he wrote, "I am afraid Wordsworth went rather huff'd out of Town – I am sorry for it."

Scottish Tour:

On March 13th, the very day that Shelley left Dover for Calais on his way to Italy, Keats was writing his friend Bailey at Oxford. He was then at Teignmouth with his brothers. By April 8th, still at Teignmouth, he wrote that Tom is getting "greatly better." It was at this point that John expressed his intention to "within a Month to put my knapsack at my back and make a pedestrian tour through the North of England, and part of Scotland ..."[17] On May 25th, Keats was back at Hampstead telling of his plans of how he was about to leave with his friend Charles Brown for their tour of Scotland, a country in which Brown's family had roots. At some point in this period his brother George announced his plans to marry, did so, and immediately took a ship for America.[18] With George off to America and John off for a pedestrian tour of Scotland, the youngest brother Tom was alone for a number of weeks at Hampstead (Well Walk). As for Keats and Brown: after traveling north, likely by coach, they were by June 27th in the north of England, "The Lake District," the home territory of William Wordsworth and Robert Southey. It is there that Keats began his journal of his walking tour.[19]

The main object for Keats and Brown was to tour Scotland, so not much time was spent in the Lake District. Within a week they had walked through the area and were nearing Scotland. On July 1st they were at Carlisle. "I fear our continued moving from place to place, will prevent our becoming learned in village affairs; we are mere creatures of Rivers, Lakes, and Mountains. ... We have now walked 114 miles, and are merely a little tired in the thighs and a little blistered; We shall ride 38 miles to Dumfries ..." By July 14th they were at Glasgow. On the 18th, at Inverary.

> We have come over heath and rock and river and bog to what in England would be called a horrid place – yet it belongs to a Shepherd pretty well off perhaps. The family speak not a word but gaelic and we have not yet seen their faces for the smoke which after visiting every cranny, (not excepting my eyes very much incommoded for writing), finds its way out at the door. I am more comfortable than I could have imagined in such a place, and so is Brown. The people are all very kind.

On July 26th, Keats reported: "We had a most wretched walk of 37 miles across the Island of Mull ... I have a slight sore throat and think it best to stay a day or two at Oban." On August 6th the pair are at Inverness: "... among these Mountains and Lakes ... I have got wet through day after day – eaten oat-cake, and drank Whisky, walked up to my knees in Bog, got sore throat ..." Illness brought an end to his pedestrian travels. (Indeed, this report of his sore throat was the beginning of the end for John Keats.) When an opportunity came to board a small sailing vessel, he did so; and in nine days time Keats was at London.[20]

Attacked:

Keats' first epic poem *Endymion*, which came out in 1818, is a story about the relationship between a goddess and her human lover. The work came about as a result of a competition between himself and Shelley.[21] Rossetti related the story, as part of his rather thorough analysis of *Endymion*, that the two should each produce such a work. In the result Shelley came out with *The Revolt of Islam* and Keats *Endymion*. Rossetti, further observed that "Shelley proved to be the more rapid writer of the two; his poem of 4,815 lines was finished by the early autumn of 1817, while Keats's, numbering 4,050 lines, went on through the winter ..." The first line of *Endymion* – "A thing of beauty is a joy for ever" – is familiar to all lovers of poetry. Clearly, *Endymion* contains lines of beauty which gives joy to those who read them, but the overall work was considered faulty. This due to the inexperience of the poet and the manner in which the work came into being: it "will be quite clear to the reader, who must soon perceive great inexperience, immaturity, and every error denoting a feverish attempt rather than a deed accomplished."[22]

In 1818, in an edition of an Edinburgh paper, the *Quarterly Review*, there appeared a critique which "branded into ignominious permanence ... the name and fame of Keats." (Rossetti.) The editor of the *Quarterly Review* was William Gifford (1756-1826) who had been its editor since 1809. It was Gifford's good fortune to be befriended by the rich and famous. As a critic "he was unduly biased."[23] In any event Gifford wrote a review of *Endymion*:

> It is not that Mr. Keats (if that be his real name, for we almost doubt that any man in his senses would put his real name to such

a rhapsody) – it is not, we say, that the author has not powers of language, rays of fancy, and gleams of genius. He has all these; but he is unhappily a disciple of the new school of what has been somewhere called 'Cockney Poetry,' which may be defined to consist of the most incongruous ideas in the most uncouth language. ... He seems to us to write a line at random, and then he follows, not the thought excited by this line, but that suggested by the *rhyme* with which it concludes. There is hardly a complete couplet enclosing a complete idea in the whole book. He wonders from one subject to another, from the association, not of ideas, but of sounds ...

– As quoted by Rossetti.

Gifford's allegations were likely correct, certainly they were to Keats' biographer, William Michael Rossetti.[24] However, Rossetti thought that Gifford's article was "an act of brutalism" a "venom of abuse" "poured into the poetic cup of Keats as an expedient for drugging the political cup of Hunt, an act of partisan turpitude."

Gifford had an ally in John Gibson Lockhart.[25] Lockhart was the editor of another Edinburgh paper, the *Blackwood's Magazine*. Lockhart readily joined in on the attack on the "Cockney School of Poetry." Actually, *Blackwood's*, this Tory (conservative) magazine out of Edinburgh had started in earlier, and, indeed, had coined the expression the "Cockney School" in its edition of October, 1817, when in its pages it inveighed against Leigh Hunt who ran the *Examiner*, a Whig (liberal) magazine out of London. With the appearance of Gifford's piece skewering poor Keats, in 1818, out came Lockhart with his vituperative piece against Keats.

To witness the disease of any human understanding, however feeble, is distressing; but the spectacle of an able mind reduced to a state of insanity is of course ten times more afflicting. It is with such sorrow as this that we have contemplated the case of Mr John Keats. ... He was bound apprentice some years ago to a worthy apothecary

> in town. But all has been undone by a sudden attack of the malady. ... For some time we were in hopes, that he might get off with a violent fit or two; but of late the symptoms are terrible. The phrenzy of the "Poems" was bad enough in its way; but it did not alarm us half so seriously as the calm, settled, imperturbable drivelling idiocy of *Endymion*.

At the conclusion of the Lockhart review the advise was given that Keats should resume his former occupation: "Back to the [apothecary] shop Mr John, back to 'plasters, pills, and ointment boxes.'"

Benjamin Haydon was to write that the articles against Keats and his poetry had a melancholic effect on the young poet. "[Blackwood's] attacks on all who showed the least liberalism of thinking or who were praised by or known to the *Examiner*.[26] ... On Keats the effect was melancholy. He became morbid and silent, would call and sit whilst I was painting for hours without speaking a word."

Keats, it would certainly appear from his correspondence at the time, could not have treated this attack in a more self-possessed, measured, and dignified spirit. He wrote: "The genius of poetry must work out its own salvation in a man. It cannot be matured by law and precept, but by sensation and watchfulness in itself. That which is creative must create itself. In *Endymion* I leaped headlong into the sea, and thereby have become better acquainted with the soundings, the quicksands, and the rocks, than if I had stayed upon the green shore and piped a silly pipe, and took tea and comfortable advice. I was never afraid of failure, for I would sooner fail than not be among the greatest." (As quoted by Rossetti.)

Sorrow, Love and the Writing of Poetry:

After his Scottish tour in 1818, John Keats went back to nursing his brother and continued to do so until Tom's death that December. Tom died of tuberculosis, just as his mother did seven years previously. Tuberculosis is a contagious disease, so the brotherly love extended during the last few month's of Tom's life, was to be the death of John Keats. Tom having died, for all practical purposes, Keats was left alone without family. His parents were dead; Tom was now dead at the age of only 20 years; George had departed for America; and "his girlish sister [was] a permanent inmate of the household of Mr. and Mrs. Abby at Walthamstow." In February of 1819, Keats wrote George, "I am still at Wentworth Place – indeed I have kept in doors lately, resolved if possible to rid myself of my sore throat."[27]

It is now time for a brief note on Fanny Brawne: As already mentioned, Wentworth Place had on the other side another dwelling which, in May of 1819, was to see new tenants move in. These tenants were Mrs Brawne (a widow) and her three children. One of these children was a young woman, Fanny Brawne, with whom Keats was to fall hopelessly in love. Keats began writing love letters to Fanny in July: "I almost wish we were butterflies and liv'd but three summer days – three such days with you I could fill with more delight than 50 common years could ever contain." As for Fanny, well, she did not seem to be quite as keen for John Keats as he was for her. However, things did progress to the point where the couple declared that they would marry. "This [the engagement] was contrary to Mrs. Brawne's liking. They appear to have contemplated – anything but willingly on the poet's part – a tolerably long engagement; for he was a young man of twenty-three, with stinted means, no regular profession, and no occupation save that of producing verse derided in the high places of criticism." (Rossetti.) It could be that Mrs. Brawne required a cooling off period but just as likely it was because Keats calculated it was time to refill his poetic vessel with the experiences to be gained by further travel. Keats separated himself from Fanny for a period of time.

In the early part of the summer of 1819, Keats traveled to the Isle of Wight, a place he had chosen to start out with when he traveled alone in 1817, and which led to the production of his first major work, *Endymion*. There at Shanklin he shared rooms, at first with his friend James Rice who was later replaced by another, Charles Brown. In a letter to his sister dated July 6th he set out his reason for his stay at Shanklin, "to try the fortune of my pen once more ... Our window looks over house tops and Cliffs onto the Sea ... We have Hill and Dale forest and mead and plenty of lobsters." Further, "I would rather be here alone at my desk than in the bustle and hateful literary chitchat." It is here, at Shanklin, that Keats wrote *Lamia*. At some point before August 14th, Keats and Brown left the Isle of Wight.

> We removed to Winchester for the convenience of a library and find it an exceeding pleasant Town, enriched with a beautiful Cathedrall and surrounded by a fresh looking country. We are in tolerably good and cheap Lodgings. Within these two Months I have written 1500 Lines, most of which besides many more of prior composition you will probably see by next winter. I have written two tales, one from Boccaccio call'd the *Pot of Basil* [*Isabella*]; and another call'd *St. Agnes' Eve* on a popular superstition; and a third call'd *Lamia* – half finished – I have also been writing parts of my *Hyperion* and completed 4 Acts of a Tragedy [*Otho The Great*].

Keats continued to write poetry at Winchester at a furious rate, as if he knew that his time for such activity was short and soon to come to an end. He continued to stay on at Winchester until October. By November of 1819, Keats was back at Wentworth Place (Hampstead) and was feeling increasingly unwell, as a dreary winter seeped in all around him.

The Death Of Keats:

During the last year of his life, 1820, Keats' health went steadily down hill. He was as much in love with Fanny as ever but he knew that their union was an impossibility. On February 4th we see that he was writing from his sick bed to Fanny Brawne who was but beyond a wall at Wentworth Place. "They say I must remain confined to this room for some time. The consciousness that you love me will make a pleasant prison of the house next to yours." On February 10th, another letter to Fanny Brawne: "On the night I was taken ill – when so violent a rush of blood came to my Lungs that I felt nearly suffocated ... I shall be looking forward to Health and the Spring and a regular routine of our old Walks." And again in another letter in the same month: "I am recommended not even to read poetry, much less write it. I wish I had even a little hope. I cannot say forget me – but I would mention that there are impossibilities in the world." In May, Keats was obliged to move from Wentworth Place to Wesleyan Place, Kentish Town. On June 23rd, he wrote his sister and told how he wanted to make a trip up town to visit his publisher as his new works (among them, *Lamia* and *Isabella*) were about to come out. However, "I set myself to come to town, but was not able for just as I was setting out yesterday morning a slight spitting of blood came on which returned rather copiously at night."

On hearing of this bad spell that Keats had in June, his friend and publisher of his poems, Leigh Hunt, determined to get involved. Hunt brought Keats into his home. Incidently, it was during the summer that Keats' last volume was published and which contained his best works.[28] In July there was talk of Keats getting himself off to the warming climate of Italy.[29] In August, Keats heard from his fellow poet, Shelley. Shelley was then in Italy. An invitation was extended by Shelley to Keats, he should come and stay with him in Italy. With this, Keats made up his mind: "There is no doubt that an English winter would put an end to me, and do so in a lingering, hateful manner. Therefore, I must either voyage or journey to Italy, as a soldier marches up to a battery."[30] It was Fanny who made the decision for Keats. John should go to Italy, in order to get better. For John, it was more, "I should go to Italy to spare Fanny the miseries of my death." His publisher, John Taylor, raised a subscription among his friends so that Keats might have the necessary money for the trip. And so it was, that in September of 1820, Keats and his friend, the painter Joseph Severn, boarded the sailing vessel, *Maria Crowther*.

Keats and Severn arrived at Naples on October 21st, 1820. John Keats at this point was a very sick man.[31] His poetry writing days were over.[32] After spending a period of time in routine quarantine the pair made their way to Rome, arriving there on November 15th, 1820. From Naples Keats might have gone up to Shelley's, who was then at Pisa, but he passed Pisa up for Rome. At Rome there was a very famous Scottish doctor, by the name of James Clark[33] with whom Keats' friends had already corresponded. Clarke determined to assist Keats and help him through his illness. Among other things,

Clarke arranged for lodgings for Keats and Severn opposite his own, in central Rome, up the Spanish Steps leading to the Trinità dei Monti.

During his last couple of months, Keats did manage to get around with the help of his friend, Joseph Severn, and explored to a small extent his immediate neighborhood usually to take the evening air. On the 10th of December, 1820, Keats suffered a serious hemorrhage. He recovered slightly for Christmas but by the 10th of January he was confined to his bed. John Keats died on February 23rd, 1821. He was buried in the Protestant Cemetery, behind the Pyramid in Testaccio. He was only 25 years old at the time of his death.[34]

Conclusion:

William Michael Rossetti—who as a critic of poets and poetry must be put in the front rank – thought that none of Keats' work has much merit.[35] Keats was, as Rossetti wrote, "many-mooded, with a tendency to perverse self-conflict. The circumstances of his brief career – his poetic ambition, his want of any definite employment, his association with men of literary occupation or taste whom he only half approved, the critical venom poured forth against him, his love thwarted by a mortal malady – all these things tended to bring out the unruly or morbid." Rossetti thought Keats' poetry was "emotional without substance, and beautiful without control."

The contemporary artist and personal friend of John Keats, Benjamin Haydon wrote:

> One day he was full of an epic poem; the next day epic poems were splendid impositions on the world. Never for two days did he know his own intentions. ... The death of his brother wounded him deeply, and it appeared to me that he began to droop from that hour.

I was much attracted to Keats, and he had a fellow-feeling for me. I was angry because he would not bend his great powers to some definite object, and always told him so. Latterly he grew irritated because I would shake my head at his irregularities, and tell him that he would destroy himself ... Poor Keats! had nature given you firmness as well as fineness of nerve, you would have been glorious in your maturity as great in your promise.

Palgrave, many years later put his figure on this same point which Haydon had made. "Marvelous Boy": This is the title that Palgrave gave to John Keats.

If the fulfillment may ever safely be prophesied from the promise, England appears to have lost in Keats one whose gifts in Poetry have rarely been surpassed. Shakespeare, Milton, and Wordsworth, had their lives been closed at twenty-five, would (so far as we know) have left poems of less excellence and hope than the youth who, from the petty school and the London surgery, passed at once to a place with them of 'high collateral glory.'[36]

Keats was a bud cut by a fatal frost. Richard Dowling[37] thought that much the same thing could be said of Shelley who also died at a young age in Italy – only 17 months after the death of Keats. They "were never regular race-horses. They were colts that bolted in their first race and ran until they dropped." The poetry of John Keats, as a body of work was too green to ever be ranked with the best, however, in his work, especially that which was his last in 1818, one sees the brilliant flashes which will live on in the hearts of poetry lovers down through the ages.[38]

When I have fears that I may cease to be
Before my pen has glean'd my teeming brain,
Before high-piled books in charact'ry
Hold like rich garners the full-ripen'd grain;

When I behold, upon the night's starr'd face,
Huge cloudy symbols of a high romance,
And think that I may never live to trace
Their shadows, with the magic hand of chance;

And when I feel, fear Creature of an hour!
That I should never look upon thee more,
Never have relish in the fairy power
Of unreflecting love – then on the shore

Of the wide world I stand alone, and think
Till Love and Fame to nothingness to sink.

– Keats.

Robert Southey

(1774-1843)

Robert Southey
(1774-1843).

"The Patriot Bard."

Thomas Southey, a Bristol linen draper, married Margaret Hill in 1772. Their son, Robert, was born to them at Bristol on August 12th, 1774, as the second and eldest surviving child.[1] In his early years Robert was mostly brought up by his mother's half sister, living in Bath, Miss Elizabeth Tyler. Bath was a center to which the rich and influential regularly retired and thus it was a cultural center. Miss Tyler was to bring her young charge to cultural events including live theater.

At the age of fourteen Robert was sent to Westminster School. This was at the expense of his uncle, Rev. Herbert Hill who was the Chaplain to the "British Factory" at Lisbon, Portugal. During his last year at school, Southey entered a period of acute adolescent rebellion, finally being expelled for a school-magazine essay condemning flogging. As a result of this expulsion Southey was refused entrance at Christ Church, Oxford, however, he was accepted at Balliol where he matriculated in November 1792. Southey's stay at Oxford was not so profitable for him, as he was later to declare, "All I learnt was a little swimming ... and a little boating."[2]

At Oxford, in June of 1794, Southey was to meet Coleridge who was then visiting from Cambridge. The two hit it off, and together with some of their fellow political dreamers, were soon making plans for a communistic settlement in America to be independent of any government except that of the settlement itself, a pantisocracy.

> Their wants would be simple and natural; their toil need not be such as the slaves of luxury endure; where possessions were held in common, each would work for all; in their cottages the best books would have a place; literature and science, bathed anew in the invigorating stream of life and nature, could not but rise reanimated and purified. Each young man should take to himself a mild and lovely woman for his wife; it would be her part to prepare their innocent food, and tend their hardy and beautiful race. — Dowden.

These lovely ideas were to become unraveled about as quick as they were knitted up. Of all the group (Coleridge, *et al.*) Southey was the first – after first suggesting as an alternative to America, that the community might be set up in Wales – to proclaim that pantisocracy was unworkable. The fundamental flaw, of course, whether they saw it this way or not, was that such schemes cannot work where everyone was expected to throw all they have into the communal pot and hope that everybody else does the same. Given the nature of man such schemes couldn't possibly work. Besides, even to get such a community set up would take a fair bit of money, money which none of these young dreamers had. However, it does seem that certain of these young pantisocrats had lined up three "mild and lovely women" for their wives: the three Fricker sisters.

These developments did not impress the Southey family. His uncle, Rev. Hill, who was very much interested in shaping things up for his young nephew, thought that Robert should go to the ministry. If not, then he should read for the bar. Hill didn't push too hard and suggested that Robert should take a little time to think about things and suggested he should go to Portugal and spend some time with him, Uncle Hill, at Lisbon. Southey agreed and gave up his ideas of pantisocracy; though he was not to give up his idea of marrying Edith Fricker (1774-1837). Aunt Tyler, incidently, was particularly disturbed over Robert's plans to marry Edith Fricker, whom she thought was but a common girl.

So it was, in 1795, that Southey was off to spend time at Lisbon. But first there was a commitment that he felt bound to honor before he left. On the 14th of November, 1795, in the parish of the Fricker family, St Mary Redcliff, Bristol, Robert Southey secretly married his love, Edith Fricker. (Better than a month earlier, I should note, in the same church, Coleridge married Sarah Fricker. At Coleridge's marriage, Robert Southey was not present as the pair were no longer on speaking terms. Coleridge, it seems, was upset with Southey because Southey had cast aside the ideas of pantisocracy.[3]) Right after the marriage ceremony, seemingly at the church door, the newly married couple said their goodbyes to one another. Edith was to go and be with the family of a friend while Southey went off to Portugal.

In September of 1796, after a six month absence, Southey returned to England and to his new wife. He and Edith soon set up housekeeping in the Bristol area. In that year there was to be a partial reconciliation with Coleridge, particularly with the birth of the Coleridges' first child on September 19th; the boy was named Hartley. Sorrow too was to come that year when his brother-in-law, a young budding poet like Coleridge and Southey, and their close friend, was to suddenly die from a fever leaving behind a young widow (one of the Fricker sisters) and a young child. During the next few years Southey did turn to the study of law, but the law was not for him. In 1797 a well heeled gentleman (C. W. W. Wynn) gave Southey a yearly pension of £160. Such a gift enabled

Southey to devote time to writing and to traveling. In 1800, both Southey and Sara traveled to Portugal to spend time with Rev. Hill. The Southeys returned to England in June of 1801.

In September of 1803, the Southeys moved to the Lake District, Keswick. It would certainly seem that they moved there at the invitation of Mrs. Southey's sister, Sara. As we have seen, Sara had married Coleridge. By 1803, Sara was in need of help. Coleridge was addicted to opium and was proving to be a failure both as a husband and a father. Further, Edith Southey was in need of some consoling, as she had lost her first born but a month before and it must have been thought that a change of scenery would help.[4] The Coleridges had moved into this large home at Keswick known as Greta Hall, and had been living there for about three years. Greta Hall was certainly big enough for both families, indeed, Greta Hall was big enough for three families: the Coleridges, the Southeys and the Lowells. Most of the members of these families lived together there at Greta Hall for a number of years. As we have seen, the three young friends (Southey, Coleridge and Lowell) had married three of the Fricker sisters. Coleridge was never to spend any great amounts of time there, indeed, in the course of events he was to take up permanent residence at London. As for Lowell, as we have seen, he died in 1795. Thus it was that the three sisters and their children were to live at Greta Hall with Southey as the male head of the entire collective.

De Quincey in his *Recollections* was to describe Greta Hall and the arrangements, therein. "The house itself – Greta Hall – stood upon a little eminence ... overhanging the river Greta. There was nothing remarkable in its internal arrangements: in all respects, it was a very plain, unadorned family dwelling; large enough, by a little contrivance, to accommodate two, or, in some sense, three families, viz., Mr. Southey and *his* family; Coleridge and *his*; together with Mrs. Lovell [Lowell], who, when her son was with her, might be said to compose a third." De Quincey wrote of the amusing jest of Southey's that he called the hill on which Greta Hall was placed, the *aunt hill*. "The house had, therefore been divided (not by absolute partition into two distinct apartments, but by an amicable distribution of rooms) between the two families of Coleridge and Southey." The two families might live apart during the day but would meet together at dinner.[5]

In comparing it to Wordsworth's, de Quincey wrote of Southey's library at Greta Hall:

> ... the two or three hundred volumes of Wordsworth occupied a little, homely bookcase, fixed into one of two shallow recesses formed on each side of the fireplace by the projection of the chimney in the little sittingroom up stairs. ... I believe Wordsworth rarely resorted to his books ... On the other hand, Southey's collection occupied a separate room, the largest, and every way the most agreeable, in the house; and this room styled, and not ostentatiously (for it really merited that name), the Library. ... The books were chiefly English, Spanish, and Portuguese; well selected, being the great cardinal classics of the three literatures.

Southey, generally, was a very organized and industrious researcher and writer.[6] Regular money came to him because of the generosity of a government pension. So it was that Southey had the leisure to fully pursue his literary interests. Augustine Birrell commented on Southey's industry and devotion:

> He [Southey] wrote poetry (as if anybody could) before breakfast; he read during breakfast; he wrote history until dinner; he corrected proofsheets between dinner and tea; he wrote an essay for the *Quarterly* afterwards, and after supper, by way of relaxation, composed the *Doctor*, a lengthy and elaborate jest. Now, what can anyone think of such a life, except how clearly it shows that the habits best fitted for communicating information, formed with the best care and daily regulated by the best motives, are exactly the habits which are likely to afford a man the least information to communicate? Southey had no events, no experiences. His wife kept house and allowed him pocket-money ...
>
> – Birrell's essay, "Walter Bagehot," *Selected Essays*.

De Quincey, who lived as a neighbor to both of them, compared Wordsworth and Southey in respect to their life styles:

> Wordsworth lived in the open air: Southey in his library, which Coleridge used to call his wife. Southey had particularly elegant habits (Wordsworth called them finical) in the use of books. Wordsworth, on the other hand, was so negligent, and so self-indulgent in the same case, that, as Southey laughingly expressed it to me some years afterwards, 'to introduce Wordsworth into one's library, is like letting a bear into a tulip garden.'

Overall, especially compared to the other romantics such as Coleridge and Lord Byron, Southey was a steady man, not given to extremes of behavior. His personality was flat, as William Hazlitt observed, not "a boon companion." The diarist, Henry Crabb Robinson, however, was charmed by Southey's person and manners. I quote Robinson's biographer, Edith Morley:

> Crabb Robinson was on cordial personal terms with Southey from the time of their first meeting at Dr. Aikin's house in March 1808, when he was 'charmed by his person and manners.' They did not agree on politics, and Crabb Robinson 'deemed him... an honest' alarmist[7]; they seldom agreed about poetry, except in so far as both

admired Wordsworth and Coleridge. But Crabb Robinson and Southey had much in common in their love of travel and their love of letters, and when, at Godwin's house in 1817, in Crabb Robinson's presence, Shelley 'was very abusive towards the laureate,' saying he had 'sold himself to the court,' the diarist is content to state that 'the friends of Southey are under no difficulty in defending him.' It is, by the way, somewhat surprising to find that Crabb Robinson noted in Shelley 'a resemblance to Southey, particularly in his voice.' This seems to have been the only occasion when the two men met, and Crabb Robinson says that Shelley made 'a pleasing impression, which was not altogether destroyed by his conversation, though he is vehement, and arrogant, and intolerant.'

Shelley was abusive of Southey, because Shelley, never did give up on the ideas on which the young revolutionaries had fed as the 18th-century closed. Ideas as were reflected in the *French Constitution of 1791*; a theory of liberty, the *Golden Rule of Liberty*: "Men are born free and equal in rights, ... Liberty, ... consists in being permitted to do anything which does not injure other people. ... The exercise of the natural rights of each man has no limits except those which guarantee to the other members of society the enjoyment of the same rights." (Articles 1 & 3.) There were young men, not only in France but in England as well, who greeted the French revolutionaries as the saviors of liberty. Among these young men would have been Southey in his early years. While the French Revolution led directly to the collapse of the rule of absolute monarchy and its attending aristocratic orders, however, in its wake there followed blood, death and misery. The events that unfolded in France shocked many people such that they were to change their views: Southey and Wordsworth were examples of such men. So too, it is to be remembered, that the events in France were to turn into international war;

to side with the French was to be on the side against England. Edmund Burke summed the matter up:

> Whatever were the first motives to the war among politicians, they saw that in its spirit, and for its objects, it was a *civil war*; and as such they pursued it. It is a war between the partisans of the ancient civil, moral and political order of Europe against a sect of fanatical and ambitious atheists which means to change them all. It is not France extending a foreign empire over other nations: it is a sect aiming at universal empire, and beginning with the conquest of France.
>
> – As quoted by Kirk.

As for Southey: well, he progressed with his thoughts and was to come to realize that when men are forced to change the result is blood and misery. Best, he concluded in time, and after some soul searching – to let things be, that things will unfold naturally as they ought to unfold. William Hazlitt wrote of Southey's earlier revolutionary thoughts and his eventual conversion to toryism:

> ... the light of the French Revolution beamed into his soul ... while he had this hope, this faith in man left, he cherished it with child-like simplicity, he clung to it with the fondness of a lover. He was an enthusiast, a fanatic, a leveler; he stuck at nothing that he thought would banish all pain and misery from the world; in his impatience of the smallest error or injustice, he would have sacrificed himself and the existing generation (a holocaust) to his devotion to the right cause. But when he once believed after many staggering doubts and painful struggles, that this was no longer possible, when his chimeras and golden dreams of human perfectibility vanished from him, he turned suddenly round, and maintained that 'whatever is, is right.'

To Hazlitt, Southey's "inquires are partial and hasty, his conclusions raw and unconcocted ... He wooed Liberty as a youthful lover, but it was perhaps more a mistress than a bride; and he has since wedded with an elderly and not very reputable lady, called Legitimacy." Hazlitt continued:

> He was born an age too late. Had he lived a century or two ago, he would have been a happy as well as blameless character. But the distraction of the time has unsettled him, and the multiplicity of his pretensions have jostled with each other. No man in our day (at least no man of genius) has led so uniformly and entirely the life of a scholar from boyhood to the present hour, devoting himself to learning with the enthusiasm of an early love, with the severity and constancy of a religious vow; and well would it have been for him if he had confined himself to this, and not undertaken to pull down or to patch up the State!'

Southey's earlier works, as he was to observe, were written "under the influence of opinions which I have long since outgrown, and repeatedly disclaimed, but for which I have never felt either shame or contrition. They were taken up conscientiously in early youth, they were acted upon in disregard of all worldly considerations, and they were left behind in the same strait-forward course, as I advanced in years." (Hazlitt, *Political Essays*.) Hazlitt was of the view that Southey, if he ever had them, sold out his principles: "he quitted his principles when he saw a good opportunity: in taking up the cause of the Allies, his principles and his interest became united and thenceforth indissoluble."

By age 38, Southey had quite given up all of the revolutionary notions that he had possessed as a young man. By then, 1812, he was "a state pensioner and a champion of the party of order in the *Quarterly Review*..."[8] What Southey, and Wordsworth too, had turned into were supporters of British society; and, certainly it is plain, that British society had become supporters of Southey and Wordsworth. Others poets, Byron for one (and he could well afford to be independent in thought) was of the view that Southey and his ilk were but "dull hirelings," "venomous apostates" and "cold blooded assassins of freedom." (Dowden.)

Any views on Southey's character, like that of Byron's, must be tempered by the fact that Robert Southey was a popular person and had many friends. He was to be admired because of his devotion to his work, his family (much extended) and his country. To be admired, as Hazlitt was to write, simply because Southey was an "industrious and calligraphic man."

> The variety and piquancy of his writings form a striking contrast to the mode in which they are produced. He rises early, and writes or reads till bedtime ... Study serves him for business, exercise, recreation. He passes from verse to prose, from history to poetry, from reading to writing, by a stop-watch. He writes a fair hand without blots, sitting upright in his chair, leaves off when he comes to the bottom of the page, and changes the subject for another, as opposite as the Antipodes. His mind is after all rather the recipient and transmitter of knowledge, than the originator of it. He has hardly grasp of thought enough to arrive at any great leading truth. His passions do not amount to more than irritability. With some gall in his pen and coldness in his manner, he has a great deal of kindness in his heart. Rash in his opinions, he is steady in his attachments, and is a man, in many particulars admirable, in all respectable — his political inconsistency alone excepted!.
>
> — Hazlitt, "Mr. Southey," *The Spirit of the Age*.

It would not appear that Southey had too many disappointments in life. He was certainly deeply affected by the loss of his ten year old son in 1816. Another blow was when, after being married to her for 39 years, in 1837, Edith Southey died. However, her loss come on in stages, the major one being in 1830 when Edith started showing signs of insanity. In the fall of 1834, Southey committed her to an asylum at York. Edith did recover sufficiently so that she came back home by the spring of 1835, so to spend her last year with her family. Southey's health quickly deteriorated after the death of Edith. He recovered, then surprisingly – though, maybe not – Southey remarried. This was to happen in 1839, exchanging vows with Caroline Bowles. Southey had but four years to live with Caroline before his death; it would appear she was more of a keeper of Southey than anything else. His mental state slipped just shortly after his marriage to Caroline and he became steadily worse. In 1843, Robert Southey died and was buried in the Churchyard of Crossthwaite near Keswick.

Lord Byron

(1788-1824)

Lord Byron
(1788-1824).

A Peer, a Poet of Revolt ...
An Aristocrat in Sentiment, a Democrat in Opinion ...

And, for the Ladies ....
"Mad, Bad, and Dangerous To Know."[1]

Lord Byron's life is a moral tale. While Byron was born an aristocrat, he led the life of a vagabond. He was a genius subject only to his own ruling passions. He was born with a malformation of one foot, which left him with a life long limp. Notwithstanding, he grew up to be a dark and handsome man; the women liked Byron and he liked the women; his sexual exploits are legend. Byron spent a significant part of his adult life on the continent, making his first trip in 1809 with his school chum, John Hobhouse. Hobhouse returned to England leaving Byron to go on to Greece by himself. During this eastern trip Byron wrote the first two cantos of *Childe Harold*, which tells the story of his tour. On his return to England, he arranged for its publication and it "took the town by storm; seven editions were sold in a month." Byron then tried to settle down into a regular aristocratic life, even to the point of getting himself married (it lasted but a few months), but for Byron, none of it worked very well. By 1821 Byron was permanently living in Italy where he became part of a romantic literary circle, one that included Shelley. After Shelly's death, Byron left Italy for Greece, arriving there in 1824. He intended to assist the Greeks in their struggle against the Turks. Shortly, thereafter, at Greece, at the age of 36, Lord Byron died.

Byron became an idol of the romantic movement, a symbol of the heady times that extended from the 1790s to the 1830s. He represented one extreme of these highly political times.[2] A model has been made of him, "The Byronic Hero": brave, proud, masterful with a general contempt for his fellows.[3]

Byron's Early Life:

Our hero's grandfather was a well respected navy man, Admiral John Byron (1723-86). The admiral had two sons and three daughters. It was the eldest son, John Byron (1751-91) who was the poet's father. John received a commission in the army and became a captain in the guards. His military career likely matched his dismal life. "Mad Jack" was an unprincipled man and had the respect of no one including the members of his family. In 1779, "Mad Jack" married his first wife.[4] Of that union came two daughters; the first died in infancy; the second, Augusta, lived on (we will take up Augusta and her relationship with her famous step brother, presently). "Mad Jack's" first wife died in the same year (1784) that she gave birth to her daughter, Augusta.

Byron's mother, Catherine Gordon of Gight (b.1765), was John Byron's second wife. She was one of the Gordons of Scotland, though, at the time Catherine first met John Byron she was residing at Bath. The two married in 1785. I am not sure when or the reasons for the move[5] but eventually "Mad Jack" took Catherine off to live on the continent. Whatever the arrangements were on the continent, they did not suit Catherine; more particularly, she likely figured out just how despicable a character "Mad Jack" really was. Catherine left "Mad Jack" to go to live with her family in Scotland.

On the 22nd January, 1788, while laying over at London on her way to Scotland, Catherine gave birth to her only child, George Gordon. Thereafter, Catherine carried on with her son to Scotland. At Aberdeen, doubtlessly with the help of her family, Catherine took a small house. “Mad Jack,” not long after, showed up on Catherine’s doorstep. The couple with the baby then lived together as a family; but not for long.[6] Being pressed by his creditors, abandoning his wife and young son, John Byron fled to Valenciennes, France, where he died in 1791. The son, the subject of this sketch, was but only three years of age at the time of his father's death.

Byron attended Aberdeen Grammar School. Due to a pronounced limp from a congenital malformation of at least one of his lower limbs,[7] Byron likely had problems with the socialization process involved with his early schooling. Difficulties in the school yard surely had an effect on his developing personality. But likely that which had more of an effect on the young Byron and the string of difficulties that he was to have in his adult life, especially with his female acquaintances, was Byron’s relationship with his mother. Catherine, was pathetic, generous and affectionate, but with a violent and uncontrollable temper; as a boy, she alternately petted and abused Byron.[8] The temper, which Byron preserved throughout the balance of his life was “passionate, sullen, defiant of authority, but significantly amenable to kindness.”[9]

More generally, as to his early schooling, John Nichol in his biography on Byron wrote:

> ... he was backward in technical scholarship, and low in his class, in which he seems to have had no ambition to stand high; but that he eagerly took to history and romance, especially luxuriating in the *Arabian Nights*. He was an indifferent penman, and always

disliked mathematics; but was noted by masters and mates as of quick temper, eager for adventures, prone to sports, always more ready to give a blow than to take one, affectionate, though resentful.

Now, what is to be told, is how this young lame boy in Scotland was to become a peer of the realm and to take all the privileges that flow from the added appelation of "Lord." Though he personally could in no way be described as such, Byron's father, as previously noted, came from a noble English family. Byron's grand-uncle was the Fifth Baron Byron of Rochdale, a hereditary title. The Fifth Baron died in 1798 leaving no direct descendants, such that, through the laws that govern succession, this hereditary peerage fell to our poet making him the Sixth Baron Byron of Rochdale. As fine a gift as a baronetcy was to the young Byron, what hope, title or no tile, did such an honor hold out where the inherited estate was all but bankrupt and where the only income to the promoter of the young lord, his mother, was a yearly income of £122, being from a small capital sum that she had managed to rescue from "Mad Jack's" spendthrift ways. What was necessary was for somebody with money and connections to take the young Lord in tow. By whatever manner, the case came to the attention of Frederick Howard, Fifth Earl of Carlisle (1748-1825), a distant relative to the ten year old Lord Byron. Friends had encouraged Lord Carlisle to take the young lord under his wing and see to his education. The first thing that Carlisle did was to use his influence to get Catherine Byron placed on the civil list which was to provide her an additional yearly income of £300. What was necessary, too, was to move the young peer to London. So it was, that Catherine and her young son moved away, as it turned out, permanently from Scotland.[10]

The reason, I suppose, that the move to London was necessary, was because an application had to be made to Chancery Court. Being a minor and a lord and without a father, Byron was automatically a ward of the court. A solicitor was employed to handle matters in respect to the applications for approval of the guardianship, etc. The solicitor employed was John Hanson, who, thereafter, took a personal interest in the affairs of the young lord, and, indeed, played a pivotal role in the balance of Byron's life.

For the next number of years, Byron and his mother lived at London. Byron was first sent to school at Dulwich[11] then to Harrow. No doubt, Byron's time at Harrow, 1801-1805, was beneficial to his budding poetic mind. He learned Latin and Greek, and dipped into the classics. Also, he came to the view, as generally all boys do who attend such schools as Harrow by measuring the esteem of each other, that he was made of special social suff.[12]

With Byron's advancement to a Baronetcy came title to Newstead Abbey, the ancestral Byron estate in Nottinghamshire. No sooner after she settled legal matters at London, Catherine took her ten year old son to Newstead Abbey, only "to find it in almost complete decay."

> Hitherto the less ruinous portions of the abbey had been occupied by a tenant, Lord Grey de Ruthven. The banqueting hall, the grand drawing-room, and other parts of the monastic building were uninhabitable, but by incurring fresh debts, two sets of apartments were refurnished for Byron and for his mother. Dismantled and ruinous, it was still a splendid inheritance. In line with the front of the abbey is the west front of the priory church, with its hollow arch, once a "mighty window," its vacant niches, its delicate Gothic mouldings. The abbey buildings enclose a grassy quadrangle

overlooked by two-storeyed cloisters. On the eastern side are the state apartments occupied by kings and queens not as guests, but by feudal right. In the park, which is part of Sherwood Forest, there is a chain of lakes – the largest, the north-west, Byron's "lucid lake." A waterfall or "cascade" issues from the lake, in full view of the room where Byron slept. The possession of this lordly and historic domain was an inspiration in itself. It was an ideal home for one who was to be hailed as the spirit of genius of romance.

– E. H. Coleridge.

On arrival at Newstead Abbey, Catherine determined to effect repairs and live there. It was soon realized, however, that fixing up Newstead Abbey was an impractical plan. They returned to London where Byron started school, as we have mentioned, at Dulwich. Catherine was a thorn in the side of the Chancery solicitor who was in charge, John Hanson, as it seems she was to everyone including her young son. She went on about more than just a better school for her son, there were other matters and Catherine was continually working her list. Finally Hanson decided to put his foot down. He limited Catherine's involvement in her young son's affairs. A compromise seemingly was worked out. Byron's enrolment at Harrow would be arranged; and – given the quarrels and difficulties between Catherine and her young son – the Hanson family would establish a second home for Byron. (The Hansons lived at Earl's Court.) Byron was to be given a choice as to, with whom he wished to spend the holidays. Therefore, after 1801, one would have seen Byron, when not boarding at Harrow, visiting with either his mother or the Hansons. In July of 1803, when Byron was fifteen years of age, his mother moved to Burgage Manor in Southwell, a village about 12 miles from Nottingham, viz. near the ancestral Byron estate, Newstead Abbey. The young Lord Byron, in between times at Harrow, in addition to his place in London (the Hansons) and his mother's place, had a third place to which he might run. Byron's mother, not able to cope with the expenses and in need of money, had rented Newstead Abbey to Henry Edward, the nineteenth Baron Grey de Ruthyn, a lease which was to last during Byron's minority. Lord Grey extended, however, an open invitation for Byron to visit his ancestral estate anytime he pleased (Lord Grey had an eye for young boys). Determined to skip the fall term at Harrow in 1803, Byron rode to Newstead where he stayed at the gate-house with Owen Mealey, the steward. It was during this time that Byron was to first experience the pangs of love, when he met his cousin, Mary Chaworth of Annesley Hall, an event we will expand upon in due course.

Cambridge and The Lord's Rejection:

Having finished up at Harrow (he apparently ran away from the place a couple of times), in October of 1805, at the age seventeen, Byron entered Cambridge (Trinity College). Byron was fast approaching the age of majority, when, without permission of the court, he could deal with his own affairs as he saw fit. Byron was particularly looking forward to taking title to Newstead Abby. Money lenders in London, now that he was approaching the age of majority, were fast becoming Byron's friends. Thus, Byron could easily raise the money to support a conventional life of extravagant dissipation. During his years at Cambridge, 1805-08, he divided his time between Cambridge, London and at his mother's house at Southwell. At times through these years he would leave Cambridge in the middle of term, or arrive late or leave early; Lord Byron was more interested in tasting life as might be had at London than keeping his nose in the books at Cambridge. Still, the allowances were coming through Hanson's hands and Byron was kept at the wheel of learning, through threats from solicitor Hanson, that, should Byron leave Cambridge, he would be cut off. These threats usually had the effect of driving Byron back to his studies at Cambridge.[13]

Quarrels through these years continued with his mother over his extravagances at Cambridge and London, and his arrangements with the money-lenders. He passed his days not so much studying as much, with his friends, shooting pistols, playing cricket, and swimming.[14] At London, Byron took fencing and boxing lessons. Notwithstanding all this activity, Byron found time to write. As early as 1806, Byron saw to the publication of his first poems, *Fugitive Pieces*. This first work was privately printed without Byron's name. Criticism of this work caused Byron to recall most of the distributed copies which he then proceeded to destroy. He then carried out "excisions and prunings" of the work and re-published it. In 1807, he brought out *Poems on Various Occasions* (January), again, privately printed (about 100 copies) and *Hours of Idleness* (June). In February of 1808, a scathing review of *Hours of Idleness* appeared in the *Edinburgh Review*, "imitative, sentimental, and mawkish." This criticism provoked Byron to reply with the publication, in 1808, of *English Bards and Scotch Reviewers*. This work was an immediate success and a sell out.[15]

In 1808, Byron entered into a time that he could fully call his own. In June of that year, Lord Grey's lease on Newstead Abbey came to an end. That July, Cambridge granted Lord Byron a degree. By September, Byron took up residence at Newstead. His mother was likely quite prepared to join him there but he managed to keep her away on the basis that repairs must first be carried out.[16] His friend, John Hobhouse,[17] joined him at Newstead and stayed until November, after which Byron continued to write in the isolation of the Abbey.[18]

Upon coming of age, Byron went through the motions of establishing himself as a high class member of society. On January 22nd, 1809, Byron became twenty-one. He traveled to London and filed his papers giving evidence of his heredity right to become a member of the House of Lords. In March of that year, Byron took his rightful seat at the House of Lords, but he was "humiliated by the manner in which he is announced." The fact is that the young lord was spurned by his fellow lords; and, Byron felt it deeply. Why was he rejected? – Was it because he was too young to join the old club. Was it because these men thought that Byron had no real power or money behind him? Was it because Byron was a man who fancied himself a poet? Was it because his father was a reprobate? Was it because he was a cripple? Byron, I am sure, turned over all of these reasons in his head. Eventually he decided that he did not need the approval of such men. He would make his way in the world on his own terms.[19]

Hobnobbing with Ali Pasha:

Trelawny recollects that in 1809 Byron first left England; rode on horseback through Spain and Portugal, four hundred miles; crossed the Mediterranean on board a frigate, and landed in Greece,[20] where he passed two years after which he returned to England.

Leaving London with John Hobhouse, in June of 1809, the pair departed Falmouth on July 2nd, on the

Lisbon packet, *Princess Elizabeth.*[21] By the 7th of July, Byron and Hobhouse were at Lisbon, and from there went by horseback to Seville and Cadiz. It is during this time that Byron swam the Tagus.[22] In time, he went by sea to the British base of Gibraltar. On the 16th of August, Byron sailed for Malta where he makes love to Mrs. Spencer Smith (the "Fair Florence" of *Childe Harold).* After three weeks in Malta the party landed at Preveza and after that, toured Albania. He met the bandit, Ali Pasha, and the two took a liking to one and other. They traveled in company to Greece[23] and Turkey (Byron swam the Hellespont). His travels with Ali Pasha included, to quote E. H. Coleridge: "a yachting tour along the shores of the Ambracian Gulf (November 8-23), a journey by land from Larnaki to Athens (December 15-25), and excursions in Attica, Sunium and Marathon (January 13-25, 1810)." Hobhouse was not so impressed with all of this as was Byron. On July 14th, 1810, Hobhouse took a passage to England, leaving Byron to go back to Greece. During this, Byron's first eastern trip, he wrote the first two cantos of *Childe Harold*, which tells the story of his tour. At Greece he composes "Hints from Horace" and the "Curse of Minerva".

Not as much is known of Byron's travels after saying his goodbyes to Hobhouse, in July of 1810. I again quote Coleridge's biography: "... he was traveling in the Morea during August and September, that early in October he was at Patras, having just recovered from a severe attack of malarial fever, and that by the 14th of November he had returned to Athens and taken up his quarters at the Franciscan convent."[24] Byron might have been in residence at a convent, the Capuchin convent; but Byron did not live the life of a monk. We see at this period of time, November, 1810 – though in bad financial shape – how Byron managed to partake of the high life in Athens. In a letter to a friend, Byron describes "a party with drunken, rowdy Turkish heads-of-state." It is thus that Byron continued on in Athens until April of 1811. It was in June that he was back in Gibraltar; in between April and June he spent a few weeks at Malta. (Ah! Yes. – Mrs. Spencer Smith.) It was after leaving Malta that Byron wrote in his journal of his general unhappiness with mankind. By July 14th, he was back in England[25] after an absence of a little more than two years. Before the month was out, Byron had met up with Hobhouse, now a captain in the Militia. The pair toured Canterbury and its vicinity. In August of 1811, Byron heard the news of his mother's ill health. Borrowing £40 from his Solicitor, John Hanson, Byron traveled home to see his sick mother. It was too late. Catherine died at Newstead on August 1st. "On arriving at Newstead, all their storms forgotten, the son was so affected that he did not trust himself to go to the funeral, but stood dreamily gazing at the cortége from the gate of the Abbey." (Nichol.)

English Love Affairs:

Very early in Byron's life, the little girls about him made his heart go pitter-patter. For instance there is, when he was but a boy of eight, the record of his first love affair. It amounted to a passionate attachment to Mary Duff, a distant cousin he met at dancing-school likely at Aberdeen. The attachment that gets more attention, however, is the one that Byron had for his cousin, Mary Chaworth of Annesley Hall, to whom we have already made reference. In 1803, the 15 year old Byron, made his first visit to his ancestral home,

Newstead Abby. He had determined to skip the fall term at Harrow, and lodged himself at the gate-house with Owen Mealey, the steward. His infatuation for Mary Chaworth ended when he overheard her mocking his lameness.[26] We read, too, that during this time that Lord Grey – remember Lord Grey, he was the one that held the lease on Newstead Abbey, but only to Byron's age of majority – Lord Grey made "some sort of sexual advance" that shocked the young Byron and led to "an abrupt and decisive break between the two." Byron's discovery of the pleasures or displeasures of sex, however, came about at an earlier point of time. When Byron was but a boy of eleven, there was in his household, a housekeeper, May Gray. Ms. Gray, it was found out, used to slip into bed with the young lord. The Chancery Solicitor who had taken Lord Byron under his wing, John Hanson, came to learn of Ms. Gray's proclivities and promptly saw to her dismissal.

After the death of his mother that August, Byron stayed on at Newstead until December when he returned to London; though, before the month was out, he was back at Newstead with friends. In January of 1812, Byron again traveled to London. This time it was for the opening of Parliament (being a lord, he had a seat in the upper chamber). On March 10, 1812, *Childe Harold*, Cantos I and II, were offered to the public for sale by John Murray. "Within three days, the first edition of 500 copies sells out." ("The Byron Chronology.") Byron's prospects were looking up. He also was in for quite a sum of money, as Byron that year had entered into an agreement to sell Newstead.[27] Thus it is, in 1812, that George Gordon Byron was widely known as a handsome lord with money. Enter, all in the month of March:

Lady Caroline Lamb, Lady Jane Oxford and Annabella Milbanke.

Lady Caroline Lamb (1785-1828) was the wife of William Lamb who was to become known as Viscount William Melbourne (1779-1848).[28] Lady Caroline was the daughter of the Earl of Bessborough and Henrietta Ponsonby, and the niece of the Duchess of Devonshire. "As a child she was a tomboy – and a spirit of recklessness and disdain for convention never left her."[29] At the time of their first meeting, in March of 1812, Byron was 24 years old; Caroline was 27 years old, married and the mother of an autistic son. They met at a function in a grand room of one of the great homes of aristocratic England, Holland House.[30] Byron used these words to describe Caroline: "She was tall and very thin, with short, curly blonde hair and hazel eyes."[31] It was not long after this first meeting when the pair were alone with a little time on their hands: we might imagine Byron slowly unbuttoning one of Caroline's pageboy outfits.

> They became lovers and shocked London with their affair through much of April and May 1812. Byron had long believed women were truly incapable of understanding male thoughts and desires. With Caroline, he was forced to abandon this notion. They read together, discussed poetry – and argued fiercely. His supposed flirtations with other women and her open affection for her husband and other admirers caused most of the fighting. Some arguments ended 'without any verbal explanation', Byron told a friend. He was particularly jealous of her waltzing with other men. And since Byron could not dance with his club-foot, Caroline now sat with him, no longer the life of her parties. When she was not invited to a party he attended, she would wait out in the street for him. If he needed money, she told him, he could pawn her jewels. ...[32]

Byron left a lifelong track record: he loved to pursue women but once he realized his goal of having them completely he then grew bored and became irritated with them. This familiar course defines the short affair he had with Caroline Lamb. To quote his biographer, Nichol: "... after the first excitement, he began to grow weary of her talk about herself, and could not praise her indifferent verses; 'he grew moody, and she fretful, when their mutual egotisms jarred.'" He too, was getting pressure from his friends such as John Hobhouse. Shocked by the open affair of Byron and a married lady of high standing, they urged him to return to Newstead Abbey and forget Caroline. Leaving Caroline in the lurch, Byron took his friends' advice and rode up to Newstead. Caroline wrote him there, letter after letter which Byron systematically ignored. Needing to attend to business, by July, Byron was back at London. Finding out that he was back, Caroline arrived at Byron's rooms. Hobhouse was there at the time and wrote of the event in his diary:

> Wednesday July 29. Went to Byron's in expectation of going to Harrow, a scheme he had resolved on to avoid the threatened visit of a Lady – at 12 o'clock just as we were going, several thundering raps were heard at the door & we saw a crowd collected about the door & opposite to it – immediately a person in a most strange disguise walked up stairs – it turned out to be the Lady in question from Brocket.[33] ... I did think that to leave my friend in such a situation, when ... every soul in the house servants & all knew of the person in disguise, and not to endeavor to prevent the catastrophe of an elopement which seemed inevitable, would be unjustifiable – accordingly I stayed in the sitting room whilst the Lady was in the bed room pulling off her disguise – under which she had a page's dress ... at last she was prevailed upon to put on a habit, bonnet & shoes – belonging to a servant of the house and, after much entreaty did come out into the sitting room. ..."[34]

In August, Caroline left her family. The call went out to Byron and he sought her out in Kensington from where he returned her to her family at Brocket Hall. Though now somewhat of a prisoner (I suppose) at Brocket Hall, Caroline continued to write letters threatening Byron with revenge; and at one point, in a yard at Brocket, Caroline Lamb burned effigies of Byron and copies of his letters, while neighborhood children danced around the bonfire. In January of 1813, Caroline managed to carry off a much valued painting of Byron and did so by forging Byron's writing in a letter directing his publisher, John Murray to give the painting to Lady Caroline. Caroline's theft of the portrait upset Byron which of course was Caroline's objective. Caroline kept up these antics for a considerable period of time. Later in the year, 1813, both Byron and Caroline were at Lady Heathcote's ...

> On 5 July, they met again at a waltzing party at Lady Heathcote's. Caroline remembered his earlier pleas for her to sit with him instead of dancing. She walked up to him and asked, 'I conclude I may waltz now.' Byron replied: 'With every body in turn – you always did it better than anyone. I shall have a pleasure in seeing you.' Later, he said to her sarcastically, 'I have been admiring your dexterity.' Caroline picked up a table knife, 'not intending anything', she later wrote. Byron was amused and contemptuous. 'Do, my dear. If you mean to act a Roman's part,' he told her, 'mind which way you strike with your knife – be it at your own heart, not mine – you have struck there already.' Caroline cried out, 'Byron!' and fled in distress. When some ladies tried to take the knife from her, she cut her hand.[35]

Byron continued to be the object of Caroline's scorn for a considerable period of time. It might have passed in a shorter time, except that Byron was bedding one of Caroline's friends, Lady Jane Oxford, an affair which Caroline came to know about, and which accounts – together with her natural proclivities – for Caroline's extreme reactions. At some point earlier, the Oxfords had befriended Byron. (His relationship with the Oxfords, I note parenthetically, drew Byron into the circle of the Princess of Wales, such that he was a regular visitor at Kensington Palace.) I am not sure of the exact circumstances, but it seems clear that Lady Oxford's affair[36] with Byron started in October of 1812, a point in time after he had broken things off with Caroline Lamb. Lady Oxford did not help matters much and goaded Byron on, in his dealings with Caroline. Caroline during this withdrawal period had written Byron asking for a lock of his hair. The letter, as was the case with others were read jointly by Byron and Jane. A lock of hair was sent to Caroline, not of his but rather of Lady Oxford's; it being determined that there was little difference in the color of her hair when compared to that of Byron's. The affair between Byron and Lady Oxford lasted but a few months.

A closing note on Caroline Lamb: she continued, to one degree or another, to be a problem for Byron until about 1815 when Caroline's attention was finally diverted. It was then that she and her mother traveled over to Europe, as her brother, Frederick Ponsonby, had been wounded at Waterloo. Caroline and her mother planned to be at Brussels to nurse him. For Caroline, as it certainly was for Byron (he was to have hundreds), what was wanted was to have a number of love affairs. Her political husband (highly successful) was to receive appointments which included stays at Paris and Brussels where there were stationed a great number of young handsome military officers. Her most famous conquest was the Duke of Wellington. Caroline became more and more distraught as her last years sped by. She separated from Lord Melbourne in 1825, though he continued to remain close, indeed, he was at her bedside when she died in 1828 at the age of 43. Lord Melbourne survived Caroline for twenty years; never married again; and went on to be the prime minister of Great Britain.

It is now time to pass on to Anne Isabella Milbanke (1792-1860), she was most always referred to as Annabella. She has her place in history as the wife of Byron. She was an heiress and a cousin of Caroline's husband, William Lamb. Annabella is one of the mysteries of Byron's life. It is reported that he was not in love with her, and there was no money to be gained by the match. It would not appear that Annabella was swooped off her feet by Byron, but like so many woman to come into his orbit, in time, succumbed to Byron's sexual charms.[37] "In his endeavours to corrupt my mind he has sought to make me smile first at Vice, saying 'There is nothing to which a woman may not be reconciled by repetition or familiarity.' There is no Vice with which he has not endeavoured in this manner to familiarize me." This much we know: in 1813, Byron proposed to Annabella and she refused him. In September of 1814, however, a further marriage proposal was accepted by Annabella. In January of 1815, Byron married Annabella; in December their daughter, Augusta Ada was born.[38] A month later, in January of 1816, the pair parted for good.[39]

It was on the 25th of March, 1812, that Byron met Annabella Milbanke at Brocket Hall, a place that is central to our story of Byron during this part of his life; it was where the Melbournes lived, near Hatfield in Hertfordshire. Lady Elizabeth Melbourne, was Annabella's father's sister. It just so happened – there is some suggestion that Lady Elizabeth arranged it – that Annabella was at Melbourne House when Byron came to visit. I am not sure how things progressed to the point, but on October 12th, Byron proposed marriage which Annabella rejected, a rejection which likely came more from Annabella's family than herself. The pair, however, kept up correspondence. Annabella's family gradually warmed up to Byron, such that in April of 1814, Byron received a formal invitation to visit Seaham Hall from Sir Ralph Milbanke, Annabella's father. Written correspondence between the two picked up through the summer. In August, Byron received a cryptic letter from Annabella in which she acknowledged an "imperfect" attachment to him. On September 9th, Byron posted a marriage proposal to Annabella. On the 19th he received Annabella's acceptance. After that the fiancés are seen to be writing daily to one another. Though Annabella wished for a large wedding, Byron insisted on a private ceremony. When Byron learned that a potential agreement of purchase and sale for Newstead fell through, he proposed to Annabella that they postpone the wedding. Byron's insistence that they will be poor until Newstead was sold, left her unconcerned. On January 2nd, 1815, the pair were bound over on their marital vows in a private ceremony in the first floor drawing room at Seaham Hall.[40] Lord and Lady Byron spent their honeymoon at the Noel estate, Halnaby.

I do not know how long the wedded bliss lasted. By February, his financial affairs were such that Byron thought it best to be in London. They eventually moved into residence at Piccadilly Terrace and were living mostly on Lady Byron's marriage settlement from her parents. That spring Annabella met Byron's half-sister, Augusta, for the first time. Augusta was Byron's – I would say – closest friend, we will come to her shortly.

Byron's finances were in a very precarious state. Creditors were stepping up the pressure. Legal writs and processes were coming at him with regularity. He feared the next steps were not far away – distrains and arrests. Though Byron's properties were then worth over £100,000, he was unable to find buyers to pay his price. Things were that disparate that he sold his library. At this point, Byron was drinking heavily.[41] Byron's rages led Annabella to believe him temporarily insane. In September, Byron wrote Augusta telling her that he believed Annabella had been searching through his papers and had broken open his writing desk. In November, Augusta, in response to Annabella's alarming letters, arrived at Piccadilly Terrace to help manage Byron's moods. On December 10th, Annabella delivered a baby girl, Augusta Ada. In January of 1816, things were such between Byron and his wife that he proposed that they break up the expensive house in London, with Annabella and the baby moving, "temporarily" to her parents' house in Kirkby Mallory.[42] Annabella and the baby made the move. When Annabella's family heard about what was going on they obliged their daughter to consult their solicitors. Soon after, legal channels were opened and by March formal terms were agreed upon.

The question that now comes to be asked, is this: What role did Byron's half-sister play in the breakdown of his marriage; or, more generally, what was the nature of the relationship that Byron had with his half-sister, Augusta Leigh (1783-1851). We first mentioned Augusta when dealing with Byron's early life. We saw where Byron was born in 1788, the son of John ("Mad Jack") Byron. Byron was the product of his father's second marriage. John's first wife died shortly after giving birth, in 1784, to a daughter, Augusta. Now I do not know where Augusta was during the years that Byron grew into manhood; she is missing from the picture. With both her mother and father being dead, Augusta, it would appear, was brought up by her mother's family.[43]

We pick up on Augusta's life at her age 20. It was in October of 1804 that General Charles Leigh objected to his son's marriage to Augusta based on the smallness of her income, £350 a year left her by her grandmother Lady Holderness. During October and November of 1804, Byron and Augusta exchanged letters in which they commiserate over their respective difficulties: those he had with his mother, she with the Leighs. The Leigh family was to eventually get over their objections to this marriage of first cousins. On August 17th, 1807, Augusta married the general's son, Colonel George Leigh.[44] Byron did not see much of Augusta after her marriage, for, maybe a five year period. There seems to be no correspondence between the two even after his return from Greece in July of 1811. If is difficult to think that he did not see Augusta at Newstead just after his mother died on August 1st, 1811. In any event, only in 1813, do we see Byron and his half-sister coming together to commiserate as they did eight years previously. Byron had just passed a year full of problems. You will remember, this was the year that Byron was trying to extricate himself from the clutches of Caroline Lamb; the year, after dropping Caroline, that he took up with Lady Oxford; the year that he first met Annabella Milbanke.

In 1813, Augusta Leigh was living with her husband at Six Mile Bottom, north of London, very near Cambridge. It was in June of that year that Augusta arrived at London for a three week visit. She came again to London on August

5th and by the 20th she was back at Six Mile Bottom. In mid-December, Augusta was again in London and after a stay of a few days was brought back to Six Mile Bottom by Byron who returned to London on December 27th. On January 17th, 1814, Byron and Augusta had set out for Newstead. On January 22nd, Byron celebrated his 26th birthday. Augusta Leigh gave birth to a daughter on April 14th, 1814. The child was named Elizabeth Medora after Byron's famous heroine in *The Corsair*.[45] In May, Byron sent Augusta £3,000 to settle her husband's debts. In August of 1814, Byron, Augusta, and the Leigh children traveled to Newstead. Augusta tried to arrange a marriage for him with Lady Charlotte Leveson Gower. It will be remembered that Byron married Annabella on January 2nd, 1815.

Well what are we to make of this recitation of the times and events in respect to the relationship between Byron and his half-sister. I think it was but a matter of a sister moving close to her brother during a time he was having troubles. There are those who would say that the two had an incestuous relationship; but, really, there is little proof of it. Ms Hellam, in her analysis wrote:

> Byron began to woo his half-sister Augusta Leigh in August of 1813. On April 15, 1814 Augusta gave birth to Elizabeth Medora who is believed to be the child of Byron's and Augusta's incestuous relationship. To end rumors that circulated about the two of them, Augusta urged Byron to marry. Annabella, due to their correspondence for the past eight months and previous romantic history, seemed the likely candidate. In September of 1814 Byron proposes and Annabella surprisingly accepts.[46]

After the marriage, in February, the wedded pair visited Six Mile Bottom, where Annabella and Augusta meet for the first time.[47] In July, 1815, Byron signed a new will stipulating that after the payment of Annabella's marriage settlement, the remainder of his estate would go to Augusta and her children.[48] Augusta, it would appear, continued to help her brother as he went through the marriage breakup. She spent time with Byron that November in response to Annabella's alarming charges that Byron had gone mad. Augusta went to London to be with Byron. He was in a bad mood and lashing out at anyone, even Augusta.[49]

Byron took the separation from his wife with great difficulty. Leigh Hunt saw him at this time and observed that Byron became ill; "his face was jaundiced with bile; he felt the attacks of the public severely; and, to crown all, he had an execution in [on] his house. I [Hunt] was struck with the real trouble he manifested, compared with what the public thought of it. The adherence of his old friends was also touching."[50] Trelawny recollects: "As to the oft-vexed question of the Poet's separation from his wife ... he treated women as things devoid of soul or sense; he would not eat, pray, walk, nor talk, with them. ... who would have marvelled that a lady tenderly reared and richly endowed, pious, learned, and prudent, deluded into marrying such a man, should have thought him mad or worse, and sought safety by flight? Within certain degrees of affinity marriages are forbidden; so they should be where there is no natural affinity of feelings, habits tastes, or sympathies."

On April 8th, 1816, Byron, Augusta Leigh, and Hobhouse (who had by then moved in with Byron) attended a party at Lady Jersey's where they met Benjamin Constant (1767-1830). Some of the fashionable set cut both Byron and Augusta ... On the 13th, Annabella snubed Augusta, by having her solicitor respond to a private note. Byron was furious; it was more than he could stand. On the 23rd, he was on a carriage headed for Dover; on the 25th he sailed for Ostend, Belgium.[51] On May 4th, Byron stood on the fields of Waterloo, bloodied the previous year. We can but only image Byron turning west away from England and the fields of Waterloo. He was soon off to Switzerland and Italy. In Italy, he took up a new life with a new circle of poetic friends.

Italy (1816-20):

As has been observed in my biographical sketch on Shelley, there are many reasons why an Englishman, back in the early part of the 19th-century, would want to settle down in Italy.[52] Marital difficulties or financial difficulties (they so often go together) are good reasons to get thyself to Italy. The living was cheaper in Italy than in England, then there is the climate (wonderful), the fresh vegetables and fresh fruit, the women, the wine, – well, you know all the usual enticements. However, I must not get too far into this part without telling of yet another woman in Byron's life: Jane Clairmont, better known as Claire. To put matters in larger perspective: Claire was the younger half-sister of Mary Godwin who ran off with Shelley in 1814. Claire and Mary, as they say, were joined at the hip.[53] Anything the one did the other came along and did likewise. When Shelley first met Mary in the spring, he determined (if they were willing) that he would abandon all and run off with them. It was in June of 1814, much before any of them made their acquaintance with Byron, that Shelley arranged for a carriage and the girls (Mary was seventeen, Claire was sixteen) slipped out of their parents' house and off they drove to Dover. They traveled through France and on to

Switzerland. By September the 13th the three were back in London. (All of this is set out in my sketch on Shelley.)

What we know for sure, is that on January 13th, 1817, in England, Claire gave birth to a child (Allegra) who, the parents disclosed, was fathered by Byron.[54] If the child went full term, then Claire and Byron were together during the month of April. Byron was off to Dover on the 23rd of April headed for Belgium, maybe after a wonderful night with Claire, who knows? That May, as it turned out, Shelley, Mary and Claire were visiting Byron at Lake Geneva. Thus it might have been that Allegra was born prematurely.

Running from his matrimonial and financial[55] troubles, on April 25th, 1816, getting to Dover by way of Canterbury, Byron with his party[56] crossed over on a sixteen hour voyage to Ostend, Belgium. On the 26th, they stayed the night at the Cour Imperiale, Bruges, from where in the morning they took the carriage to Ghent. At Ghent they stayed at the Hotel des Pays Bays. On the evening of April 29th, they arrived at Antwerp where the next day the group visited the basins built for Napoleon's navy as well as the principal churches and museums. After lunch, the party traveled to Mechlin (Malines). On route, the carriage broke which necessitated repairs to be carried out, which was done at Brussels. There at Brussels, Byron met Major Pryse Lockhart Gordon, a friend of his mother. The party stayed over to May 4th, at which time Byron visited the fields of Waterloo with Gordon as his guide. During that time from May 10th to the 16th, Byron and party traveled the Rhine, visiting Bonn, Coblenz, the Castle of Drachenfels, and Mannheim. On the 18th Byron and his party were at Basel, Switzerland. It was at this time that Shelley, needing a break from his particular set of matrimonial and financial troubles, together with Mary and Claire arrived at Geneva with the express purpose of meeting up with Byron. It was there, in May of 1816, that Shelley and Byron met for the first time. Shelley and Byron, though possessing quite different personalities hit it off.[57] The four – Shelley, Byron, Mary and Claire – for the most part, had a wonderful time while together at Lake Geneva. These four months on Lake Geneva are very important months to the world of literature. Byron wrote *Prisoner of Chillon*; Shelley wrote *Mont Blanc* and the *Hymn to Intellectual Beauty*; Mary Godwin (Shelley) wrote *Frankenstein*; and Claire was busy writing out fair copies of Byron's third canto of *Childe Harold*. They played and they wrote and they visited the noblesse of Geneva.[58] As the summer wore on Byron and Shelley returned to an earlier established pattern of daily boat rides. By July of 1816, Byron had cast the pregnant Claire aside and refused to see her alone. Then, after considerable discussion which I do not believe demonstrated any animosity, Shelley and the two girls determined to return to England. On August 29th, they set out.[59]

That September, after the Shelley party had left, Byron and Hobhouse set out for Italy touring the Alps on route. On October 12th they were at Milan; November 6th, Verona; November 10th, Venice.[60] "Byron takes lodgings over the shop of a draper named Segati for 20 francs a day. He is quickly entranced by Segati's wife, Marianna.[61] Hobhouse takes different lodgings."

In the new year, Claire was delivered of Byron's child, Allegra. The birth happened in England, where, just then, a general resurgence of Byron's popularity was occurring. That past November and December, John Murray, Byron's publisher, got into the shops *Childe Harold* (canto III), and the *Prisoner of Chillon* and Other Poems. Murray wrote and advised Byron that he sold 7,000 copies of both publications. Back in Italy, Byron and Hobhouse left Venice for a tour of Italy, a tour that apparently lasted a few months. In the spring of 1817, April 29th, Byron caught up with Hobhouse at Rome, apparently having become separated at an earlier point. That May, still having Marianna Segati on his mind, Byron hurried back to Venice. That June, Byron took up residence at the Villa Foscarini, "a large house on the river near La Mira outside of Padua." That summer he was back at *Childe Harold* finishing canto IV in July. In August Byron took up with Margarita Cogni,[62] while still involved with Marianna Segati. In October, he finished *Beppo*.

In January of 1818, Hobhouse left for England taking with him Byron's latest manuscripts. Just after this Byron accepted an invitation extended by Countess Albrizzi; it was there in the Albrizzi Ballroom that Byron met Countess Teresa Guiccioli. She was the daughter of Count Ruggero Gamba. She was, when first she met Byron, the young wife (only 18) of a sixty year old nobleman. Nothing came of this first meeting, though it seems the couple went for a walk together in the gardens or was it a museum – reference was made to Canova's bust of Helen of Troy. And that was it, they did not see one another after that, until April the 2nd or 3rd, 1819. It was then that Byron and his friend Alexander Scott paid a visit to the Countess Benzoni's conversazioni, there Byron and Teresa Guiccioli met again. During this meeting the two were able to sit down with one another and have a discussion about Italian poetry. No arrangements were made to meet further; then ten days later they met, quite by chance. It was when their gondolas passed on one of the lagoons of Venice. What transpired in the following days, I do not know. The Guicciolis were only on a visit to Venice, a trip away from their home at Ravenna to which they returned. Before leaving however, Byron and Teresa agree to secretly exchange private letters.

On their return home to Ravenna the Guicciolis traveled by carriage over rough roads; it was then that Teresa fell ill. Incidently, Teresa was then, I think by her husband, three months pregnant. The count and his attendants did manage to get Teresa back home to Ravenna, but she miscarried. On June 10th, Byron traveled to Ravenna. He was responding to an invitation from Count Alborghetti, Secretary General of the Government of Lower Romagna, to attend a theater performance. At the theater Byron learns to his great distress that Teresa is ill. The next day Byron visits Teresa. For the next week he visits her daily; her health improves dramatically. On the 15th, though Teresa is still sick, she is well enough to ride in her carriage with Byron. I am not sure of all the movements or what messages might have been passed, but, on August 9th, the Guicciolis go to Bologna. The next day, at 3 o'clock in the morning, Byron rides out of Venice for Bologna there to take up residence at his old rooms at the Pellegrino. At this point, it seems that Byron was chumming together with both the Count and the Countess, as for example the three of them went to view Alfieri's Mirra at the Arena del Sole Theater. The Count, like all cuckolded or about to be cuckolded husbands, took a while to come to the realization that another was bedding or about to bed his wife. Quarrels broke out between the Count and the Countess. After a particularly bad bout on August 12th, Teresa fell ill and required the care of Dr. Aglietti in Venice. The Count and Countess travel to Venice for the necessary medical consultations. It seems that a lengthy course of treatment was prescribed which would require Teresa's constant attendance at Venice. The Count had a home at Venice (Palazzo Malipiero) so staying at Venice posed no great problem, however, political troubles back at Ravenna meant the Count had to travel back and forth. Her opportunities now being more frequent, Teresa began to see a lot of Byron, indeed for periods of time she would stay over with Byron at La Mira, though, they kept separate while traveling in public. In October, Byron was caught in a drenching rain storm from which he took a chill and came down with a fever. Teresa found him ill and packed him back to her place to nurse him. On November 1st, Count Guiccioli arrived early at home and came upon a bad scene. There then followed quarrels between the Count and his young wife. At the end of ten days, Teresa agreed to return to her husband's house in Ravenna. On November 10th, Count Guiccioli and Teresa returned to Ravenna. Upon her return home, Teresa again fell ill. By December 11th, Teresa was so ill that her father, with the agreement of the Count, requested that Byron return to Ravenna. Byron agreed. Upon Teresa hearing that Byron was coming to see her she had a marked improvement in her health; it was then clear to everyone that her heart was set on Byron. Before December was out Byron was by Teresa's side but there was always company around, always company. It appears that Byron was back and forth to see Teresa and before the winter was out took up accommodations, which the Count kindly rented out to him, the upper floor of his home, the spacious Palazzo Osio. Now under the same roof, the couple were to regularly see one another, though the two were frustrated because of their inability to be alone with one another. Tensions continued to increase. During March of 1820, Byron and Count Guiccioli quarreled violently. On April 2nd, Count Guiccioli broke into Teresa's writing-desk and took all her letters. During the middle of May, the Count confronted Byron once again. The Count's violent behavior frightened Teresa. The next morning she called her father (Count Gamba) and her brothers to the Palazzo and asked to return to their protection. Byron at this point stepped up to the family and stated that, to protect Teresa's marriage, he would leave Ravenna; the only alternative he could see to that, would be a separation between the Guicciolis. The Gamba family at this time was very powerful and what Count Gamba wanted, he usually got. Before the month was out, Count Gamba applied to the Pope for a separation for his daughter, which on July 6th was granted. Amongst the ecclesiastical terms was that while separated from her husband she was to be under the protection of the Gamba family, that is to say, pretty much be living with them. The count, no matter his part in the matter, was required to pay Teresa an allowance of 100 scudi a month (the English equivalent of £1000 a year, a large sum). On July 13th, 4 p.m. Teresa returned to her father's house at Filetto, 15 miles southwest of Ravenna.

During the time that the ecclesiastical separation was arranged, Byron stayed clear of the two families, the Guicciolis and the Gambas. Byron held back for better than a month, then, on August 16th, he made his visit to Teresa's father's house. The Gamba family accepted Byron's presence (the old count gave into the cries of his young daughter at least to that extent) as long as the terms of the Papal order were upheld, that Teresa must continue to live with her family, the Gamba family. The Gambas, like most very rich families have a number of residences, so Teresa had a couple of choices open to her. During November, 1820, she moved into her father's house in town. All this seem to work until July of the following year, 1821, when the estranged husband came to the view that things had just gone too far with Byron, and matters were such, that it could no longer be concluded that Teresa was living with her family. Thus, Count Guiccioli moved to force Teresa to return to him or he would see to her placement in a convent. The Gamba family at this point was fully behind their Teresa, so she and a number of the family members received visas good for four months and moved out of Count Guiccioli legal clutches. It is to be remembered that the country of Italy did not yet exist, it was, back in those times, a collection of sovereign states many of whom were feuding with one another. During all of this, for reasons to be better understood by one who has knowledge of the complicated Italian political situation of the time, the Gamba family ran out of favor in certain quarters.[63]

Another old friend during this period dropped in on Byron for a visit in Italy, Tom Moore (1779-1852) a fellow poet. This was at a point when Byron was at Venice and Moore found that Byron had "grown fatter ... he appeared more humorous." Humorous, indeed, in the widest sense of that word. Byron was subject to moods, moods that ranged over the full spectrum full of humors which were fanciful, capricious, whimsical, sometimes downright odd and/or fantastic. This might be demonstrated by his love of exotic animals, the more exotic the better.

This tenancy to keep exotic animals around first showed itself during his university days at Cambridge where he use to keep a bear on a leash.[64] When in Italy – he was to call it "Byron's Zoo" – Shelley listed "ten horses, eight enormous dogs,[65] three monkeys, five cats, an eagle, a crow and a falcon; and all of these, except for the horses, walk about in the house, which every now and then resounds with their unarbitrated quarrels, as if they were the masters of it." Shelley recounted what he observed when he went on a visit to Byron's and saw that upon leaving, his list was not complete for he "met on the grand staircase five peacocks, two guinea hens, and an Egyptian crane" and wondered who "all these animals were before they were changed into these shapes."[66] Shelley's biographer, Edmund Blunden tells the story on how Byron had ordered up a goose which, it was intended, should be roasted for a holiday meal. The goose arrived ahead of time, alive of course that being the best way to keep it fresh. During the period of time spent fattening the bird (a month), the goose and Byron had become friends and he did not go into Byron's oven, another just before the event was brought in. Countess Guiccioli found this to be all very amusing.

The Last Years of Byron (1821-24):

In the summer of 1821 on a visit to Byron, Shelley observed: "Lord B. is greatly improved in every respect – in genius, in temper, in moral views, in health and in happiness. His connection with La Guiccioli has been an inestimable benefit to him. He lives in considerable splendor, but within his income ...."[67] That was the year Byron was at Pisa, having followed his Countess there. At Pisa a circle of English romantic poets had gathered.

There, at Pisa, Byron had for neighbors the Shelleys, the Hunts (with their six children) and Trelawny.

Edward John Trelawny (1792-1881) was a friend of both Byron and Shelley. Before meeting them, however, Trelawny's life included episodes of naval service and of privateering in the Indian Ocean. He entered the navy when but a boy of eleven. At some point he deserted his Majesty's navy and went off to become a pirate, or as *Chambers* states, "lived a life of desperate enterprise in Eastern seas." In 1821, he made the acquaintance of both Shelley and Byron at Pisa; he was probably just traveling through, coming from one adventure to the next. How they met, or in what order, I do not know; but they all became friends. Trelawny was associated more with Byron than with Shelley, indeed, it appears that Trelawny was a general factotum to Lord Byron.

Leigh Hunt was one of a pair of brothers (John the other) who in 1808 involved themselves in a new journalistic effort, a political weekly, the *Examiner*, this was in London. The British authorities thought that what the brothers printed was subversive, especially during a time of war. The government eventually charged both of the Hunts. The matter was heard by a court of law during 1812, and, on February 3rd, 1813, they were convicted of libel and sent off to prison for two years. While in prison – the Hunt Brothers cause, being one supported by all true artists and freedom fighters – Byron, that April, paid a visit to Leigh Hunt taking him some books. I think that was probably the only time the two met until they met again in Italy in 1821.

Shelley and Byron (it was more Shelley's idea) determined to set up a magazine to be put together in Italy for the market back in Britain. Their new journal was to be called *The Liberal.*[68] If they were to get this scheme off the ground it would be necessary to have an experienced English editor and one that knew the printing business. The two poets agreed that Leigh Hunt was their man, if only they could get him to come to Italy. Shelley got a letter off to Hunt with a proposal and Hunt sent a letter right back saying that he would come to Italy[69] and assist in bringing out the new magazine but that he was without the funds to pay for the passage for himself and his large family. Shelly and Byron went into the huddle and in the result another letter was sent off to England with some money and a promise of further support when the family arrived in Italy. In July of 1822, having sailed from England, the Hunt family, escorted by Shelley who had met them at the coast, arrived at Pisa. The Hunt family, at Byron's invitation, moved into the lower level of Byron's large premises, Casa Lanfranchi; Byron and Countess Guiccioli occupied the second floor. It proved almost immediately to be very awkward for them all, mainly because Byron took a hardy dislike to Mrs. Hunt and her uncontrollable brood.[70]

We saw earlier where Byron and Shelley had met. It was back in 1816 when Shelley, Mary Godwin and Claire Clairmont ran away from England to spent that wonderful spring and summer of 1816 with Byron who was then at Lake Geneva. Leaving Byron to continue his continental adventures, Shelley and the girls left Geneva for England at the end of the summer. Claire was pregnant with Byron's child. Shelley came back to face a couple of difficult years during which his wife committed suicide and her family had the children taken away from Shelley by court order. In 1818, Shelley, now married to Mary, moved to Italy to live permanently. Accompanying the Shelleys were Claire and the children (three of them: Shelley's 26 month old William and 6 month old Clara,[71] and Claire's child fathered by Byron, 14 month old Allegra). In May of that year, 1818, we just might mention, Byron had moved into the Palazzo Moncenigo, on the Grand Canal, Venice. On hearing of her arrival in Italy, though refusing to see Claire personally, Byron sent for Allegra. Actually, the little girl was not long at Byron's place – just as well, considering the kind of life that he led. Allegra was boarded with the family of the English Consul at Venice, Richard Hoppner.[72]

In August of 1821, Shelley paid a visit to Byron at Ravenna. Shelley believed that he and Byron could work together in getting their collected works published. What would be necessary was for Byron to move to Pisa to be near Shelley, Byron shrugged off the suggestion of moving to Pisa. On Shelley's return he located a residence for Byron, the Casa or Palazzo Lanfranchi, a 16th-century palace on the Lungarno, a wonderful place but it was not enough to make Byron move. Then, that September the Gamba family moved to Pisa. Byron followed within the month arriving at Pisa "with his troop of carriages, horses, dogs, fowls, monkeys, and servants." That November, "The Pisa Circle" was fully formed: The Shelleys moved from San Giuliano to Pisa taking a flat in the Tre Palazzi di Chiesa. Byron's Casa Lanfranchi was across the bank of the Arno from the Shelleys. Teresa and her family, having received visas, resided at the Casa Parra only ¼ of a mile from Byron's (Byron visited Teresa everyday). Shelley's friends, Edward and Jane Williams also moved to Pisa, and were introduced to Byron. Trelawny, I might add, did not join the circle until 1822. During this period they all visited one another and rode frequently, especially Teresa, Mary Shelley and Edward Williams (Shelley and Jane Williams got off alone with one another quite regularly). Byron had weekly dinners for the men in the group. During the days shooting parties were organized. Byron continued to have an eye out for the attractive peasant girls which upset Teresa. Through all of this, Byron remained under constant police surveillance.

In the spring of 1822, both Byron and Shelley had an "old naval friend" of Trelawny's, Captain Roberts at Genoa, build "an open boat for Shelley, and a larger decked one for Byron." Shelley called his the *Don Juan*; Byron called his the *Bolivar*.[73] Shelley took delivery of his boat in May of 1822. Earlier we saw where, in July of 1822, having sailed from England, the Hunt family arrived in Italy. Shelley had rented a summer place[74] up along the coast on the Bay of Spezzia not far from Leghorn (Livorno), the port at which the Hunts arrived. Shelley, that July, sailed across the Bay of Spezzia in the *Don Juan* and put in at Leghorn. There he met the Hunts and escorted them over to Pisa where the family was to move into the lower level of Byron's large premises, Casa Lanfranchi. Shelley did not stay to settle the Hunts in, as he was anxious to return home to Mary who had not been feeling well. It was on the return trip from Leghorn in the *Don Juan*, a storm having over taken his small sailing vessel, that Shelley loss his life in the Bay of Spezzia. It was a few days before Shelley's body was discovered on the shore. It was on the beach where Shelley's body had been discovered that Trelawny, Hunt and Byron built a funeral pyre.[75]

Shelley's sudden and unexpected death, in 1822, was to have the effect of breaking up the circle of English romantic poets that had been living in and around Pisa since 1818. Mary Shelley and her half-sister, Claire, within a day of hearing of the loss of Shelley, moved from Casa Magni. Mary had some money and soon made arrangements to return to England which she did in 1823 together with her only surviving child by Shelley, a son, three year old Percy Florence. So too, Mary paid for the expenses so that Claire could join her brother Charles in Vienna. So soon they were all gone.

Byron stayed around the Pisa area for a while longer, resuming his work on his ongoing poem, *Don Juan*.[76] That September, he too left Pisa.[77] Just then, the Greeks were waging a fierce war of independence against the Turks and Byron wanted to go and support the Greek cause, as Trelawny put it, "his last Quixotic crusade in Greece."[78] Teresa was told to return to her family who were then at Ravenna and to stay with them until his return from Greece.[79] Teresa was upset with Byron leaving her, and, at his request, Mary Shelley arrived to stay with Teresa for a period of time to comfort her. On June 18th, a 120-ton English ship, the *Hercules*, was chartered for a two month period. Byron ordered uniforms and helmets for himself and others on the expedition. The *Hercules* set sail from Italy on the 16th of July, 1823. The Byron party included: Trelawny, Pietro Gamba (I think Teresa's brother), Byron's faithful valet Fletcher, and the bearded Tita.[80] On August 3rd, after a slow trip down and around the boot of Italy and across the Adriatic, the *Hercules* arrived at Argostoli Harbor. News that a rich English lord had arrived spread quickly. An increasing number of ambassadors from the various Greek regions arrived with requests and petitions for money. During this time Byron stayed aboard the *Hercules* but by September he discharged the vessel and hired a house for himself and Pietro Gamba at Metaxata. Trelawny[81] traveled on to Pyrgos leaving behind at Metaxata Byron, Pietro Gamba and Dr. Bruno. The three men passed their time pleasantly, in "conversation and reading."[82] In December, a decision was taken to go to Missolonghi; Byron hired two boats for the journey.[83] On January 4th, 1824, Byron arrived at Missolonghi, to a 21-gun salute. Byron found lodgings on the second floor of the house of Apostoli Capsali. Byron did not have much in the way of physical forces or supplies so to go into battle. The Greek government volunteered 3,000 men for an expedition against Lepanto. What the Greeks thought was that Byron should keep such an army in the field; well, while Byron had some money he did not have that much. Fights broke out between the local Greek (Suliote) fighters[84] who were of the view they should be paid greater sums; it struck them that Byron was the man with the money. At one point, fearing for his life, Byron ordered that cannon be placed at his gates and he hired ten German mercenaries as bodyguards. Then, a fatal turn of events.

On the 9th of April, 1824, Byron took a long ride with Gamba and a few of the remaining Suliotes. Just a few days before he had "intervened to prevent an Italian private, guilty of theft, from being flogged by order of some German officers."

> ... after being violently heated, then drenched in a heavy shower, persisted in returning home in a boat, remarking with a laugh, in answer to remonstrance, 'I should make a pretty soldier if I were to care for such a trifle.' It soon became apparent that he had caught his death. (Nichol.)

Byron's last couple of days were described by Dale:

Next morning (17th) ten ounces of blood were drawn.[85] The patient sat up and read a little but becoming weak was assisted to his bed. Dr. Treiber, Dr. Millingen's assistant, and Dr. Vaya, physician to Prince Mavrocordato, were called in consultation. Again Bruno clamored for blood, but he was overruled by the other doctors. Shortly after the consultation Byron fainted, his pulse became weak, and his hands and feet grew cold. He was given green tea with laudanum, following which medication he fell asleep. His respiration was jerky and he moaned with each expiration. Leeches were applied to his temples and were thought to have helped. At four o'clock in the afternoon of April 18 he appeared to be sinking and two hours later he fell asleep. He slept all night and the next morning could not be aroused. In the afternoon his respirations grew progressively shallower and faster; at six-fifteen o'clock he died.[86]

Trelawny, his friend who had seen Byron through so much in the last couple of years was not there at the time of Byron's death. Byron had died just as Trelawny was making his way back to Missolonghi from another part of Greece. Byron died on the 19th of April, just five days before Trelawny made it back to Missolonghi. Missolonghi had just come through a great deal, and it showed the effects of not only war but also of natural disasters that had rolled through the place in the previous months consisting of both a flood and an earthquake. Trelawny was to describe what he faced as he came back into Missolonghi:

It was the 24th or 25th of April when I arrived; Byron had died on the 19th. I waded through the streets, between wind and water, to the house he had lived in; it was detached, and on the margin of the shallow slimy sea-waters. For three months this house had been besieged, day and night, like a bank that has a run upon it. Now that death had closed the door, it was as silent as a cemetery. No one was within the house but Fletcher, of which I was glad. As if he knew my wishes, he led me up a narrow stair into a small room, with nothing in it but a coffin standing on trestles. No word was spoken by either of us; he withdrew the black pall and the white shroud, and there lay the embalmed body of the Pilgrim – more beautiful in death than in life.

Though it was thought to just bury Byron, maybe Athens, a movement grew to get Byron's body back to England. *The Florida* (the ship that brought Byron's body back to England) reached the Thames on the 29th of June. By the 5th of July Byron's remains had arrived and were laid out at London for a period of time. It is interesting to note that on the 9th of July Mary Shelley made a visit and paid her respects. On the 11th, Byron's old companion, Hobhouse, paid his last respects. On 12th, a funeral procession was made up in London and it began its four day journey to the family vault located at Hucknall in the yard of St. Mary Magdalen Church.[87]

Final words:

What we come away with, from a study of Byron's life, is that he was governed by no law but the impulses of his own will. He was a lord as well as a poet and he considered "his brother authors as a Grub-street crew." He thought himself alone to be all-accomplished. He had an "insufferable pride and self-sufficiency."[88] The great Macaulay wrote that the 19th-century romantics drew from Byron's poetry "a system of ethics compounded of misanthropy and voluptuousness a system in which the two great commandments were to hate your neighbor and to love your neighbor's wife."[89] That such might be drawn from Byron's poetry,[90] maybe so – I have made no study of it – that such a conclusion may come from a study of Byron's life, most certainly. Macaulay's description is as apt a description of the "Byronic Hero" as may be found anywhere.

Macaulay continued:

> He was naturally a man of great sensibility; he had been ill-educated; his feelings had been early exposed to sharp trials; he had been crossed in his boyish love; he had been mortified by the failure of his first literary efforts; he was straitened in pecuniary circumstances; he was unfortunate in his domesticated relations; the public treated him with cruel injustice; his health and spirits suffered from his dissipated habits of life; he was, on the whole, an unhappy man. He early discovered that, by parading his unhappiness before the multitude, he produced an immense sensation. The world gave him every encouragement to talk about his mental sufferings. The interest which his first confessions excited induced him to affect much that he did not feel; and the affection probably reacted on his feelings. How far the character in which he exhibited himself was genuine, and how far theatrical, it would probably have puzzled himself to say.

I suppose we might develop any number of theories as to what drove Byron, the man; but none could explain the mythological mystery of Byron.[91] "Byron was not, to the imagination of most of England, a man; he was a miracle. He was lightning and thunder, he was love and beauty, he was a dynast; and of course he was only following the Olympian traditions when in his glorious way he made female loveliness bow at his feet, or exercised his caprice at the cost of petty men."[92]

Notes

Notes: "William Wordsworth"

1 We may mark the beginning of the English Romantic Period with the year 1793, the year William Godwin brought out his work, *Political Justice*; the end came with the passing of the great *Reform Bill of 1832*.

2 See Bagehot's piece, "Wordsworth, Tennyson, and Browning ..." (1864) as found in Jones.

3 In 1783 Dorothy was once again shifted. She went to live, "for the sake of economy," with her maternal grandparents, the Cooksons, at Penrith. There she was "brought up in the tradition of blue-stockings, Dissenters and the evangelicals of that age. In 1788, it would appear, she was moved once again. She was rescued by her uncle, William Cookson who was then a fellow of St. John's College, Cambridge.

4 De Quincey in his *Recollections* was to observe that the arrangements at Hawkshead "was chiefly Etonian, even more so; for in both places the boys, instead of being gathered into one fold, and at night into one or two huge dormitories, were distributed amongst motherly old 'dames.'" These dames, with maternal tenderness and with a professional pride would see to the comfort of their young flocks and protect the weak from oppression.

5 Lefebure. It should be noted that about this time both Malthus and Coleridge also attended Cambridge. It is not likely that Wordsworth was to make the acquaintance of Malthus and Coleridge. Though Malthus and Coleridge, it is to be observed, did have dealings with one another.

6 Wordsworth gives his poetic impressions of London in *The Prelude*, Seventh Book. As his biographer, Burra observed, "Hardly even the novelists have described with so much meaning in their zest such a London as Wordsworth gives ... from the daily street scene to the fantasy of Bartholomew Fair; from the life of the River, Westminster, St. Paul's, Parliament, and the Pulpit, the Courts, to all its most curious entertainments – Theatres, Circuses, Panoramas, and Pantomime; and all things combined at once in the place he loved ..."

7 Much of the evidence of Wordsworth's love affair with Annette Vallon did not come to light until the 20th-century. Annette wrote a number of letters to Wordsworth, some of which might have gotten through to England (the two countries were then at war). One letter which shed considerable light on the relationship was located late in the 19th-century at the Blois Record Office, in a pile of letters which the war censors had set aside. While obliged because of the outbreak of war to return to England, Wordsworth tried to keep in touch with Annette, and, indeed, tried to get back to her in France. In spite of repeated attempts, the war stymied him.

8 Burra. De Quincey in his remembrances wrote that Wordsworth "spent his time for a year and more chiefly in London, overwhelmed with shame and despondency for the disgrace and scandal brought upon Liberty by the atrocities in that holy name." (*Recollections* ....)

9 The European liberalism of the 19th-century was first formally proclaimed in the French constitution of 1791. It was a theory of liberty, the "Golden Rule of Liberty." "Men are born free and equal in rights, ... Liberty, ... consists in being permitted to do anything which does not injure other people. ... The exercise of the natural rights of each man has not limits except those which guarantee to the other members of society the enjoyment of the same rights."(Articles 1 & 3 of the 1791 French Constitution.)

10 In England, without the shedding of blood, the *Glorious Revolution* had done away with the notion of an absolute monarchy, but rather that it was subject to the "people's parliament."

11 From *Regicide Peace*, as quoted and cited by Kirk.

12 During these years, because of its life and death struggle with Napoleon, the government of England had placed ideas of liberty very low down on the scale of things. As mentioned in the text, in 1793, the very year that *Political Justice* made its appearance, the "Reform-martyrs" were transported to Botany Bay. Therefore, it is surprising that Godwin did not run afoul the authorities. The book was dressed as a learned treatise and was to be sold for a price much out of the reach of many, unlike the penny pamphlets of the day. The story is that when the book was brought to the attention of William Pitt, the prime minister, who might easily have set the wheels in motion for a charge of

sedition to be laid, dismissed the suggestion, saying, "a three guinea book could never do much harm among those who had not three shillings to spare." (As quoted by Brailsford.)

13 Indeed, for a period of time, that sacred writ of the law, *Habeas Corpus* was suspended. Numbers of men against whom there was no evidence languished in prison during the last years of the century.

14 Calvert's legacy amounted to £900, a very substantial sum in those days. In leaving this inheritance to Wordsworth, whether he had a plan in mind or not, Calvert gave to England one of her most loved poets.

15 As quoted by Burra. "A few months of hesitation followed Raisley's death, during which the plan was mooted of their living in London as journalists; but William found that the restlessness of that life was wholly uncongenial to more serious composition ..."

16 There is some suggestion that Coleridge and Wordsworth were to meet at London as early as 1795. In December of 1796, Coleridge with his family had settled at Nether Stowey, Somersetshire. In 1796, it is to be noted, Coleridge brought out his first book of poems, *Ode to France*. We might suppose that Wordsworth obtained a copy and would have been most anxious to meet this published poet. Burra, Wordsworth's biographer, wrote, "It is strange that the beginning of so great a friendship is not exactly known."

17 As quoted by Burra. As it happened, on November of 1796, their childhood friend, Mary Hutchinson, was to come and visit the Wordsworths at Racedown. Mary was to stay with the Wordsworths for approximately four months, leaving in March of 1797. It was just after Mary had left the Wordsworths that Coleridge came calling.

18 It is not clear to me how many visits were paid back and forth by Coleridge and the Wordsworths. It seems that Wordsworth was to visit Coleridge as early as March of 1797. In late March "Wordsworth and his friend Basil Montagu, on their way to Bristol from Racedown where the Wordsworths were then in residence, visited STC at Stowey." (Lefebure.)

19 De Quincey in his *Recollections* made reference to Thomas Poole. "He was almost an ideal model for a useful member of Parliament. I found him a stout, plain-looking farmer, leading

a bachelor life, in a rustic, old-fashioned house; the house, however, upon further acquaintance, proving to be amply furnished with modern luxuries, and especially with a good library, superbly mounted in all departments bearing at all upon political philosophy; and the farmer turning out a polished and liberal Englishman, who had traveled extensively, and had so entirely dedicated himself to the service of his humble fellow-countrymen – the hewers of wood and drawers of water in this southern part of Somersetshire – that for many miles round he was the general arbiter of their disputes, the guide and counselor of their difficulties; besides being appointed executor and guardian to his children by every third man who died in or about the town of Nether Stowey."

20 We have already made reference to the Rousseauish sensibility that had swept certain of the younger set. The Wordsworths and the Coleridges were of this set. They reveled in walking out into the country with the express intention of viewing the scenery. It struck the traditionalists – to be found in abundance around Nether Stowey – on seeing these nature lovers going by with their camp stools and their mirrors, that these people were very strange, indeed.

21 It did not help any, that Coleridge at this time was to entertain one his friends, John Thelwall (1764-1834) who came to pay him a visit. (Lefebure.) Thelwall was one of the twelve reformers who were tried in 1794 on the charge of high treason. (The twelve were acquitted.)

22 These Rousseauan romantics could usually be immediately identified by their behavior. They reacted to things with complete spontaneity and spoke with total frankness. "In the context of personal relationships Romantic sensibility implied a special kind of sympathy: a warmth of tenderest understanding, a reciprocal feeling with, as well as for, a person, a loving more profound, more delicate, more sensitive, more innocent, more true than the love which the vulgar, lacking sensibility, were capable of experiencing." (Lefebure.)

23 "Mrs. St. Aubin, who did not like what she heard of her tenants, would not be persuaded to renew the year's lease." (Maclean.)

24 These were years of war and travel had to be difficult and expensive. At this point, early fall of 1798, things were looking up for England. Nelson had re-entered the Mediterranean in

May, 1798, and in August had destroyed Napoleon's fleet at the *Battle of the Nile*. Nelson's victory had the effect of considerably changing the complexion of the war in Europe. To begin with Napoleon was locked up in Egypt without a fleet to get himself and his army back home. This gave the timid princes of Europe the courage to form the "Second Coalition": England, Austria, and Russia. The Russians drove the French out of northern Italy while Nelson gave aid to the counter-revolutionaries in the south.

25 "From Temple Sowerby they made their way to Bampton, from Bampton along Hawes Water to Windermere and Hawkshead." (Maclean.)

26 I see from Maclean, at about the same time the Wordsworths moved to Grasmere, the Hutchinsons moved from their farm at Stockton to another near Scarborough, Gallow Hill.

27 It was Dorothy, who was involved with the fixing up and the maintaining of Dove Cottage, not so much William. She showed a particular interest in the garden: "Dorothy found that almost every day she could find some treasure for the garden she was shaping – mosses from Easedale, wild thyme and wild columbine from the hill above the cottage, orchises from the lakeside, foxgloves and primroses from the Bainriggs wood." (Maclean.)

28 By 1805, there had been four editions of *Lyrical Ballads*. With each new edition there was new material added. The success of *Lyrical Ballads* was to bring out imitators. For example there was Mrs. Robinson's *Lyrical Tales* which was published by Longmans.

29 The suggestion is, that for a period of time they carried on a incestuous relationship. (See, Lefebure.)

30 De Quincey's *Recollections of the Lakes and the Lake Poets*. De Quincey made the observation, that, like Charles Lamb, Dorothy had a bit of a stammer.

31 As quoted by Trickett in her introduction to *Dorothy Wordsworth's Lakeland Journals*.

32 The *Treaty of Amiens*, 1802, left France supreme in Western Europe and England supreme on the oceans of the world. "Amid all the triumphs of the revolutionary war, the growth of the British empire had been steady and ceaseless. She was more than ever mistress of the sea. ... She was turning her command of

the seas to a practical account. Not only was she monopolizing the carrying trade of the European nations, but the sudden uprush of her industries was making her the workshop as well as the market of the world." (Green.)

33 The Wordsworths, apparently traveled no further than the French port of Calais. Annette, with whom the Wordsworths had kept up a written correspondence over the years, did not want them to travel to her home, still, presumably, Blois; she and Caroline, now ten years of age, and not ever having been seen before by her father, would travel to Calais and there they would meet. Annette, it is plain, had her mind made up to tell William that she did not intend to exercise any hold that she may have had over him. "Somehow, during the troublesome times, she had earned the reputation of widowhood, and she was anxious to avoid any risk of losing it. She remained the 'Widow Williams' until her death in 1841." (Burra.) Incidently, Burra wrote that Caroline was to marry, in 1816, at Paris, to Jean Baudouin.

34 As quoted in Lefebure.

35 The Wordsworth were to have five children: John (1803), Dora (1804), Thomas (1806), Catherine (1808) and William (1810). Two of them died early in life, both in 1812: four year old Catherine and six year old Thomas.

36 "Miss Wordsworth was always ready to walk out – wet or dry, storm or sunshine, night or day; whilst Mrs. Wordsworth was completely dedicated to her maternal duties, and rarely left the house, unless when the weather was tolerable, or, at least, only for short rambles." (De Quincey, *Recollections ...* .)

37 Burra. It is speculated that the Wordsworths had given to John some money which he was going to invest in the trip, one to the far east, and with his return they would all be able to retire in style. Well, the trip hardly got under way before these dreams were quite literally dashed against the hard rocks of a leeward English shore.

38 On reading of de Quincey, though it is not clear, the death of four year old Catty came about because of a misadventure, some negligence of an older and parentless child which the Wordsworths had taken in under their roof as a charity case.

39 In 1818, Wordsworth, in connection with the general election of that year, was, once again, to support the aristocratic and

powerful Lowther family. Again, for Wordsworth, this support was to pay off: he was appointed a Justice of the Peace.

40 Southey, though he was but a dozen miles away at Keswick, did not likely pay too many visits to the Wordsworths, as, Southey and Wordsworth were not always on good terms with one another. De Quincey was to say, "... Wordsworth and Southey never had one principle in common; their hostility was even flagrant. ... Wordsworth disliked in Southey the want of depth, or the apparent want, as regards the power of philosophic attraction. Southey dislikes in Wordsworth the air of dogmatism, and the unaffable haughtiness of his manner." (*Recollections* ... .)

41 Robinson led the crusade to get legislation relief to those who were subject to various and galling legal disabilities, all, simply because they were not members of the Church of England. Wordsworth thought no such change was needed. Robinson commented: "He [Wordsworth] has lost his love of liberty; not his humanity, but his confidence in mankind." (See Morley.) As Robinson was to observe, Wordsworth's home, Rydal Mount "is animated by High Church and Tory feelings, and though I force them to tolerate my heresies by a half-grave and half-serious assertion, yet the perpetual effort to preserve my independence becomes at time wearisome..."

42 "Feast of the Poets," as first printed in the *Reflector*.

43 As quoted by P.P. Howe, *The Life of William Hazlitt*.

44 www.blupete/Literature/Essays/Hazlitt/SpiritAge/Wordsworth.htm

45 In a letter dated 21st February [1818?], from Keats to his brothers, as quoted by Howe.

46 "The Rime of the Ancient Mariner" is a work, which some considered to be the only worthwhile work ever put out by Coleridge. For example, Hazlitt: "His *Ancient Mariner* is his most remarkable performance, and the only one that I could point out to anyone as giving an adequate idea of his great natural powers." (See Hazlitt's "Lectures on the English Poets.")

47 See "Mr. Wordsworth" and "Mr. Jeffrey" in Hazlitt's *The Spirit of the Age*. Of Wordsworth's poems, Oliver Wendell Holmes was to write, "Trivial in subject, solemn in style, vivid in description, prolix in detail."

48 Francis Jeffrey (1773-1850). Jeffrey was one of its founders and the editor/manager of *Edinburgh Review*, the "Great Gun" of the Enlightenment, and was so through to 1829.

49 As quoted by Howe. Hazlitt should not be accused of hyperbole. In 1807 Crabb Robinson wrote his brother of his impressions of Wordsworth gained at their first meeting: "His manners are not prepossessing... tho' not arrogant yet they indicate a sense of his own worth; he is not attentive to others and speaks with decision his own opinion. He does not spare those he opposes: he has no respect for great names, and avows his contempt for popular persons as well as favorite books. ... Yet with all this, I should have a bad opinion of that person's discernment who should be long in his company without contracting an high respect, if not a love for him. Moral purity and dignity, and elevation of sentiment are the characteristics of his mind and muse." (Morley.)

50 Both Dorothy and Mary were to survive beyond William; Dorothy died in 1855 and Mary in 1859.

Notes: "Samuel Taylor Coleridge"

1 The expression, "wrecked in a mist of opium," is from Matthew Arnold's Essays in Criticism, second series, 1888.

2 De Quincey's *Recollections* ....

3 "His father was described to me [de Quincey], by Coleridge himself, as a sort of Parson Adams, being distinguished by his erudition, his inexperience of the world, and his guileless simplicity." (*Recollections* ...) Parson Adams, incidentally, is a simple-minded country clergyman of the 18th-century, as referred to in Henry Fielding's, *Joseph Andrews*.

4 "The years there had developed in him all the classical symptoms of what might be termed the English-school syndrome. In his worst nightmares he was to dream that he was back there; his outstanding memories of the place included savage floggings, semi-starvation, acute home-sickness, loneliness ..." (Lefebure.)

5 In the University of Cambridge, and at Trinity College, Dublin, an undergraduate member admitted under this designation and receiving an allowance from the college to enable him to study was known as a sizar. Incidentally, Malthus, having become a fellow of the College in 1793, was to act at one point as a judge and sentencer of a junior student who had been absent without leave from the College. The young student was Coleridge.

With this background, one might better appreciate Coleridge's comment on Malthus' second edition of his work: "Verbiage and senseless repetition ..." What is certain is that Coleridge was no friend of Malthus.

6 Sarah was not to be Coleridge's first love. While at Cambridge he was to make the acquaintance of the Evans family; I think likely because he knew the son, Tom. Well, Tom had a sister, Mary, for whom Coleridge had developed quite a hankering; but things just didn't seem to work out between the pair of them. Coleridge was in love with Mary Evans but thought she was unresponsive. After going back to Bristol and getting himself engaged to Sarah Fricker, only then did he receive a letter from Mary saying she loved him, but by then it was too late – hence his sad little poem, "On a Discovery Made Too Late," and his later remarks, whenever Bristol was mentioned, "And there I had the misfortune to meet my wife." Sarah, aged 21, little, blue eyed, plump, and fresh, was very much in love with Coleridge, and he tried to persuade himself he loved her. In 1795, Coleridge was to get the news that Mary had married another; and thus there is speculation that Coleridge married Sarah on the rebound.

7 Coleridge charmed people with his talk; he was a "brilliant conversationalist." It was one of the reasons, in later years that he was such a hit on the lecture circuit. Hazlitt expressed the view that Coleridge might have been a better author, if, he had taken more time with his writing rather than spending the time going about impressing people with his talk. He laid down his pen to talk, "and mortgages the admiration of posterity for the stare of an idler." ("Mr. Coleridge.")

8 Hazlitt wrote of the time when Coleridge, then at Shrewsbury, was to receive word of the Wedgwood gift. "My father was a Dissenting Minister, at Wem, in Shropshire; and in the year 1798 ... Mr Coleridge came to Shrewsbury, to succeed Mr Rowe in the spiritual charge of a Unitarian Congregation there. He did not come till late on the Saturday afternoon before he was to preach; and Mr Rowe, who himself went down to the coach, in a state of anxiety and expectation, to look for the arrival of his successor, could find no one at all answering the description but a round-faced man, in a short black coat (like a

shooting-jacket) which hardly seemed to have been made for him, but who seemed to be talking at a great rate to his fellow-passengers. Mr Rowe had scarce returned to give an account of his disappointment when the round-faced man in black entered, and dissipated all doubts on the subject by beginning to talk. He did not cease while he stayed; nor has he since, that I know of. He held the good town of Shrewsbury in delightful suspense for three weeks that he remained there, 'fluttering the proud Salopians, like an eagle in a dove-cote' ...

When I came down to breakfast, I found that he had just received a letter from his friend, T. Wedgwood, making him an offer of £150 a-year if he chose to waive his present pursuit [to be a minister in the Dissenting Church], and devote himself entirely to the study of poetry and philosophy. Coleridge seemed to make up his mind to close with this proposal in the act of tying on one of his shoes. ... being settled, the poet-preacher took leave, and I accompanied him six miles on the road. It was a fine morning in the middle of winter, and he talked the whole way." ("My First Acquaintance with Poets.")

9 "... STC never ceased to pay tribute to her dedicated and tireless devotion as mother to his children and her exceedingly capable management of the always meagre financial resources. Her absolute purity of mind won enduring tribute from him, as did her discretion." Lefebure continued, and made the observation that Sarah was "giddy, gad-fly, happy-go-lucky," which enchanted Coleridge at the first but was soon to wear thin.

10 The Lake District is a scenic mountain region situated in north-west England. The high point in the range is Scafell Pike, 3,210 ft (978 m). The district is an inland strip, about 30 miles (50 km) wide, and includes 15 lakes, among them Ullswater, Derwentwater and Windermere.

11 "... all went well for a fortnight, when Coleridge made up his mind to leave his companions and their gig, and to return on foot by himself. Mr. Campbell supposes that he 'had found the close companionship incompatible with that free indulgence in narcotics which had become to him a necessity of pleasurable or even tolerable existence.' At any rate, after walking hundreds of miles on his own account, he was back at Greta Hall on 15 September." (Howe.)

12 Just that previous fall (September 7th, 1803) Southey had moved to the Lake District with his family to move into the Coleridge residence, Greta Hall. The Coleridges had moved into this large home at Keswick three years previously. Greta Hall was certainly big enough for both families, indeed, it was big enough for three families: the Coleridges, the Southeys and the Lowells. The members of these families were to live together there for a number of years. As we have seen, the three young friends (Southey, Coleridge and Lowell) had married three of the Fricker sisters. Coleridge was never to spend any great amounts of time there, indeed, in time, he took up a permanent residence in London. Lowell died in 1795. Thus it was that the three sisters and their children were to live at Greta Hall with Robert Southey as the male head of this collective.

13 "STC had dreamed of returning from Malta with his debts paid off, with copious material for journalism and literature, with recovered health and freed from drug slavery. Instead he had lost [a regular excuse for Coleridge when he missed a deadline] nine-tenths of his papers and manuscripts, had no more than two or three guineas in his pocket, no decent hat on his head, nor shoes to his feet. He was in worse health [due to his extensive use of opium while at Malta, alone, in his room] ... than when he left England. [And] He had no home to go to." (Lefebure.)

14 The quoted words are Howe's. We write of Charles ("Elia") Lamb (1775-1834). Incidently, when Coleridge sailed from Portsmouth on his way out to Malta in March of 1804, Lamb was among a number that saw him off. Charles Lamb lived in London and was a writer of prose, a journalist. His pen name was "Elia"; his writing is known for its humor, whimsy, and faint overtones of pathos.

15 Opium and all of the concoctions made from it were unrestricted until 1868, when the first *Pharmacy Act* in Great Britain became law.

16 See Virginia Berridge's *Opium and the People, Opiate Use in Nineteenth-Century England.* There was one popular mixture called Chlorodyne, it being composed of chloroform, morphia, tincture of Indian hemp, prussic acid, and other substances.

17 *Biographia Literaria*, it would appear, was Coleridge's only attempt at getting his prose into print. It includes accounts of

his literary life and also critical essays; it appeared in 1817. Coleridge's borrowings from German idealist philosophers, it was thought, bordered at times on plagiarism. It is said (Lefebure) that chapters 12 and 13, in *Biographia Literaria*, are "long, literally verbatim quoted passages from Schelling and Mass."

18 Lefebure makes the point, then proceeds to refer to Carlyle's view (*The Life of Stirling*) that Coleridge's contribution both in literature and philosophy was "small and sadly intermittent." It was Hazlitt's view that *Ancient Mariner* was the only work that expressed the "extraordinary powers" possessed by Coleridge. "His *Ancient Mariner* is his most remarkable performance, and the only one that I could point out to anyone as giving an adequate idea of his great natural powers." Hazlitt's comments are consistent with the comments of others, that Coleridge's best work was done in his early years. I think it fair to say that even *Ancient Mariner* was not well received at the time of its publication. Indeed, Coleridge knew it and amused himself by inserting in the *Morning Post* the following lines: "To the author of the *Ancient Mariner*.

Your poem must eternal be,
Dear Sir! it cannot fail,
For 'tis incomprehensible,
And without head or tail.

The first edition of the *Ancient Mariner* took but five months to write, but Coleridge regularly reworked certain of its parts throughout the balance of his life.

19 See Introduction to *Biographia Literaria*.

20 *The Spirit of the Age*, "Mr. Coleridge." The quote is from Shakespeare's *Two Gentlemen from Verona*, Act 2, Sc. 7, line 34.

21 Coleridge named his first and second sons, "Hartley" and "Berkeley."

22 J. Shawcross in his introduction to Oxford University Press' ed. (1969) *Biographia Literaria*.

23 The opium-taking Coleridge "sponged on them and lied to them ... he insulted them; he fled from them; he returned to them. ... [He had to be] very hard to love; yet they continued to solace, comfort and support him." (Lefebure.)

24 It is not thought that Gillman ever was to get Coleridge off of opium, but it was measured out to him so that he could carry on in life being reasonably productive and socially acceptable.

25 These last couple of quotes came from Morley.

26 It was Coleridge's daughter, virtually abandoned by her father, who is responsible for Coleridge's now lasting reputation. She sacrificed most of her life to compiling various books, including his *Biographia Literaria*, *Table Talk*, *Collected Poems*, *Literary Remains*, *Constitution of Church and State*, and *Lectures on Shakespeare*. This she did out of the primeval chaos of his unpublished papers, thus rescuing Coleridge from oblivion and, as it were, inventing Coleridge as the master of philosophy and prose.

27 Coleridge was buried in Highgate Churchyard.

Notes: "Percy Bysshe Shelley"

1 As quoted by Trelawny, *Recollections* ....

2 John, Bysshe and Piercy; thus we see how our poet came by his Christian names.

3 Timothy and Elizabeth had seven children: Percy Bysshe, Elizabeth, Mary, Helen who died in infancy, another Helen, Margaret and John. The last of these, John, was born in 1806. Incidently, the family was to call our poet, "Bit."

4 In referring to Shelley's experiences at Eton, Blunden wrote: "Upon the whole not much in the curriculum turned Shelley's tastes and inquiries from the classical texts which thus established themselves firmly beneath a great part of what he was to write in his own tongue." (*Shelley* ....)

5 In Hogg's *Life of Shelley* (1858), as reproduced, in part, by Hughes.

6 The last quote comes from Blunden, *Shelley* .... Brailsford wrote: "In the world of prose he [Shelley] called himself an atheist. He rejoiced in the name, and used it primarily as a challenge. 'It is a good word of abuse to stop discussion,' he said once to his friend Trelawny, 'a painted devil to frighten the foolish, a threat to intimidate the wise and good. I used it to express my abhorrence of superstition. I took up the word as a knight takes up a gauntlet in defiance of injustice.'"

7 It seems that Harriet's sister, Eliza, 14 years older, permanently associated herself with the couple and moved right in with them and stayed until the marriage had broken down; no doubt, much because of the meddlesome Eliza.

8 After being expelled from Oxford, Hogg and Shelley lived together in London (Poland Street) but not apparently for long. Hogg went on to York and a legal career. We can see that Shelley, at least in the early years, kept in touch with Hogg. In 1858, well after Shelley's death and at a time when Shelley was to became a popular public figure, seemingly cashing in on his earlier acquaintance with Shelley, Hogg wrote his *Life of Shelley*.

9 *Queen Mab* is Shelley's first long poem which he privately printed in 1813. The work opens with a sleeping maiden whose spirit is transported to Queen Mab's court located in deep space. The queen is quite impressed with the maiden's grasp of the condition of humanity and how, the maiden supposes, all will be changed in time to a new moral, social and economic order. In this work Shelley vented about what is and what should be and expounded on a number of subjects including: law, warfare, marriage, free love, religion, atheism, vegetarianism, etc. The work only became widely read a decade or so after Shelley's death. (It is often referred to as the Chartist Bible. "Chartists" were a body of 19th-century political reformers who claimed that they represented the working classes.) *Queen Mab* is a juvenile work which William Michael Rossetti described as being "absolute and heinous rubbish, the 'clotted nonsense' of a boy." (In Rossetti's Preface to *The Complete Poetical Works of Percy Bysshe Shelley*.)

10 It is reported (Green) that Napoleon was to brag, "Let us be masters of the channel for six hours and we are masters of the world." But, France, and for that matter no enemy of Great Britain was ever to go through her "wooden walls."

11 Brailsford wrote: "The *Vindication* is certainly among the most remarkable books that have come down to us from that opulent age. It has in abundance most of the faults that a book can have. It was hastily written in six weeks. It is ill-arranged, full of repetitions, full of digressions, and almost without a regular plan. Its style is unformed, sometimes rhetorical, sometimes familiar. But with all these faults, it teems with apt phrases,

telling passages, vigorous sentences which sum up in a few convincing lines the substance of its message." Its message, of course, was that there should be equality of the sexes. This was a message which was novel back then; and which, only in the last couple of decades of the 20th-century, has taken hold. Brailsford continued: "The chief merit of the *Vindication* is its clear perception that everything in the future of women depends on the revision of the attitude of men towards women and of women towards themselves." Wollstonecraft "exposed the whole system which compels women to 'live by their charm.'" As Wollstonecraft was to write (see Brailsford): "Females have been insulated, as it were, and while they have been stripped of the virtue that should clothe humanity, they have been decked out with artificial graces that enable them to exercise a short-lived tyranny."

12 As for Mary Jane Clairmont: She was a "vulgar and worldly woman." (Brailsford.) She was a "stepmother of convention, and treated both Fanny Imlay and Mary Godwin with consistent unkindness." The disasters which by and large all of the children came to, was not so much brought about by the "new philosophy" of William Godwin as some have observed but rather from the presence of Mary Jane Clairmont in their lives, "who flattered, intrigued, and lied." As for the children of the Godwin household (we will read of Mary and Jane further on): Fanny killed herself in Wales, in 1816. Charles Clairmont left early and struck out for Vienna "where he became a successful teacher of languages." (Cameron.) Godwin's son, William, who himself turned to novel writing, died in 1832.

13 "I am the son of a man of fortune in Sussex. The habits of my father and myself never coincided. Passive obedience was inculcated and enforced in my childhood ... I am heir by entail to an estate of £6,000 per annum." (As quoted by Blunden, *Shelley ...* .)

14 Godwin, for a period of time had gone into the publishing business. It began in 1805. He specialized in school books and children's tales. Godwin wrote much of the material under the name of "Edward Baldwin." He never seem to make any money at his business. In 1822, the business came to an end. The conclusion is, that Godwin was not a person one wanted to be around with, not for long, and certainly it was not thought wise

for one to introduce a friend to him, for, in short order, he would corner the fellow looking for money. Henry Crabb Robinson, a diarist who knew many of these political and literary characters of the age, thought that Godwin's "acquaintance was of the least agreeable kind. He made me feel my inferiority unpleasantly, and also in another way disagreeably, by demands on my purse for small sums and trying to make use of me with others." (*Diary, Reminiscences and Correspondence of ...*)

15 In the days of Shelley, the law of inheritance was different. Now, one can disinherit a disobedient son; but not back then. Shelley was the oldest son and he would inherit upon his father's death the "landed estate," viz. Field Place. The law was such that the interests of these large estates could not be splintered and thus would come down whole, devolving from the eldest son to the eldest son. The estate was thus entailed and could not be bequeathed at pleasure by any one possessor but was to come through the generations in a fixed or prescribed line of devolution. Thus Shelley, as the oldest son, always held the trump card, as he was going to inherit on his father death whether the family liked it or not. Bankers knew that Shelley would come into money some day, so he borrowed money against his prospects. Of course, Shelley could always sign his rights away; and, it would appear that he did so at one point or other in exchange for yearly payments, viz. a life pension with periodic payments beginning immediately.

16 In a letter dated March 16th, 1814, just four days before the re-marriage at St. George's, Shelley wrote his school chum, Tom Hogg: "It is a sight which awakens an inexpressible sensation of disgust and horror, to see her [Eliza] caress my poor little Ianthe ... I sometimes feel faint with the fatigue of checking the overflowings of my unbounded abhorrence for this miserable wretch. But she is no more than a blind and loathsome worm, that cannot see to sting." (Reproduced in part in by Cameron.)

17 A considerable amount on that occasion, £3,000.

18 As for Mary, Shelley was hers and she would do anything Shelley wanted. And, if Mary Godwin was involved in anything, so was her half-sister, Jane Clairmont. "What Miss Godwin wanted Miss Clairmont also wanted, adventure above all. ... [Jane] was more a child of the warm south than Shelley had yet come upon. Quick in conversation, adroit in the common round, she well knew

the advantage that she had in her physical vitality and invitation." (Blunden, *Shelley* ....) In 1816, Jane (Clair), then in Italy, formed an unhappy attachment with Lord Byron. Claire became pregnant by Byron. At some point, so it is claimed, she also became pregnant by Shelley (see Blunden). Both of these children ended up in orphanages and died young. (Johnson.)

19 Though some sort of arrangement was made by his father in the spring of 1814, during a time when Shelley was going through the motions of changing his life around so to better suit the expectations of both the Shelley and Westbrook families, it was not until 1815, with the death of his grandfather, was there to be any regular money coming in for Shelley. Up to that point, it would appear, he relied on funds coming from loans that he made against his inheritance. Throughout these years, Shelley was always in need of money to satisfy his creditors, and, to satisfy the dunning demands of Godwin.

20 Shelley was obliged, in these two principal female relationships in his life, the one with Harriet Westbrook, the other with Mary Godwin, to take a sister in, in each case. There was Eliza Westbrook who Shelley came to despise. During his marriage to Harriet, Eliza was a constant fixture in the house who undoubtedly was ready with a commentary on any proceeding in which Shelley might be involved. And then with Mary he was to have Claire, Mary's half-sister. The effect that Claire was to have on the Shelley/Mary relationship was not as disagreeable, but still she proved to be a problem at times. Shelley's biographer, Edmund Blunden explains: "Sometimes Claire Clairmont was entirely agreeable and alluring, sometimes the opposite; Shelley felt then that she was incapable of friendship; but she was always present. From the first she had been hardly less interested in Shelley than Mary was, she was by nature possessive, and she did not mean to spend her life in Godwin's house. It was not easy to arrange that she should live anywhere else but with Mary, since her escapade in France made the Godwins unwilling to receive her on reasonable terms and she had no money. She began to fasten upon Shelley by her process of being sullen and sunny in turn ..." (*Shelley* ... .)

21 Mary's first child, Clara, was born prematurely on February 22nd, 1815, and died March 6th.

22 Godwin, this viper, as soon as he heard that Shelley had finally settled, got in on the act. Shelley gave Godwin £1,000 that spring. It will be remembered that the year before, he had given Godwin £3,000. These were very great sums of money in those days. Other sums were also handed over to Godwin through the years. Godwin expressed little gratitude, indeed, he was disdainful to Shelley, thinking him to be a man that lustfully took his two daughters away while at the same time deserting a wife and child. Shelley, however, as if in amends, continued for the balance of his life to pay sums of money to Godwin. In 1820, Shelley, then in Italy and yet still sending money, in a letter to Godwin, wrote, "I have given you the amount of a considerable fortune, and have destituted myself of nearly four times the amount." (*OED*, under "destitute.")

23 "... many readers have judged its [*Alastor's*] politics as a quietistic [of passive devotional contemplation] contrast to the outspoken radicalism of *Queen Mab*." ("Irony and Clerisy," by Linda Brigham, Kansas State University, URL:http://www.rc.umd.edu/praxis/irony/brigham/alastor.html : January 27th, 2006.)

24 Claire was impregnated by Byron. We cannot be exactly sure when this event occurred? Claire had apparently met Byron in England before he left the country. It could be that while Shelley enjoyed travel and wanted to meet Byron, one of the objects of going to Switzerland was for Claire to meet once again with Byron so that he could get the "good" news directly from Claire. Claire had been delivered of a child on January 13th, 1817. (We might observe that if Claire went full term, she was impregnated when first meeting Byron in Italy that spring.) Claire gave the little girl the name of "Alba" ("Dawn"); Byron gave her the name "Allegra." Byron eventually installed Allegra at an Italian convent; she died there at the age of five.

25 It was there at a villa, in the encouraging company of Byron and Shelley, that Mary Shelley wrote the book for which she became famous, *Frankenstein*.

26 One of the matters was for Shelley to deal with Byron's publishers who were eagerly waiting for Byron's work. Shelley carried with him on his return from Italy the manuscripts of *Prisoner of Chillon* and further cantos of *Childe Harold*.

27 It must not be thought that Mary's father, William Godwin approved of the union of Shelley and Mary. He thought it was just so much lust on each of their parts. "He forbade Shelley his house, and tried to make a reconciliation between him and Harriet. ... Godwin felt and expressed the utmost disapproval, and for two years refused to meet Shelley ..." (Brailsford.) The two never were to make up until Shelley's marriage to Mary in December of 1816, at which time Godwin walked Mary down the isle.

28 Harriet's apparent suicide came on the heels of another suicide in the clutch of females that Shelley had attracted. Fanny Imlay, Mary's other half-sister (a child which Mary Wollstonecraft had by Gilbert Imlay) had killed herself that October. They found her in a hotel room with an empty bottle of laudanum (opium) and a farewell note by her side. Fanny, yet another young woman of the Godwin household, was as much attracted to Shelley as was Mary and Claire. (The speculation is that at various times Shelley had sexual relations with all three. See Johnson.)

29 In August the children were delivered to Dr. and Mrs. Hume who lived at Hanwell in the western suburbs of London. The arrangement held until just after Shelley's death. In 1823, Harriet's sister (Eliza) was to finally get official custody of Ianthe, then age nine; with young Charles (age seven) to go to live with his grandfather at the Shelley estate, Field Place. Sadly, Charles died in 1826 but twelve years of age. Ianthe grew to womanhood and married, in 1837, Edward Jeffries Esdaile and lived to 1876. I understand that Ianthe and Edward had two sons and a daughter.

30 This was quite the house, that at Great Marlow. He apparently took it on a long lease and when the decision was made to leave England for Italy, he was obliged to rent it. The ad read in part, "containing a good dining-room, library 36 feet by 18, drawing-room 30 feet by 18, study, 5 best bedrooms, 2 large nurseries, each 30 feet by 20, water closet, 6 or 7 attics, convenient offices, good garden and pleasure-ground ..."

31 It should not be construed that Shelley spent money lavishly, certainly not on himself. Trelawny recollects: "An Italian who knew his way of life, not believing it possible that any human being would live as Shelley did, unless compelled by poverty, was astonished when he was told the amount of his income ..."

32 Blunden writes (*Shelley* ...): "It may be due to the disappearance of family papers that among Shelley's latest doings in England nothing shows him making an attempt to see either his family at Field Place or his children and Harriet's."

33 The first accounts that the Shelleys and Claire got of Allegra, thereafter, were encouraging. "They dress her up in little trousers trimmed with lace and treat her like a little princess." (See Blunden, *Shelley* ... .) Actually, the little girl was not long at Byron's place – just as well, considering the kind of life that he led. Allegra was boarded with the family of the English Consul at Venice, Richard Hoppner.

34 Shelley wrote of Pisa: "Stand on the marble bridge, cast your eye if you are not dazzled on its river glowing as with fire, then follow the graceful curve of the palaces on the Lung' Arno till the arch is naved by the massy dungeon-tower, forming in dark relief, and tell me if anything can surpass a sunset at Pisa." (As quoted by Blunden, *Shelley* ... .)

35 Being shocked at Lord Byron's profligate way of living, Shelley, as a consequence, wrote *Julian and Maddalo*.

36 In letter to a friend back home (Peacock) dated 22nd December, 1818, Shelley writes his impressions of Rome. "Rome is a city, as it were, of the dead, or rather of those who cannot die, and who survive the puny generations which inhabit and pass over the spot which they have made sacred to eternity. In Rome, at last in the first enthusiasm of your recognition of ancient time, you see nothing of the Italians." (As reproduced by Hughes.)

37 In Greek mythology, Prometheus was a demigod; and, though a mere demigod, was fabled to have made man out of clay. He then stole fire from Olympus and taught men how to use it. For this act (but not just this act as he did other things to upset the gods such as deflowering Minerva) Prometheus was punished by Zeus. The punishment was that he was bound down by chain to a rock in the Caucasus where his liver was preyed upon every day by a vulture. The original story was dramatized by the Greek poet, Aeschylus (525-456 BC). Shelley sought to get his political message across with the writing of his, *Prometheus Unbound*. Shelley's Prometheus was aware of the miseries heaped on him because of the modern state of society and Shelley took the "magic-wand approach," *à la Godwin*. The work, as a piece of poetry, is considered (*Cambridge Guide*) to be Shelley's

masterpiece, especially the first two acts. *Prometheus Unbound*, however, as a whole, is not one that can be much appreciated by a person who simply wants to browse poetry. Mary Shelley, after her husband's death, was to write in 1839: "It requires a mind as subtle and penetrating as his own to understand the mystic meanings scattered throughout the poem. They elude the ordinary reader by their abstraction and delicacy of distinction, but they are far from vague." (As quoted, Blunden, *Shelley* ....)

38 Trelawny recollected that "Shelley never flourished far from water. When compelled to take up his quarters in a town, he every morning, with the instinct that guides the water-birds, fled to the nearest lake, river, or sea-shore, and only returned to roost at night. If debarred from this, he sought out the most solitary places." Further, Trelawny wrote: Shelley had a "habit of eternally brooding on his own thoughts, in solitude and silence ... Like many other over-sensitive people, he thought everybody shunned him, whereas it was he who stood aloof. To the few who sought his acquaintance, he was frank, cordial, and, if they appeared worthy, friendly in the extreme; but he shrank like a maiden from making the first advances."

39 The poem came about because of Shelley having met a young woman, Contessina Teresa Emilia Viviani, the daughter of the governor of Pisa. Emilia had been placed in a convent against her will. Then when it came time for her to marry she was forced into one of convenience. Shelley was upset on how custom and parental power locked this beautiful woman up both physically and mentally. More particularly, Shelley was fascinated by the beauty of this young woman.

"There – One, whose voice was venomed melody
Sate by a well, under blue nightshade bowers:
The breath of her false mouth was like faint flowers,
Her touch was as electric poison – flame
Out of her looks into my vitals came,
And from her living cheeks and bosom flew
A killing air, which pierced like honey-dew
Into the core of my green heart, ..."

40 Keats had arrived in Italy the previous fall, a very sick man. He had come there with his artist friend, Joseph Severn; all were hoping against hope that the spending of that winter under the Italian sun would some how revive Keats who was suffering

from tuberculosis. Shelley knew that Keats was in Italy and had invited him to stay with him at Pisa, but Keats couldn't make the trip because of his health, and, it seems, that Shelley could not make the time to get up to Rome.

41 "Shelley and Keats were never regular race-horses. They were colts that bolted in their first race and ran until they dropped." (Richard Dowling, "My Copy Of Keats," www.blupete.com/Literature/Essays/Best/DowlingMyCopyKeats.htm)

42 As quoted by Blunden, *Leigh Hunt* .... In addition to the £150 sent by Shelley, Byron made a loan to Hunt in the amount of £220. (*Ibid.*)

43 Jane Williams, a neighbor first introduced Shelley to Trelawny. Trelawny gave an accounting of the event. Shelley had come to pay a call, but hesitated at the door, "Come in, Shelley; it's only our friend Tre just arrived." Trelawny thoughts were: "Swiftly gliding in, blushing like a girl, a tall thin stripling held out both hands; and although I could hardly believe as I looked at his flushed, feminine, and artless face, that it could be the Poet, I returned his warm pressure. After the ordinary greetings and courtesies he sat down and listened. I was silent from astonishment: was it possible this mild-looking, beardless boy, could be the veritable monster at war with all the world? ... denounced by the rival sages of our literature as the founder of a Satanic school?" Mrs. Williams, to break the spell, requested Shelley to read from a book that he had named and that he had carried into the room. "Oh, read to us!" Shelley cracked the book and read to them and was instantly "oblivious of everything but the book in his hand. It happened to be a Spanish book and Trelawny was impressed with "his lucid interpretation of the story, and the ease with which he translated [it] into our language ..." Shelley finished and Trelawny continued in his trance, then looked up. Shelley was gone. He asked of Jane Williams, "Where is he?" To which she replied, "Who? Shelley? Oh, he comes and goes like a spirit, no one knows when or where."

44 As quoted by Blunden, *Shelley* .... As the entry in *Chambers* discloses, Trelawny was entered in the navy rolls at a young age but deserted and for many years lived a life of "desperate enterprize in Eastern seas." After accompanying Byron to Greece and staying after Byron's death he traveled widely seeking adventure. He lived on for many years going into

retirement back in England where he "amused, shocked, excited and alarmed Victorian dinner-parties and roared down all who did not please him." (Blunden, *Shelley* ... .)

45 An area of Italy, at that time, where "the only indication of human habitation was a few miserable fishing villages scattered along the margin of the bay [Spezzia]. Near its centre, between the villages of Saint' Arenzo and Lerici, we came upon a lonely and abandoned building, called the Villa Magni, though it looked more like a boat or bathing house than a place to live in. It consisted of a terrace or ground-floor unpaved, and used for storing boat-gear and fishing tackle; and of a single story over it divided into a hall or saloon and four small rooms which had once been whitewashed; there was one chimney for cooking ... it had a verandah facing the sea ..." (Trelawny.)

46 That spring both Byron and Shelley had an "old naval friend" of Trelawny's, Captain Roberts at Genoa, build "an open boat for Shelley, and a larger decked one for Byron." Shelley called his the *Don Juan*; Byron called his the *Bolivar*. It would appear that Trelawny sailed the *Bolivar*, as her captain, more then did Byron. Shelley took delivery of his boat at Casa Magni in the month of May. Trelawny wrote that she was a ticklish boat to manage, "very crank in a breeze," though, fast and strongly built. Both Shelley and Williams were quite pleased with the *Don Juan*. Shelley writes: "Williams declares her to be perfect, and I participate in his enthusiasm, inasmuch as would be decent in a landsman. We have been out now several days, although we have sought in vain for an opportunity of trying her against the feluccas or other large craft in the bay. She passes the small ones as a comet might pass the dullest planet of the heavens."

47 Trelawny wrote: "Shelley returned to Leghorn, and found Williams eager to be off. We had a sail outside the port in two boats. Shelley was in a mournful mood, his mind depressed by a recent interview with Byron."

48 We quote Hunt from his *Autobiography*: "He [Trelawny] and his friend Captain Shenley were first upon the ground, attended by proper assistants. Lord Byron and myself arrived shortly afterwards. His lordship got out of his carriage, but wandered away from the spectacle, and did not see it. I remained in the carriage, now looking on, now drawing back with feelings that were not to be witnessed." Afterwards, Byron and Hunt

"dined a little and drank too much." Later they drove through the outskirts of Pisa in their carriage – "We sang, we laughed, we shouted." What the driver of the couch thought, they did not care. Shocking was the scene, "a ghastly trio," but the "event was real and a relief."

49 Trelawny described the scene: "... more wine was poured over Shelley's dead body than he had consumed during his life. This, with the oil and the salt, made the yellow flames glisten and quiver. The heat from the sun and the fire was so intense that the atmosphere was tremulous and wavy. The corpse fell open, and the heart was laid bare. The frontal bone of the skull, where it had been struck with the mattock [the digging tool used to unearth Shelley's body and which had struck Shelley's head], fell off; and, as the back of the head rested on the red-hot bottom bars of the furnace, the brains literally seethed, bubbled, and boiled, as in a cauldron, for a very long time."

50 See Hughes' Introduction to *Shelley*. Edward Dowden in his biography on Southey wrote, "Shelley's opinions were crude and violent, but their spirit was generous, and such opinions held by a youth in his teens generally mean no more than that his brain is working and his heart ardent."

51 "Shelley, while there was still time, would pour his words on paper, and put in the repairs and supplements when 'the thing had gone from him'; but writing thus unsteadily, as if art and impulse were at odds, he would mar his pure flame-like diction and the structure of entire poems (excepting *Adonais* and many of the lyrics) with looseness and wastefulness." Matthew Arnold, the professor of Poetry at Oxford, 1857-67, thought Shelley had missed his medium and was meant by Nature to write music. "The critics complain that the passion blazes but does not glow, that the lover knows not whom to love, but wastes his ardour on wind and cloud and metaphysical being." (Hughes' Introduction to *Shelley*.)

52 From William Hazlitt's, "On Paradox and Common-Place." Matthew Arnold, incidently, wrote that Shelley was "a beautiful and ineffectual angel beating in the void his luminous wings in vain." (As quoted by Brailsford.)

53 Brailsford wrote of Mary that she was rich with "generous vitality." That she won the hearts of all that knew her "because her own affections were warm and true. She was a good sister,

a good daughter, a passionate lover, an affectionate friend, a devoted and tender mother."

54 In *The Aspern Papers*, first published in 1888 in *The Atlantic Monthly*, Henry James wrote a story about an unscrupulous critic who attempted to pry loose papers possessed by an old woman which relate to a deceased Romantic poet, Jeffrey Aspern. James based his story on Shelley and Claire Clairmont.

Notes: "Leigh Hunt"

1 William Michael Rossetti (1829-1919), brother to Christina and Gabriel. I quote from William's work, *Life of John Keats*.

2 The American artist Benjamin West also fled Philadelphia and moved to London. West was to later marry Elizabeth Shewell, the sister of Isaac Hunt's father-in-law. Thus Mary Hunt was Elizabeth's niece. Mary and Elizabeth were not too far apart in age; they were friends. For a period of time Isaac and Mary lived with the Wests in London. [Leigh Hunt's "New World Forebears" by Desmond Leigh-Hunt, Iowa 40 (April 1984) The University of Iowa, URL: www.lib.uiowa.edu/spec-coll/Bai/leigh-hunt.htm : January, 2007.]

3 Hunt wrote in his *Autobiography*: "Christ's Hospital is a nursery of tradesmen, of merchants, of navel officers, of scholars; it has produced some of the greatest ornaments of their time; and the feeling among the boys themselves is, that it is a medium between the patrician pretension of such schools such as Eton and Westminster, and the plebeian submission of the charity schools. ... Christ's Hospital, I believe, towards the close of the last century [1700], and the beginning of the present [1800], sent out more living writers, in its proportion, than any other school."

4 The well recognized uniform of the boys from Christ's Hospital was a long blue habit and yellow stockings. As set out in my biographical note on Coleridge: "The discipline at Christ's Hospital in those days was ultra-Spartan, the mood monastic. All domestic ties were to be put aside." In Blunden's work (*Leigh Hunt and his Circle*) we see this: "The system of education was simpler than what has been attempted in later days without more convincing results. A Blue either spent his school life in the Writing School, where he would normally become a master of counting-house rules and fearsomely fine longhand; or in the

Mathematical School, there to vanquish the ogres of latitude, azimuth, parallax; or in the Grammar School, with 'insolent Greece and haughty Rome.'" Hunt was to spend his time at Christ's Hospital in the Grammar School, there, under a very well remembered Reverend James Bowyer. ... In the truly great poets, Bowyer would say, there is a reason assignable, not only for every word, but for the position of every word ..."

5 Hunt explained: "The Upper Grammar School was divided into four classes or forms. The two under ones were called Little and Great Erasmus; the upper were occupied by the Grecians and Deputy Grecians. ... When a boy entered the Upper School, he was understood to be in the road to the University, provided he had inclination and talents for it; but, as only one Grecian a year went to College, the drafts out of Great and Little Erasmus into the writing-school were numerous. A few also became Deputy Grecians without going farther, and entered the world from that form. Those who became Grecians always went to University ..." (*Autobiography*.)

6 The essayist Charles Lamb and the poet Samuel Taylor Coleridge, it is to be remembered, were also "Blue coat boys," though at earlier points in time. Lamb was eight years older than Hunt, Coleridge twelve.

7 Once the paper was on its feet, in about a year or so, Leigh Hunt left his job at the war office.

8 The *Examiner* was a weekly, published on Sunday, of 16 pages and only two columns a page, which made it more legible than most dailies. Its circulation gradually rose to 7,000 – 3,000 to 5,000 was the usual break-even range – and, as Jeremy Bentham observed, the *Examiner* was a highly regarded weekly among those interested in politics. (See Johnson.)

9 "Great is Journalism. Is not every Able Editor a Ruler of the World, being a persuader of it?" (Carlyle.)

10 Burdett, of course, is Sir Francis Burdett, and, as a parliamentarian, campaigned for parliamentary reform; Hunt is Henry Hunt (1773-1835) (no relation to Leigh Hunt) who was considered to be a dangerous radical who advocated annual parliaments, universal suffrage, the secret ballot and the repeal of the Corn Laws.

11 The authorities – maybe thinking the sentence severe – passed the message down to the prison authorities that they should try

to make Hunt's stay as comfortable as possible. An unused ward of the prison infirmary consisting of two rooms was assigned to him. The rooms were painted and decorated to his taste; the walls were papered with rose trellising and the ceiling was "colored with clouds and sky." Hunt's family was allowed to stay with him, though it would not appear that his wife stayed with him for the entire two year period. He had his library books with him and on top of the bookshelves was a bust of Homer; in the corner he had a piano; Charles Lamb was to declare that "there was no other such room except in a fairy-tale." A small part of the prison yard was fenced off just for him where he established a garden.

12 In his prison Hunt carried on with his journalistic practice and received visitors. It became fashionable to be seen in his prison and to send hampers of delicacies. The parliamentarian and jurist, Henry Brougham paid a visit. The essayist, William Hazlitt spent time with Leigh Hunt. History painter and diarist, Benjamin Haydon (1786-1846) was allowed to bring into Hunt's prison quarters Haydon's 12-foot *Judgment of Solomon* just to show Hunt. Lord Byron came to visit and declared that Hunt was "the wit of in the dungeon." (Johnson.) Hunt wrote that the "Lambs came to comfort me in all weathers, hail or sunshine, in daylight and in darkness ..." (*Autobiography*.) Jeremy Bentham came too, who Hunt described as one who united "the wisdom of a sage with the simplicity of a child."

13 "A Portrait of Leigh Hunt," The University of Iowa, www.lib.uiowa.edu/spec-coll/bai/portrait.htm (January, 2007).

14 It was in October of 1817 that John Gibson Lockhart, then, but age 23, at Edinburgh, with his platform being *Blackwood's Magazine*, began to fulminate against "The Cockney School of Poetry." Lockhart in particular attacked Keat's *Endymion* and Coleridge's *Biographia Literaria*.

15 Though Hunt wrote little in his *Autobiography* about his Marianne, he did write, at least this much: "My wife was a woman of great generosity, great freedom from every kind of jealousy ... she was uncomplaining."

16 Italy was represented, by a mutual friend of both Shelley and Hunt, as a place where one "will find no nuisance but the litter of the rose-leaves and the noise of the nightingales." (As quoted by Blunden, *Leigh Hunt and his Circle*.)

17 All uncredited quotes in this piece on Leigh Hunt are those of Blunden, or those quoted by Blunden in his work, Leigh *Hunt and his Circle* as listed in the table of references at the back of this book.

18 Actually the family, together with a goat for fresh milk, had set out to sail to Italy during November of the previous year (1821), but, due to stormy weather, the vessel did not get beyond the English Channel. The Hunts, after having been tossed about for weeks, came ashore to seek some comfort, and, it seems, in the process, forfeited their passage money.

19 Byron's loss of interest in the publication of *The Liberal* can be laid to the fact that Shelley, its chief proponent, had died. But also, it is to be noted that Byron took a dislike to Hunt, or more particularly to Hunt's family. The Hunt family had initially lodged itself in the downstairs area of Byron's palace at Pisa. Byron greeted the Hunt family at his place as like he would the arrival of the plague. In a contemporary letter from E. E. Williams to his wife, we read (Williams died in the boating accident with Shelley on the Bay of Spezzia but days later): "Lord B.'s reception of Mrs H. was, as S. tells me, most shameful. She came into his house sick and exhausted, and he scarcely deigned to notice her; was silent, and scarcely bowed. This conduct cut H. to the soul ..." (Trelawny.) Byron himself was to write of the Hunt children that they "are dirtier and more mischievous than Yahoos. What they can't destroy with their filth they will with their fingers ... six little blackguards." Of Hunt himself, Byron, at least in the earlier years, liked him well enough: In December of 1813, Byron was to make this note in his diary: "An extraordinary character, and not exactly of the present age. He reminds me more of Pym and Hampden times – much talent, great independence of spirit, and an austere yet not repulsive aspect. If he goes on *qualis ab incepto*, I know few men who will deserve more praise or obtain it. I must go see him again ..."

20 *The Liberal*, it appears, consisted of but four numbers, with the last coming out in 1823. (See Appendix I, Blunden, *Leigh Hunt and his Circle*.)

21 The actual ownership of the *Examiner* was obscure, the older brother, John Hunt thought he certainly had a better right to it. While Leigh was in Italy, and while he did submit the

occasional piece, John did all the work of getting it to the streets. Further, Leigh continued to expect that his brother John should continue to make remittances to his "co-owner" in Italy. Blunden observed "that a difference between these two brothers began, and widened into a coldness." (*Leigh Hunt and his Circle.*)

22 To round out this romantic group of early 19th-century English literature we mention Shelley and Byron, who did not accept government patronage, but they did not have to, they were supported to one degree or another by their aristocratic families.

23 Dickens, however, twenty-six years junior to Hunt, proved to be of considerable support to Hunt. It was Dickens and other friends that agitated for the payment of a government pension which, finally, in 1847, was granted to Hunt. On Hunt's death in 1859, Dickens was to sing the praises of Leigh Hunt and his regret that so many of Hunt's critics took up and echoed his description of Hunt in the fictional character, Skimpole; Hunt, as Dickens pointed out, showed his "graces and charms" by his continued forbearance in saying anything about Skimpole. Further Dickens was to declare: that the imprisonment of Leigh Hunt because of remarks about the king's son, in 1813, was, a national disgrace. The poet Swinburne wrote (*Quarterly Review*, July, 1902): "The simple and final reply should have been that indolence was the essential quality of the character and philosophy of Skimpole, and that Leigh Hunt was one of the hardest and steadiest workers on record, throughout a long and checkered life, at the toilsome trade of letters: and therefore to represent him as a heartless and shameless idler would have been as rational an enterprise, as lifelike a design after the life, as it would be to represent Shelley as a gluttonous, canting hypocrite, or Byron as a loyal and unselfish friend."

24 Ann Blainey, "A Portrait of Leigh Hunt," The University of Iowa.
www.lib.uiowa.edu/spec-coll/bai/portrait.htm : January, 2007).

25 Haydon and Hunt, in the earlier years, were the best of friends, but at some point had a falling out over Mrs Hunt. Keats explained (Keats died, tragically young, in 1821): "The quarrel with Hunt I understand thus far. Mrs H. was in the habit of borrowing silver of Haydon – the last time she did so, Haydon

asked her to return it at a certain time – she did not – Haydon sent for it – Hunt went to expostulate on the indelicacy, etc. – they got to words and parted for ever. All I hope is at some time to bring them all together again." (In a letter to his brothers dated 13th of January, 1818.) In later years, the Hunts were friends of the Carlyles. Mrs Carlyle was to write: "She [Marianne Hunt] is every other day reduced to borrow my tumblers, my teacups; even a cupful of porridge, a few spoonfuls of tea, are begged of me ... She actually borrowed one of the brass fenders the other day, and I had difficulty in getting it out of her hands; irons, glasses, teacups, silver spoons are in constant requisition; and when one sends for them the whole number can never be found."

26 "Mr. T. Moore – Mr. Leigh Hunt"; also, see Hazlitt's comments in "On the Conversation of Authors," viz. Leigh Hunt has "a fine vinous spirit about him, and tropical blood in his veins: but he is better at his own table."

Notes: "John Keats"

1 Keats, "I stood Tip-toe" (1816).

2 "The maternal grandfather was a Mr. Jennings, who kept a large livery stable, called the Swan and Hoop, in the Pavement, Moorfields, London, opposite the entrance to Finsbury Circus." (Rossetti.)

3 The father died 16th of April, and, on June 27th, the mother, Frances Keats, married William Rawlings. The marriage to Rawlings did not last, and, at the time of her death, Frances Keats was living with her mother and her children.

4 Charles Cowden Clarke (1787-1877) became a book dealer in London in 1820. He went on, together with his wife, Mary Victoria Novello (1809-1898), to become well known Shakespearean scholars.

5 It almost seems as if the family sold the fifteen year old; but apparently Keats was happy enough with the arrangement, at least at first.

6 Keats' line from, "Where's the Poet?" – "Poorest of the beggar-clan." Keats "denied that he abandoned surgery for the express purpose of taking to poetry: he alleged that his motive had been the dread of doing some mischief in his surgical operations." (Rossetti.)

7 It would not appear that Keats and Shelley came to Hunt's home at the same time. First Shelley arrived whom Hunt had met previously, then came Keats. I do not know, before they met up at Hunts' home, if the two had previously met up with one another, or not. In any event both young poets received the same warm reception with Hunt throwing his house completely open to the two young men.

8 Shelley was humored by his rich and aristocratic parents who encouraged him and paid for the publication of certain of his juvenile literary efforts. After being expelled from Oxford and becoming estranged from his family, Shelley, when but twenty-one, wrote and saw to the private publication of *Queen Mab*, a visionary philosophical and political poem in nine cantos. (As *Chambers* observed, the work is "Godwin versified.") *Queen Mab* opens with a sleeping maiden whose spirit is transported by a magical chariot to the palace of the Fairy Queen. This is an opening not unlike that of Keats' *Endymion*.

9 Keats and Shelley at some point during the winter of 1816/17, or maybe the spring of 1817, were, in fact, to challenge one another to produce, each, a poetic fantasy. In the result Shelley came out with *The Revolt of Islam* and Keats with *Endymion*.

10 In a letter to Benjamin Haydon dated April 8th, 1818, Keats expressed his intentions to travel, "to make a sort of prologue to the Life I intend to pursue – that is to write, to study and to see all Europe at the lowest expense." (*Letters of John Keats*.)

11 I write of Benjamin Robert Haydon (1786-1846). I am not sure under what circumstance or when Keats first met Haydon, but it can be said, that Haydon was a sure and good friend of Keats.

12 Bailey was at the time he met Keats attending Oxford. That Bailey was admitted to Oxford says as much about his family as it does about Baily himself. He must have been a younger son as he was studying for the church. At the end of 1817, Bailey obtained a curacy at Carlisle, and we see where in 1819 Bailey married the daughter of the Bishop of Stirling.

13 On September 10th, 1817, Keats, from Oxford, wrote his fourteen year old sister, "Dear Fanny," which letter is addressed in care of, "Miss Kaley's School, Walthamstow, Essex." Now, Walthamstow seems, from the map I consulted, in the north end of London, not far I suppose from the original Keats home and on a direct line between Canterbury and Oxford, so it seems

likely that John called by to see his young sister. He wrote: "When I saw you last I told you of my intention of going to Oxford and 'tis now a week since I disembark'd from his Whipship's[?] coach the Defiance in this place [Oxford]. I am living in Magdalen Hall on a visit to a young Man [Benjamin Bailey] with whom I have not been long acquainted, but whom I like very much – we lead very industrious lives he in general Studies and I in proceeding at a pretty good rate with a Poem [*Endymion*] ..." On September 28th, still at Oxford, we see where Keats wrote Haydon.

14 "After a tolerable journey, I went from Coach to Coach to as far as Hampstead where I found my brothers ... went to Lambs Conduit Street [Reynolds family]... From No 19 went to Hunt's and Haydon's who now live neighbours [Great Marlborough Street]."

15 Charles Armitage Brown (1786-1842) was the son of a London stockbroker originally from Scotland. Charles was sent to St. Petersburg to manage a business there but things did not work out. By 1810 Charles was back at London where he turned to writing for periodicals. His death occurred in New Zealand.

16 Since 1925, Wentworth Place, Keats Grove, NW3 has been operated as a museum administered by the London Metropolitan Archives.

17 As we can see from his correspondence, on January 23rd, when then at London, Keats sent *Endymion* to Taylor and Hessey. This work did not go through the press until after April 10th, for that is the date which Keats used at the end of his short and apologetic preface: "Teignmouth, April 10th, 1818." With that final little bit done, and with Tom "greatly better," Keats felt he could get on with his travels, though, as we can see, two more months were to pass before he got away to the north of England.

18 In his letter to Bailey, May 25th, 1818, Keats tells of how he will spend the next couple of weeks with George before he goes aboard his American bound ship with his new bride (Georgiana Augusta Wylie). That was not the last time that the brothers were to see one another. In January of 1820, George came back from America to deal with the maternal grandfather's estate – I believe that John generously signed off on everything and upon doing so George returned to his American home. Incidently,

George settled in Louisville, Kentucky, where he became a successful mill owner and was active in the civic and cultural life of that community.

19 We see from the correspondence that on June 10th Keats was at London. Then, on June 25th, he was at Enfmore, very near Kendal. The pair, Keats and Brown, called on Wordsworth who was then at Rydal but no one was at home. "I wrote a note and left it on the Mantel-piece." He apparently did get to see Southey, however, I have read no record of that meeting. Southey, it will be remembered, by then, had been the Poet Laureate of England for five years. Southey was, in 1818, 44 years of age; Keats, 23.

20 "... thought it best to get home as soon as possible and went on board the Smack from Cromarty. We had a nine days passage and were landed at London Bridge yesterday." (Letter to sister Fanny, dated August 18, 1818.) A Mrs. Dilke, related to his friend Charles Dilke, was to immediately take Keats into her care, and wrote of her impressions on seeing Keats: "arrived here last night, as brown and as shabby as you can imagine: scarcely any shoes left, his jacket all torn at the back, a fur cap, a great plaid, and his knapsack." (As quoted by Rossetti.)

21 "Keats did not take to Shelley as kindly as Shelley did to him." (Hunt's *Autobiography*.)

22 Rossetti. "Its general purport was that the poem was faulty, but the author would not keep it back for revision, which would make the performance a tedium to himself, 'I have written to please myself, and in hopes to please others, and for a love of fame.'" A contemporary criticism came from Shelley – who was no great fan of Keats, nor for that matter, was Keats of Shelley. Shelley thought that *Endymion*, while it "is full of some of the highest and the finest gleams of poetry" the work as a whole should not have been printed. (As quoted by Rossetti.)

23 Leigh Hunt observed, in his *Autobiography*, that William Gifford was a mixture of "implacability and servility": "... his *Review* spared neither age nor sex as long as he lived. What he did at first out of a self-satisfied incompetence, he did at last out of an envious and angry one; and he was, all the while, the humble servant of power, and never expressed one word of regret for his inhumanity."

24 Even Shelley, as we have already mentioned, thought that the work, while having flashes of poetic brilliance, as a whole should not have been sent to the press.

25 John Gibson Lockhart (1794-1854): *Blackwood's* had hired this young man in 1817, when he was but 23 years of age. Lockhart, spent his boyhood at Glasgow, at age 13 he went up to Oxford and by 19 had taken a first in classics. After a tour of the continent Lockhart went to Edinburgh, there to study law; while he never took up the practice of law he was called to the Scottish bar in 1816. At *Blackwood's* he was able to pursue what he wanted, a literary life. Incidently, he met Walter Scott in 1819 and was to marry, in 1820, Scott's eldest daughter, Sophia. In 1825, Lockhart came to London to become the editor of the *Quarterly Review* and there remained in that capacity until 1853. Lockhart's masterpiece is the *Life Of Scott* called the greatest biography in English after Boswell's *Johnson.*

26 The *Examiner*, it will be recalled, was Leigh Hunt's paper; it was Hunt who discovered Keats. Hunt did not think that Keats took this criticism much to heart.

27 Dr. Dale in his work, *Medical Biographies* wrote: "There is an ominous significance to persistent sore throat in a young person who has been heavily exposed to tuberculosis as Keats was. It is likely to mean laryngeal tuberculosis, a serious and painful disease which occurs rarely except as a complication of tuberculosis elsewhere in the respiratory tract. Until recent years laryngeal tuberculosis was of deadly portent."

28 This is in Rossetti's view, viz. "*Lamia*, *Hyperion*, and all his best works." *Hyperion*, as the poet Algernon Charles Swinburne (1837-1909) thought, was a triumph, completely so as much as *Endymion* was a failure.

29 July 5th: Letter to Fanny Brawne: "They talk of my going to Italy." July 5th: Letter to sister Fanny: "I have no return of the spitting of blood, and for two or three days have been getting a little better. My Physician tells me I must contrive to pass the winter in Italy." Italy was, of course, a place which Keats had wanted to go ever since Shelley had departed for the place in March of 1818. In a letter to his friend John Reynolds, dated April 10th, 1818, in referring to where he was staying at the time, Teignmouth, Keats wrote: "Who would live in the region of Mists, Game Laws, indemnity Bills, etc., when there is such a place as Italy?"

30 August 20th: Letter to Charles Browne. After telling of his resolve to go to Italy, "I think there is a core of disease in me

not easy to pull out ... if I should die ... I shall be obliged to set off in less than a month."

31 On October 24th – trying to spare Fanny – Keats wrote Mrs. Brawne. Naples Harbour, "I cannot say a word about Naples; I do not feel at all concerned in the thousand novelties around me."

32 Keats did succeed in writing one letter to his friend Charles Brown on November 30th: "I can scarcely bid you goodbye even in a letter. I always made an awkward bow."

33 This is, of course, Sir James Clarke (1788-1870). Clarke had studied medicine at Edinburgh and London and then became a surgeon with the navy. He practiced in Rome during this period. In 1826 Clarke moved back to London. He was to become the personal physician to the Duchess of Kent, Queen Victoria's mother, and in time, the "physician-in-ordinary" to Queen Victoria. Whatever he was to become to these royal personages, Dr. Clarke did not prove to be of much help to Keats; though, in such a late stage of consumption, it is not likely that anyone could have helped Keats. It seems that Clarke did not think that Keats had tuberculosis, for he prescribed regular outings and exercise, contrary to the normal prescription of rest.

34 Keats' death was brought about because of tuberculosis, though there were those who thought he went to an early grave because of the writings of cruel paper-men. Shelley, for example, was of the view that the "agony of his sufferings at length produced the rupture of a blood-vessel in the lungs, and the usual process of consumption to have begun." (As quoted by Rossetti.) At the last of it, however, Keats was in great misery, more because of his loss of his Fanny than the physical pain of a consumptive death.

35 "Let us say then, once and for all, that, whatever may be the praise and homage due to Keats for ranking as one of the immortals when he died aged twenty-five, no sort of encomium can be awarded to him on the ground that, when first began, he began early and well." (Rossetti.) The judgment of Robert Seymour Bridges (1844-1930) in his essay on Keats, is that "we may unhesitatingly accept" that the best of Keats' work is "of the highest excellence, but the mass of it disappointing." (See Bridges Introduction *The Poems of John Keats*.)

36 See Palgrave's *The Golden Treasury*. Francis Turner Palgrave (1824-1897) was the Professor of Poetry at Oxford.

37 See Dowling's essay, "My Copy Of Keats." www.blupete.com/Literature/Essays/Best/DowlingMyCopyKeats.htm

38 It remains for me to add a short note that his contemporary, William Hazlitt made concerning Keats: "I cannot help thinking that the fault of Mr. Keats's poems was a deficiency in masculine energy of style. He had beauty, tenderness, delicacy, in an uncommon degree, but there was a want of strength and substance. His *Endymion* is a very delightful description of the illusions of a youthful imagination given up to airy dreams – we have flowers, clouds, rainbows, moonlight, all sweet sounds and smells, and Oreads and Dryads flitting by – but there is nothing tangible in it, nothing marked or palpable – we have none of the hardy spirit or rigid forms of antiquity. He painted his own thoughts and character, and did not transport himself into the fabulous and heroic ages. There is a want of action, of character, and so far of imagination, but there is exquisite fancy. All is soft and fleshy, without bone or muscle. We see in him the youth without the manhood of poetry. His genius breathed 'vernal delight and joy.' 'Like Maia's son he stood and shook his plumes,' with fragrance filled. His mind was redolent of spring. He had not the fierceness of summer, nor the richness of autumn, and winter he seemed not to have known till he felt the icy hand of death!" www.blupete.com/Literature/Essays/Hazlitt/TableTalk/Effeminacy.htm

Notes: "Robert Southey"

1 The Southeys were to have nine children, five of whom died young leaving four boys: Robert (the subject of this biographical sketch), Thomas (b.1777), Henry Herbert (b.1783-1865) and Edward.

2 Wordsworth didn't think that Southey had quite the right personality to get much out of his university experience; he lacked "the congregating temper that pervades our unripe years." (Wordsworth, 1805 *Prelude*, III.)

3 As the passing times were to show, Coleridge was less upset with Southey because of the aborted ideas of their youth, but continued to bear a grudge because (so Coleridge thought) Southey had forced Coleridge to marry a girl that he did not love.

4 In September of 1802, the Southeys' first child was born, Margaret Edith; she was to die in August of the following year. There were to be others: Edith May (b.1804), Herbert (b.1806-1816), Emma (1808-1809), Bertha (b.1809), Katherine (b.1810), Isabel & Cuthbert (b.1819).

5 To be thrown in with the mix of adults and children, were the dogs. Southey was a lifelong dog lover and had in succession, as Johnson observed, pointers called Rover and Dapper.

6 Southey's writing can be broken down into two chief periods – "a period during which poetry occupied the higher place and prose the lower, and a period during which this order was reversed." (Dowden.) Besides his poetry (not much read any more) Southey wrote biographies, including: *Nelson*, *Wesley*, *Joan of Arc* and *Cowper*. He also wrote histories, including: *Brazil*, *Portugal*, *Paraguay*, *Peninsular War* and *The English Navy*. Southey was to never leave a letter unanswered for long, with the result that his correspondence now fills volumes.

7 Southey was of the view that the government was seriously endangered by the writings of William Cobbett, and still more by Leigh Hunt of the *Examiner*.

8 "Southey and the *Quarterly Review* were often spoken of as a single entity." (Dowden.)

Notes: "Lord Byron"

1 This is what Lady Caroline Lamb wrote in her diary in March of 1812, just after she first met Byron.

2 Sir Walter Scott likely represented the other extreme: servile to nature and to opinion.

3 Macaulay was to write: "From the poetry of Lord Byron they drew a system of ethics, compounded of misanthropy and voluptuousness, a system in which the two great commandments were, to hate your neighbour, and to love the neighbour's wife." (Macaulay's essay, "Moore's Life on Lord Byron," June, 1831.) The essayist, John Morley, was to write that Byron was an "English aristocrat who became the favorite poet of all the most highminded conspirators and socialists of continental Europe for half a century ... Subtlety may miss them [the multitude], graces may miss them, and reason may fly over their heads, but the words of a generous humanity on the lips of poet or chief have never failed to kindle divine music in their breasts." ("Byron" as found in Morley's *Nineteenth Century Essays*.)

4 "Mad Jack's" first wife had been married to a Marquis. She apparently was with her husband, the Marquis, when John Byron, this Captain of the Guards, came along. After John seduced her, the pair ran off to the continent. Only after the divorce of the first wife came through in 1779, did the pair get married.

5 The impression I have, after reading a number of works on Byron, is, that after their marriage "Mad Jack" spent most all of the wealth that Catherine had brought into the marriage. After the ready cash disappeared, "Mad Jack" proceeded to run up bills with his creditors. Increasing financial pressure caused him to run away with Catherine to the continent. (They did not have the bankruptcy laws which we have these days, debtors back then were put in prison.)

6 "She half worshipped, half hated the blackguard to whom she was married ..." (John Nichol's biography of Byron as found in Morley's *English Men of Letters*.)

7 Dale says, club foot or maybe club feet.

8 Catherine "was not a bad woman, but she was not a good mother. Vain and capricious, passionate and self-indulgent, she mismanaged her son from his infancy, now provoking him by her foolish fondness, and now exciting his contempt by her paroxysms of impotent rage." (Biography of Byron by E. H. Coleridge and as was published in *The Encyclopedia Britannica*, 1905.)

9 Nichol's biography.

10 "In the autumn of 1798 the family, i.e. his mother — who had sold the whole of her household furniture for £75. — with himself, and maid, set south." (Nichol's biography.)

11 "The master [of Dulwich], Dr Glennie, perceived that the boy liked reading for its own sake and gave him the free run of his library. He read a set of the British Poets from beginning to end more than once." (Coleridge's biography in *The Encyclopedia Britannica*.)

12 I am reminded of what Thomas Paine wrote in his *Common Sense*, "Men who look upon themselves born to reign, and others to obey, soon grow insolent; their minds are early poisoned by importance." Byron no doubt took away with him from Harrow an imprint of aristocratic prejudices which he bore in all his

dealings with others throughout his life, though he had little sympathy for the Tory cause.

13 In July of 1808, Cambridge somehow managed to grant a degree to Byron. "Cambridge University, which Byron attended between 1805 and 1807, was a training-ground for Anglican priests, and thus a hotbed of cant, obfuscation and hypocrisy. Little learning and still less research occurred there. There was, for example, a Chair of Physics, but no lectures in that subject had been given by the Professor of Physics since the 1730s. Byron went to Trinity, one of the two largest and most prestigious colleges (he had a room in Neville's Court). As a nobleman, he was not asked to go to lectures, nor to submit to the indignity of a public examination. He didn't even have to undergo the viva which his friends had to attend. A quiet, terminal chat with his tutor was all that was needed to assure him of his degree. But he did a huge amount of unsystematic reading, and perfected his skills in swimming, fencing with the broadsword, pistol-shooting, and boxing."
(www.hobby-o.com : January, 2007)

14 At Newstead, Byron and his selected friends were to have great parties. Nichol wrote in his biography of Byron, after an excursion outdoors, Byron would enter the mansion "between a bear and wolf, amid a salvo of pistol shots; sitting up to all hours, talking politics, philosophy, poetry ... drinking their wine out of the skull-cap which the owner had made out of the cranium of some old monk dug up in the garden; breakfasting at two, then reading, fencing, riding, cricketing, sailing on the lake or playing with the bear or teasing the wolf."

15 Byron brought *English Bards and Scotch Reviewers* out in March of 1809; Cawthorn printed 1,000 copies. William Hazlitt described it as a "satire of a lord, who is accustomed to have all his whims or dislikes taken for gospel, and who cannot be at pains to do more than signify his contempt or displeasure ... it is the satire of a person of birth and quality, who measures all merit by external rank, that is, by his own standard." Your compiler has an early copy of the work, which was printed for James Cawthorn, 1810. It was described by the dealer as "an example of the 7th Spurious Reprint of the 3rd Authorized edition."

16 "Dear Mother, If you please, we will forget the things you mention. I have no desire to remember them. When my rooms are finished, I shall be happy to see you; as I tell but the truth, you will not suspect me of evasion. I am furnishing the house more for you than myself ..." This letter is dated November 2nd, 1808, Newstead. His true feelings were probably expressed in a letter to his half-sister written a few weeks later, dated November 30th, Newstead.

17 It was at Cambridge where Byron met John Cam Hobhouse (1786-1869; afterwards Lord Broughton). These two were to become constant friends and remained so throughout Byron's life.

18 Well, not so isolated that there weren't servants. Indeed, Byron took his pleasure with one of them, Lucy, a maid at Newstead. She became pregnant by Byron. Arrangements were ultimately made through Hanson for the continuing maintenance for Lucy and the child.

19 As we will see, Byron's patrician background impacted greatly on his life and his work. It was Hazlitt who said that when a man is tired of what he is, he pretends to be something else. A poet may pretend to be a philosopher and a lord to be just one of the people. It is not likely that too many of the privileged class become bored with their lives; poets, I should observe, as a general rule, do not come from the privileged classes. Byron was either not in reality from the privileged class, or was an exception to the rule.

20 Who is to say what got Byron interested in the countries of the near east. We know that in 1802, when yet a boy of 14, on Christmas holidays from Harrow, he stayed over with his mother at Bath, long the social center of the smart set. Lady Riddel gave a masquerade, and Byron went with his mother dressed as a Turkish boy. ("The Byron Chronology," www.rc.umd.edu/reference/chronologies/byronchronology/index.html : January 8th, 2007.)

21 Accompanying them were Byron's servants: his valet William Fletcher, old Joe Murray, Robert Rushton, and Friese, a German servant whom a Dr. Butler had recommended. By August, Byron had sent all his servants (save for Fletcher) home to England, this was just before he boarded a vessel for Malta.

22 In the first two cantos of *Childe Harold,* Byron set out the principal events of his travels during 1809 and what he thought of them. E. H. Coleridge writes that Byron's "descriptions of places and scenes, of 'Morena's dusky height,' of Cadiz and the bull-fight, retain their freshness and their warmth.

23 In December of 1809, Byron's party on horseback arrived at Delphi, which Byron found to be but a dirty village. Before the month is out the party, still on horseback, arrived in Thebes and carried on after that to Athens.

24 One of the tales that has survived is this one: "On a trip back to the monastery, Byron finds himself in the midst of an execution of a girl he knew from the village. Brandishing his gun and offering bribes, Byron stops the killing and sends the girl to freedom." ("The Byron Chronology.")

25 He arrived back in London with 4,000 lines of poetry, "a collection of marbles, and skulls, and hemlock, and tortoises, and servants ..." (Nichol.)

26 "Two years his senior, she [Mary Chaworth] was already engaged to a neighboring squire. There were meetings half-way between Newstead and Annesley, of which she thought little and he only too much. What was sport to the girl was death to the boy, and when at length he realized the "hopelessness of his attachment," he was "thrown out," as he said, "alone, on a wide, wide sea." She is the subject of at least five of his early poems, including the pathetic stanzas, "Hills of Annesley," and there are allusions to his love story in *Childe Harold* and in "The Dream" (1816). Notwithstanding, that Byron might have thought himself to be "alone, on a wide, wide sea," the very next year the young Byron was again casting his heart about. In July of 1804, the 16 year old Byron traveled up from London with his mother to stay with her during the holidays at Southwell. It was then that he involved himself, at different times, with two girls: Elizabeth Pigot and Julia Leacroft. Pigot leaves for an extended absence which throws Byron into a bit of a fit. In no time after that, Leacroft came along. Byron was immediately in love again. He courted her, leading her family to think that Byron intended marriage; "he narrowly escapes both entrapment and a duel with her brother." (See generally: "The Byron Chronology.")

27 Thomas Claughton purchased Newstead Abbey, the furniture, and remaining timber for £140,000. By October of 1812, Murray reported that booksellers had purchased 878 copies of the 5th edition of *Childe Harold*. To carry this through: in February of 1814, Byron's new work, *The Corsair* sold 10,000 copies on the first day, and over 25,000 copies in seven editions in the first month. ("The Byron Chronology.")

28 Melbourne, a Whig, was the Prime Minister of England in 1834, and again during 1835-39, and then again during 1839-41; he was the favorite of the young Queen Victoria from whom she learned valuable lessons in statecraft.

29 "Lady Caroline Ponsonby Lamb," www.englishhistory.net/byron/lclamb.html : January 7th, 2007

30 The opportunity for Caroline to first meet Byron, a poet who was just then very much in vogue, had arisen earlier; but at the last moment Caroline made an exit just as Byron made his entrance. It was maybe then that she wrote in her diary that night about Byron: "Mad, Bad, and Dangerous To Know."

31 "Lady Caroline Ponsonby Lamb," www.englishhistory.net/byron/lclamb.html : January 7th, 2007

32 *Ibid.*

33 The Melbourne estate is near Hatfield in Hertfordshire, Brocket Hall.

34 As quoted in "Lady Caroline Ponsonby Lamb," www.englishhistory.net/byron/lclamb.html : January 7th, 2007 In a letter dated June, 1813, Byron complained to Lady Melbourne, I suppose Caroline's mother-in-law: "You talked to me about keeping her out. It is impossible; she comes at all times, at any time, and the moment the door is open in she walks. I can't throw her out of the window: ..." ("The Byron Chronology.")

35 As quoted in "Lady Caroline Ponsonby Lamb," www.englishhistory.net/byron/lclamb.html : January 7th, 2007. Nichol referred to more events such as the time that Caroline threatened "to stab herself with a pair of scissors, and ... offering her gratitude to any one who would kill him."

36 Jane Elizabeth Scott (1774-1824) was married by her father, the vicar of Itchin, Hampshire, in 1794 to Edward Harley, the fifth Earl of Oxford. It was a loveless match. They had children but the likelihood is that they were not fathered by Edward but rather by other men whom she took to bed with her. At the time of their sexual relationship, Byron was 24, Jane was 38.

37 So what was it that swung these women around, there never was a realistic prospect that Byron would go the distance with any of them. Nichol wrote of Byron's irresistible attraction to the fairer sex: "His rank and fame, the glittering splendour of his verse, the romance of his travels, his picturesque melancholy and affection of mysterious secrets, combined with the magic of his presence to bewitch and bewilder them." (Nichol.)

38 Augusta Ada Byron King, Lady Lovelace (1815-1852).

39 This separation "and his engaging in widely publicized immorality abroad branded the Romantic movement as inherently wicked." (Johnson.)

40 Byron's friend, Hobhouse, in his *Recollections of a Long Life* left an account of the proceedings: "I dressed in full-dress, with white gloves, and found Byron up and dressed ... Lady Milbanke and Sir Ralph soon came, also dressed. Her Ladyship could not make tea, her hand shook. ... we walked up into the drawing-room, and found kneeling-mats disposed for the couple and the others. The two clergymen, the father and mother, and myself, were in waiting when Miss Milbanke came in, attended by her governess, the respectable Mrs Clermont. She was dressed in a muslin gown trimmed with lace at the bottom, with a white muslin curricle jacket, very plain indeed, with nothing on her head. Noel [Byron] was decent and grave. ... Miss Milbanke was as firm as a rock, and, during the whole ceremony, looked steadily at Byron. She repeated the words audibly and well. Byron hitched at first when he said, "I, George Gordon," and when he came to the words, "With all my worldly goods I thee endow," looked at me with a half-smile. They were married at eleven ... The little bells of Seaham church struck up after the wedding, and half a dozen [men] fired muskets in front of the house." Note Hobhouse's reference to Byron as Noel, which he did, I think, to get a dig in at Byron. In 1815, Lady Byron's uncle, Lord Wentworth died. The Milbankes, especially Lady Byron, took very good care of the lord in his last days. Lady Byron was the principal beneficiary of Lord Wentworth's will, however there was a proviso. The Milbankes were to change their name to Noel. Byron too added Noel to his name becoming George Gordon Noel Byron.

41 It would be an incorrect image of Byron to see him as a man with a steady drinking habit. Byron never smoked and he was,

as Trelawny wrote, "exceedingly abstemious in eating and drinking." Nichol, while confirming his general abstemiousness, observed that Byron drank a pint of gin and water over his verses at night, in the morning he took claret and soda. Marshall Dale wrote that Byron regularly went into "a self-imposed regimen designed to preserve the slimness of his figure and enhance the delicacy of his features. It consisted of three Turkish baths weekly, the imbibing of large quantities of water tinctured with vinegar, and an exclusive diet of boiled rice."

42 Since the marriage of their daughter to Byron, Lady Judith and Sir Ralph had moved to Kirkby Mallory. It came to them as part of Lord Wentworth's estate, which, upon Wentworth's death in 1815, passed to his sister Judith Milbanke, Annabella's mother. It is to Kirkby Mallory, that Lady Byron took her daughter, there to live with her parents. And, what a place: "... a Ballroom (34 x 14ft.), plus a Library (34 x 14ft.) the latter having a secret doorway leading to a lobby and private staircase. ... there were 9 principal bed and dressing rooms av. (20 x 20ft), 6 secondary bed and dressing rooms av. (17 x 9ft), 5 Maid servants bedrooms, 5 men servants bedrooms and 5 spacious attic and box rooms. The ground floor contained the domestic offices, Servants Hall and Kitchen (21 x 18 ft.), Servants Sitting Room, a Scullery, Butlers pantry, Plate room, Still Room, 2 Larders, a China Cupboard, 2 Housemaids Cupboards and a Boot Hole. Underground, were wine, beer, mineral water and storage cellars also an Outside Game Larder and Ice House." (See www.btinternet.com/~john.pge/kirkhal.html : January, 2007.) I do not know that this description fitted the place as of 1815, but nearly, I suppose. Kirkby Mallory was demolished about 1950.

43 There is reference in the works to Lady Holderness as the person who raised Augusta. Augusta's mother was Amelia Darcy, who was the daughter of Robert Darcy, 4th Earl of Holderness (d.1778). It could have been the 4th Earl's wife, Mary Doublet who was the one who raised Augusta but reference is also made to one of the Byron aunts, Francis Leigh. If it was Francis Leigh, then she was raised by her future husband's mother. These genealogical lines are readily available on the 'net.

44 The general's wife (General Charles Leigh) was Frances Byron who was the sister of John Byron, Augusta's and Byron's father.

45 Byron's work, *The Corsair* came out that February, 1814, and sold 10,000 copies on the first day, and over 25,000 copies in seven editions in the first month.

46 "The History Behind Byron's 'Fare Thee Well' by Amelia Hellam
www.clayfox.com/ashessparks/reports/amy.html : January, 2007

47 Just before his marriage that December, Byron went alone to visited Colonel Leigh and Augusta at their home at Six Mile Bottom.

48 The new will revoked his earlier will of September 29th, 1813. Hobhouse and Hanson were named as Byron's executors.

49 A last word on Augusta: She had seven children: Georgiana Augusta Leigh (b. 1808), Augusta Charlotte Leigh (b. 1811), George Henry John Leigh (b. 1812), Elizabeth Medora (b. 1814 [Byron's daughter?]), Frederick George Leigh (b. 1816), Amelia Marianne Leigh (b. 1817) & Henry Francis Leigh (b. 1820). In 1815, Augusta became Lady of the Bedchamber to Queen Charlotte, a year later she said her goodbyes to her brother who, in 1816, left England never to return. Byron kept up his correspondence with Augusta when in Europe. She was the conduit through whom he was able to get information on Annabella and his daughter, Augusta Ada. We see that at one point, in October of 1822, Byron was writing his sister, Augusta, to consider moving herself, husband, and children to Italy at his expense. No such move took place. In later years, just before her death, Augusta tried to patch things up with Annabella, but Annabella expected an admission that Augusta had turned Byron against her, an admission that was not forthcoming. Augusta died in 1851 and was buried at Kensal Green Cemetery in London.

50 Hunt's *Autobiography*. All of Byron's marital difficulties were making headlines, and, the public which had been following Byron's literary career with enthusiasm, was now against him as a mad man who used women badly and was now deserting his wife and child. It is thought, that this – together with his financial difficulties – as we shall soon see, was what drove Byron away from England.

51 Travel on the continent, in 1816, was easier then it had been for 20 odd years. The removal of traveling restrictions followed along after Napoleon's defeat in 1815.

52 Italy, "A country of fiddlers and poets, whores and scoundrels." When Robert Southey wrote this in 1813, *Life of Nelson*, he no doubt had Byron in mind, the two disliked one another.

53 "What Miss Godwin wanted Miss Clairmont also wanted, adventure above all. ... [Jane] was more a child of the warm south than Shelley had yet come upon. Quick in conversation, adroit in the common round, she well knew the advantage that she had in her physical vitality and invitation." (Blunden, Shelley, *A Life Story*.)

54 Claire gave the little girl the name of "Alba" ("Dawn"); Byron gave her the name "Allegra." In 1818, Claire then in Italy, delivered up the child to Byron. Allegra was eventually installed in an Italian convent (Cavalli Bagni in the Romagna); she died there at the age of five.

55 As soon as the group left Piccadilly Terrace, the bailiffs entered and seized all that remained.

56 "Byron takes with him Dr. Polidori and three servants: Robert Rushton, who had attended Byron as far as Gibraltar in 1809; William Fletcher, Byron's valet; and a Swiss servant named Berger." ("The Byron Chronology.")

57 The fact is, though they were attracted to one another, Shelley and Byron had different characters, held different beliefs, and led different lives. Lord Byron's biographer, John Nichol wrote: "The attitude of the two poets towards each other is curious; the comparatively shrewd man of the world often relied on the idealist for guidance and help in practical matters, admired his courage and independence, spoke of him invariably as the best of men, but never paid a sufficiently warm tribute in public to his work. Shelley, on the other hand, certainly the most modest of the great poets, contemplates Byron in the fixed attitude of a literary worshiper."

58 One of the notable persons who then lived at Geneva, and with whom Shelley and Byron dealt, was Madame de Staël (1766-1817). De Staël was the cosmopolitan daughter of the Genevan banker, Necker, and wife of the Swedish Ambassador. Madame de Staël, incidently, attempted to effect a reconciliation between Lady and Lord Byron. But, there never was a chance of that.

59 Shelley and Byron continued to be on good terms, the terms for Shelley were as good as might be had with Byron. Byron

entrusted Shelley with his manuscripts to London and to give them to his publisher, John Murray. Byron left it to Shelley to negotiate and settle a price for the work. Shelley did a very good job for Byron, getting "2000 guineas" for *Childe Harold* (canto III) and *Prisoner of Chillon*, a high price which even surprised Byron.

60 Trelawny recollects that Byron "passed through the Netherlands, went up the Rhine, paused for some months in Switzerland, crossed the Alps into Italy, and never left that peninsula until the last year of his life."

61 "The Byron Chronology." Byron described Marianna Segati "as an antelope with oriental eyes, wavy hair, a voice like the cooing of a dove, and the spirit of a Bacchante [a female votary of Bacchus, the god of wine], he remained on terms of intimacy for about eighteen months ..." (Nichol.)

62 Nichol wrote a few entertaining paragraphs about Margarita Cogni. "A handsome virago, with brown shoulders and black hair. She moved in with Byron and lived with him for 12 months. She was every bit the army sergeant and ordered everybody about with considerable efficiency. She eventually became more of a problem than Byron could stand, throwing plates about, in any direction, when she was upset which she was mostly all the time. When out with Byron, Cogni would snatch the hats right off other women should they look at Byron. There was a scene of large proportions when Byron was trying to remove her from his place. "Byron told her she must go home; whereupon she proceeded to break glass and threaten 'knives, poison, fire;' and on his calling his boatman to get ready the gondola, threw herself in the dark night into the canal. She was rescued, and in a few days finally dismissed; after which he only saw her twice, at the theatre."

63 I can only but mention as an aside Byron's involvement in the revolution that was just then going on in that part of Italy. He was undoubtedly drawn in by the Gamba family and he ended up storing guns in his house for the use of the rebels. There were battles between armed groups, indeed, there was a skirmish that took place just outside of Byron's door. It did not take long for the stronger party to put the rebellion down. The authorities were then at their leisure and were systematically

picking up sympathizers. It was then that Byron was to see his "ferociously bearded but kind-hearted Venetian servant Tita" arrested. Certain members of the Gamba family were taken into custody and banished. Byron and his Countess, however, seemed to have come through all of this, OK. As Johnson observed, "As a rich English nobleman with European fame, Byron was immune, but he felt it safer to transfer himself in the autumn to Tuscany, now the least-oppressive state in Italy, and rent a palace in Pisa." I might observe that Byron soon had his trusted servant, Tita, back with him as Byron was able to call in a few political favors.

64 Lord Byron wrote: "I have a new friend, the finest in the world – a tame bear. When I brought him here (Cambridge), they asked me what I meant to do with him, and my reply was, 'He should sit for a fellowship.' This answer delighted them not." (As quoted by Nichol.)

65 Byron had a great affection for dogs. Here are a couple of lines of his from *Don Juan*, Canto I, st. 123:

Tis sweet to hear the watchdog's honest bark
Bay deep-mouthed welcome as we draw near home;
'Tis sweet to know there is an eye will mark
Our coming, and look brighter when we come.

Of the many dogs which Byron owned one was named Pompey, and another called Bosun, a Newfoundland dog. Another, a big Saint Bernard that he got in Switzerland was called Mutz. Mutz, according to Byron was a very obedient and smart dog, why, "Mutz will shut the door when he is told." (Johnson recounts the story of how one day a wild pig made its way into the Byron yard and caught Mutz chewing on a leg of mutton, the pig laid a claim to the meal, Mutz took issue but the pig's razor teeth caught the dog in a vulnerable spot and Byron was left with a dead dog. The dog was solemnly laid to rest by Byron and on the dog's stone was written: "Near this spot are deposited the remains of one who possessed beauty without vanity, strength without insolence, courage without ferocity, and all the virtues of Man, without his vices."

66 Shelley's letter to Peacock from Ravenna, dated August (likely the 10th), 1821, as reproduced in Hughes.

67 Blunden, Shelley, *A Life Story*.

68 The tragic death of Shelley likely delayed the new publication, *The Liberal*. That October, back in London John Hunt (Leigh's brother) published the first number of *The Liberal*, with Byron's *Vision of Judgment* at its front. Also Byron gave John Hunt further business; he was to "publish the existing six cantos of *Don Juan*, *Werner*, and *Heaven and Earth*." John Murray, who had pretty much published all of Byron's work up to this point, did not take the news kindly. Murray thought Byron made a "dreadful" connection calling the Hunt brothers "outcasts from Society." This likely was so much sour grapes for Murray, as, after criticizing the characters of the Hunt brothers, he then determined to be critical of Byron and his work. *The Liberal* consisted of but four numbers, with the last coming out in 1823.

69 Leigh Hunt was being chased by creditors. To add to his difficulties at this time, Hunt was fighting with his brother John as to who was doing most of the work (John), and who owned the business. It seems clear that Leigh Hunt was happy to run to Italy to get away from his problems; but only if his family could go and he was able to keep them fed and housed while there. Though their joint publication venture failed, to his credit, Byron kept the Hunt family going until they left Italy in 1823.

70 Byron himself was to write of the Hunt children that they "are dirtier and more mischievous than Yahoos. What they can't destroy with their filth they will with their fingers ... six little blackguards." (As quoted by Blunden, *Leigh Hunt and his Circle*.) As for what Hunt thought of Byron: Byron had a certain "over-communicativeness" which was just "one of those qualities of his lordship, which, though it sometimes became the child-like simplicity of a poet, startled you at others in proportion as it led to disclosures of questionable propriety." (Hunt's *Autobiography*.) As for what Byron thought of Hunt: In December of 1813, Byron was to make this note in his diary: "An extraordinary character, and not exactly of the present age. He reminds me more of Pym and Hampden times – much talent, great independence of spirit, and an austere yet not repulsive aspect. If he goes on *qualis ab incepto*, I know few men who will deserve more praise or obtain it. I must go see him again ..." (As quoted by Blunden, *Leigh Hunt and his Circle*.)

71 Both of Shelley's children by Mary, Clara and William die not long after arriving in Italy.

72 Byron eventually placed Allegra in a convent; she died in 1822.

73 It would appear that Trelawny sailed the *Bolivar*, as her captain, more then did Byron.

74 Shelley's summer place, Casa Magni, was at San Terenzo, Lerici. Shelley and Mary shared the seaside place with Claire, and with Edward and Jane Williams. The Williamses and the Shelleys had become fast friends earlier that year, indeed, they occupied the ground floor of where the Shelleys had lived at Pisa, Tre Palazzi. It was just shortly after they had moved into Casa Magni that news had come that the five year old Allegra, Claire's child by Byron, had died at the convent in which Byron had eventually placed her. This news had set a very sombre mood for the household that fateful day when Williams and Shelley set out in the *Don Juan* to sail to Leghorn.

75 I go into the details of these sad events in my biographical sketch on Shelley.

76 It can be argued that *Don Juan* is Byron's masterpiece. I make reference to John Gibson Lockhart (1794–1854), the son-in-law and biographer of Sir Walter Scott. He was the editor of and contributor to the *Quarterly Review* (1825–53). He became known as "The Scorpion" because of the fierceness of his criticism. In June of 1821 Byron received a letter from Lockhart: "Stick to *Don Juan*: it is the only sincere thing you have ever written. . . . *Don Juan* . . [is] out of all sight the best of your works; it is by far the most spirited, the most straight-forward, the most interesting, and the most poetical; and every body thinks as I do of it, although they have not the heart to say so." Hazlitt was to write that *Don Juan* has "great power." It is "sometimes serious and sometimes trifling, sometimes profligate and sometimes moral..." (*The Spirit of the Age*.) Nichol wrote: "Neither *Childe Harold*, nor the most beautiful of Byron's earlier tales, contain more exquisite poetry than is to be found scattered through the cantos of *Don Juan* ..."

77 Byron, his possessions and hangers-on proceeded in a caravan consisting of two carriages and his coach (described as a "Napoleonic coach") set out for another location in Italy. The entourage eventually found its way to Genoa where he

rented Casa Saluzzo. The Leigh Hunt family, together with Mary Shelley took a large house about a mile from Byron, Casa Negroto

78 Nichol wrote that Byron was "disgusted with his periodical [*The Liberal*], sick of his editor, tired of his mistress, and bent on any change, from China to Peru, that would give him a new theatre for display."

79 At one point Shelley described the Countess: "... a very pretty, sentimental, innocent Italian, who has sacrificed an immense fortune for the sake of Lord Byron and who, if I know anything of my friend, her and human nature, will hereafter have plenty of leisure and opportunity to repent her rashness." (As quoted by Johnson.)

80 "Byron finally sails to Greece in the company of Trelawny, Count Pietro Gamba, Dr. Francesco Bruno, Constantine Skilitzy, and three servants: his gondolier, Tita Falcieri; his valet Fletcher; and his steward Lega Zambelli; as well as five or more additional servants. Byron also takes five horses, his bulldog Moretto, and the Newfoundland Lyon." ("The Byron Chronology.") We learn from Nichol: "They had on board two guns, with other arms and ammunition, five horses, an ample supply of medicines, with 50,000 Spanish dollars in coin and bills."

81 "As I [Trelawny] took leave of him, his last words were, 'Let me hear from you often, – come back soon? If things are farcical, they will do for *Don Juan*; if heroical, you shall have another canto of *Childe Harold*." (*Recollections of the Last Days of Shelley and Byron*.)

82 On November 22nd, Byron was joined in Metaxata by Colonel Leicester Stanhope (1784-1862), who had been sent by Byron's friends in London to be his assistant. Byron formed a low opinion of Stanhope and his "high-flown notions from the sixth Form at Harrow or Eaton." (Johnson.)

83 "On the light, fast boat with Byron are Dr. Bruno, Fletcher, and Loukas Chalandritsanos, and Byron's Newfoundland dog Lyon. On the larger supply boat are Gamba, Lega Zambelli, Trelawny's negro servant whom Byron has hired, and Byron's other servants as well as the horses, baggage, the Greek Committee printing press, and Byron's bulldog, Moretto."

84 "An inhabitant of the Suli mountains in Epirus, of mixed Greek and Albanian origin."

85 The drawing of blood or the bleeding of the patient was thought to be, back then, an effective tonic or cure to the sick. Like many, Byron had his doubts. When Dr. Bruno, Byron's personal physician who traveled about with him, said that there was no more he could do, other physicians were called in, who, apparently were all of the same opinion, bleed the patient. Byron refused, saying to Bruno, "If my hour has come I shall die, whether I lose my blood or keep it." Byron got sicker and the medical advice continued to be the same. "Bleed the patient." Byron continued to wave them off. The pleas of the doctors and of his friends finally took effect. On the last occasion the doctors pleaded with Byron, he flung his arm out. "There! you are, I see, a dammed set of butchers. Take away as much blood as you like, and have done with it. And so they blooded him and blistered him, and Byron simply got worse. The remedies, as Nichol observed, "was either too late or ill-advised."

86 The conclusion is that Byron died of malaria. And further, "... the patient's life might have been saved if the physicians had thought to administer cinchona (quinine) and added whatever the disease may have been, it was surely abetted by the 'remorseless bleeding' of the patient and the almost total disregard of the elementary principles of medical care."

87 Mary Shelley saw the funeral procession when it passed her house, so too did Byron's former lover, Lady Caroline Lamb. Caroline saw the procession and enquired about it. She was unaware that Byron had died; when told, she fainted dead away.

88 Hazlitt's "Characteristics" (1823).
www.blupete.com/Literature/Essays/Hazlitt/Characteristics.htm

89 Macaulay's essay, "Moore's Life on Lord Byron," June, 1831.

90 "... if you want imaginative satire, or bitter wailing, you must go to the writings of Lord Byron; if a thoughtful, dulcet, and wild dreaminess, you must go to Coleridge; if a startling appeal to the first elements of your nature and sympathies (most musical also), to Shelley; if a thorough enjoyment of the beautiful – for beauty's sake – like a walk on a summer's noon in a land of woods and meadows, you must embower yourself in the luxuries of Keats." (Quoted by Blunden, *Leigh Hunt and his Circle.*)

91 "Subtlety may miss them [the multitude], graces may miss them, and reason may fly over their heads, but the words of a generous humanity on the lips of poet [in speaking of Byron] or chief have never failed to kindle divine music in their breasts." (John Morley's essay, "Byron" as found in Morley's *Childe Harold*.)

92 Blunden, *Leigh Hunt and his Circle*.

REFERENCES

(Note: see www.blupete.com for specific page references.)

Arnold, *Essays in Criticism*, second series, 1888.

Berridge, *Opium and the People, Opiate Use in Nineteenth-Century England* (London: Allen Lane, 1981).

Birrell, *William Hazlitt* (London: MacMillan, 1902).

—, *Selected Essays* (London: Nelson, 1908).

Blunden, *Leigh Hunt and his Circle* (London: Harper Brs., 1930).

—, *Shelley, A Life Story* (London: Collins, Readers Union, 1948).

Burra, *Wordsworth* (London: Duckworth, 1936).

Byron, *English Bards, and Scottish Reviewers* (London: Printed for James Cawthorn, 1810).

—, *The Poetical Works of Lord Byron* (London: Frederick Warne, nd)

—, *The Selected Letters of Lord Byron*, Sel. by Barzun (New York: Farrar, Strauss & Young, 1953).

Brailsford, *Shelley, Godwin, and Their Circle*, 1913 (New York: Holt, nd).

Cambridge Guide to Literature in English, The, (Cambridge University Press, 3rd Ed., 1989).

Cameron, *Romantic Rebels: Essays on Shelley and his Circle* (Harvard University Press, 1973).

Carlyle, *The French Revolution*, 1837.

Castelar, *Life of Lord Byron* (London: Tinsley, 1875).

Chambers Biographical Dictionary (Edinburgh, 1990).

Clairmont, *The Clairmont Correspondence* (Baltimore and London: John Hopkins University Press, 2 vols., 1995).

Coleridge (E. H.), See *The Encyclopedia Britannica*, 1905, under Byron.

Coleridge & Wordsworth, *Lyrical Ballads*, 1798.

Coleridge, *Biographia Literaria*, 1817, (Oxford University Press, 1969).

—, *Golden Hours* (London: Collins, nd).

—, *On the Constitution of Church & State*, 1830.

Coote, *Byron the Making of a Myth* (London: Bodley Head, 1988).

Dale, *Medical Biographies* (University of Oklahoma Press, 1987).

De Quincey, *Recollections of the Lakes and the Lake Poets* (Edinburgh: Adam Black, 1862).

Dowden, *Southey* (New York: Harper, nd).

Encyclopedia Britannica, 1905.

Garrod, *Wordsworth: Lectures and Essays*, 1923 (Oxford University Press, 1958).
Green, *History of the English People*, 1877-80.
Guiccioli, *My Recollections of Lord Byron* (London: Richard Bentley, 1869).
Hazlitt, *Political Essays*, 1819. www.blupete.com/Literature/Essays/TableHazIII.htm
—, *The Spirit of the Age*, 1825. www.blupete.com/Literature/Essays/TableHazII.htm
Haydon, *Autobiography* (Oxford University Press, nd).
Herford, *The Age of Wordsworth* (London: Bell, 1916).
Hobhouse, *Recollections of a Long Life* (London: John Murray, 1909).
Holmes, Coleridge, *Early Visions* (New York: Viking, 1989).
Howe, *The Life of William Hazlitt*, 1922 (Penguin, 1949).
Hughes, *Shelley Poetry & Prose,* 1931 (Oxford University Press, 1973).
Hunt, *Imagination & Fancy*, 1844.
—, *Men, Women, and Book; A Selection of Sketches, Essays, and Critical Memoirs* ... (London: Smith, Elder & Co., 2 vols., 1847).
—, *A Jar of Honey* (London: Smith, Elder & Co., 1848).
—, *Tales* (Walter Scott Pub. Co., nd).
—, *Essays* (London: Scott, nd).
—, *A Book for a Corner* (London: Bohn, 1870).
—, *Table Talk* (London: Smith, Elder, 1882).
—, *Prefaces* (Port Washington, N.Y.: Kennikat Press, 1967).
—, *The Autobiography of* ..., 1850 (London: Smith, Elder & Co., 1870).
James, *The Aspern Papers*, 1888.
Johnson, *The Birth of the Modern* (New York: HarperCollins, 1991).
Jones, *English Critical Essays*, Sel. & Ed. by, (Oxford University Press, 1968).
Keats, *The Poems of John Keats* (London: Lawrence & Bullen, 2 vols., 1896).
—, *Letters of John Keats*, Sel. & Intro. by Fausset (Nelson, 1938).
Keynes, *Essays in Biography* (Toronto: MacMillan, 1933).
Kirk, *Edmund Burke: A Genius Reconsidered* (Arlington House, 1967).
Lefebure, *A Bondage of Opium* (New York: Stein & Day, 1974).
Lowell, *John Keats* (Houghton Mifflin, 2 vols., 1925).

Macaulay, *Critical, Historical and Miscellaneous Essays*, (New York: Sheldon, 6 vols., 1862).

Maclean, *Dorothy Wordsworth: The Early Years*, (New York, The Viking Press, 1932).

Morley, (Edith), *The Life and Times of Henry Crabb Robinson* (London: Dent, 1935).

Morley (John), *Nineteenth Century Essays* (University of Chicago Press, 1970).

—, *English Men of Letters* (Byron, Cowper & Burke) (New York: The Publishers Plate Renting, nd).

Nichol, See John Morley *English Men of Letters.*

Oxford English Dictionary (*OED*).

Palgrave, *The Golden Treasury* (Collins, nd).

Robinson, *Diary, Reminiscences and Correspondence of* ... (Boston: Fields, Osgood, & Co., 1869).

Rosebery, *Pitt* (London: MacMillan, 1891).

Rossetti, *Life of John Keats* (London: Walter Scott, 1887).

Selincourt, *Wordsworthian and Other Studies* (Oxford University Press, 1947).

Shelley, *The Complete Poetical Works of Percy Bysshe Shelley* (London: Reeves & Turner, 3 vols., 1878).

Shelley (Mary), *Frankenstein*, 1816.

Southey, *Poems of Robert Southey* (Oxford University Press, 1909).

Symonds, *Shelley* (New York: Harper & Bros., 1879).

Trelawny, *Recollections of the Last Days of Shelley and Byron* (1858) (Boston: Ticknor & Fields, 2nd ed., 1859).

Trevelyan (George Macaulay), *British History in the Nineteenth Century* (London: Longmans, Green; 1924).

Trickett, *Dorothy Wordsworth's Lakeland Journals* (Diamond Books, 1992).

Wollstonecraft, *Vindication of the Rights of Women*, 1792.

Wordsworth (Dorothy), *Dorothy Wordsworth's Lakeland Journals* (Diamond Books, 1992).

Wordsworth & Coleridge, *Lyrical Ballads*, 1798.

Wordsworth, *The Complete Poetical Works of* ..., Intro. by John Morley, (New York: Crowell, nd).

Index

www.ingramcontent.com/pod-product-compliance
Ingram Content Group UK Ltd.
Pitfield, Milton Keynes, MK11 3LW, UK
UKHW040014200726
13854UKWH00001B/203

9 781425 128593